Praise for Barbara Sjoholm

For *The Pirate Queen:*

"Sjoholm brings to life many remarkable stories of maritime women in this fascinating book."
—*The Oregonian*

"Sjoholm's imagination is so fertile she takes on new personas during her journey."
—*The Seattle Times*

"Barbara Sjoholm is a skilled and stylish writer. . . . I fell for her hook, line, and sinker from the first page."
—*Bitch* magazine

"The story [is] truly amazing. . . . Sjoholm's account of her own travels along the Irish coast, the Shetland and Faroe Islands, as well as Iceland and Norway, adds to the enjoyment."
—*Contra Costa Times*

"Her descriptions of land and seascapes are rhapsodic and vivid, and her evocation of people is uncanny."
—*The Sun* of Bremerton, Washington

"A great read all around . . ."
—*Bloomsbury Review*

For *Blue Windows:*

"Barbara Wilson's precise, unsentimental prose delineates a decades-long journey toward self-knowledge and peace with her past: It's a very American saga, sensitively told."
—Amazon.com

"Wonderfully lucid . . . scrupulously fair-minded . . . The best sort of childhood memoir: It reaches beyond the troubled family . . . to illuminate a whole society. . . . Like a pebble tossed into a pond, *Blue Windows* resonates in ever-widening circles."
—*New York Newsday*

"A memoir of exceptional sensitivity and intelligence."
—*The New Yorker*

"Graceful, superbly written . . . In an age when the memoir has become transcendent, *Blue Windows* is among the best."
—*The Seattle Times*

"Painfully searching, honest, and, ultimately, inspiring . . . [this] courageous and moving memoir evokes a world of childhood faith and healing."
—*The Women's Review of Books*

"A brave memoir . . . Wilson movingly explores her childhood."
—*The Cleveland Plain Dealer*

INCOGNITO STREET

INCOGNITO STREET

HOW TRAVEL MADE ME A WRITER

BARBARA SJOHOLM

SEAL PRESS

Some of the material in this book previously appeared in a different form in "A Glacier Summer," in *Another Wilderness,* edited by Susan Fox Rogers (Seal Press, 1994), and "Incognito Street," in *The American Scholar,* Summer 2003.

Incognito Street
How Travel Made Me a Writer

Published by
Seal Press
An Imprint of Avalon Publishing Group, Incorporated

AVALON
publishing group incorporated

1400 65th Street, Suite 250
Emeryville, CA 94608

ISBN-13: 978-1-58005-172-9
ISBN-10: 1-58005-172-3

9 8 7 6 5 4 3 2 1
Library of Congress Cataloging-in-Publication Data

Sjoholm, Barbara, 1950-
Incognito Street : how travel made me a writer / Barbara Sjoholm.
p. cm.
Includes bibliographical references and index.
ISBN-13: 978-1-58005-172-9 (alk. paper)
ISBN-10: 1-58005-172-3 (alk. paper)

1. Sjoholm, Barbara, 1950—Travel—Europe. 2. Sjoholm, Barbara, 1950—Childhood and youth. 3. Authors, American—20th century—Biography. 4. Americans—Europe—History—20th century. 5. Authorship. I. Title.

PS3573.I45678Z46 2006
813'.54—dc22
[B]
2006012043

Cover design by Kimberly Glyder
Interior design by Megan Cooney
Printed in the United States of America by Worzalla
Distributed by Publishers Group West

To Nancy Pollak

❧ CONTENTS ❧

PART I

ONE	Faith	3
TWO	The Vagabond	23
THREE	Mediterráneo	41
FOUR	George Sand's Cigar	63
FIVE	Saffron	83
SIX	Iberia	103
SEVEN	The Garden of Forking Paths	127
EIGHT	Bleak House	147
NINE	The Looking Glass	171

PART II

TEN	Incognito Street	179
ELEVEN	A Glacier Summer	199
TWELVE	Winter in Granada	215
THIRTEEN	al-Andalus	239
FOURTEEN	Simultaneous Translation	257
FIFTEEN	Cante Jondo	277
SIXTEEN	Ripples from the Storm	297
SEVENTEEN	O Pioneers!	319

PART I

❧ ONE ❧

Faith

A FEW TEARS of farewell were still damp on my face as I settled into my window seat on the charter flight from Los Angeles to London one morning in December. Just beyond the tarmac, palms rustled with expectation in the artificial wind of takeoffs and landings. It was 1970 and I was twenty, on my way to spend two months in Europe. I'd just said a wrenching goodbye to my boyfriend, Rob, and now wondered if I'd done the right thing.

An actor and a mime, Rob excelled at dramatic attitudes and soulful expressions. Back when we were both acting in high school, our drama teacher was always reminding him that he was not the lead (he was too short), and he should not always be trying to upstage the rest of us. This morning he'd been nerve-rackingly silent driving me from the tiny seaside apartment in Long Beach that we shared with his magician friend Jeff. Silent and radiating misery and disapproval. *You're always going away,* his pale, tense hands on the wheel seemed to say, mime-like. And that was true: I was always trying to gather up enough escape velocity to leave him and California.

Two years ago I'd flown up to Seattle to attend the University of Washington. Last year I'd worked in Germany for several months. Even when we'd tried settling together in Monterey at the beginning of this year, I'd bounced constantly around Northern California, visiting friends and demonstrating against the war in Vietnam. Rob, meanwhile, had been offered a job at the newly fledged South Coast Repertory Theater back in Southern California. His career was beginning to thrive and he wanted me around to support him. Now, just when he thought we were back on track, I was leaving again. I'd be spending two weeks in London, two weeks in Paris, and then I'd meet my friend Laura for a month in Spain.

"I need to do this," I'd told him. "It will help me as a writer."

To that, he'd said nothing. Rob no longer believed in me—as an actor, an artist, or a writer—though he thought I could still be his muse. In high school he'd praised my painting and acting. He'd loved my poetry. Now, immersing himself in Beckett and Pinter, he found everything I attempted too wordy, too girlish, too predictable. It had been a long time since I'd finished a poem or a story, a long time since I'd attempted one.

Rob wouldn't look at me as he drove through the heavy freeway traffic, or as we sat holding hands in the terminal, but just before I was to board the plane, his black-lashed green eyes filled and he whispered in his slightly stagy deep voice how much he loved me. He urged me to make the most of my trip and to return to him as soon as I could. "If you don't like it over there, come back sooner. You don't have to stay two months if you're homesick. I'll be here, longing for you," he reminded me, pressing me to him fiercely.

Once, I'd lived for such moments, entranced by the sense of being so utterly adored, so completely desired. But more recently I'd begun to feel that our life together was a play that I watched from the audience. I could never be sure whether Rob was acting or not, or what he really felt about me. If he loved me, if we were the soul mates he claimed we were, why had he been unfaithful so often? Why had he so rarely written me when I was away from home and so often ignored me when I was around? Rob had become a very good actor because he believed in himself. He was determined to become a leading man, in art as well as life. I'd learned I could never be the heroine in our play; in fact, I felt more and more like the girl tied to the train tracks in a Victorian melodrama. No one was going to untie the ropes for me. I'd have to do it myself, before I was crushed.

"The time will pass quickly," I said. "You'll be so busy at the theater. And you know, I can't really disappoint Laura. She's working two jobs to save up enough money to join me."

It wouldn't have occurred to Rob to be jealous of Laura, even though he knew I found her attractive. So did he. He had no idea, when I said I wanted to travel to Europe to find myself as a writer, that I was also dreaming of being alone with Laura. I'd told him nothing about what had happened between the two of us a few months ago in September. If he could keep secrets, so could I.

Rob was only a little taller than me; his muscular body had the comforting smell of family, and his damp green eyes looked so innocent and lost that I almost turned back right there, almost said, "I made a mistake. Let's go home." I'd known him since I was seventeen. I couldn't bear the moment of saying goodbye to those I cared about; it felt so final, so death-like.

"I'll miss you every day and I'll be back before you know it," I promised, before I reluctantly boarded the plane in tears.

The plane gained altitude, the palms and airport fell away, and then the endless city and even the churning cold green Pacific, and suddenly we shot through the dirty winter cloud cover into the radiant blue above. I pulled out my traveling book—the only book I'd brought with me, and for some time my favorite companion—*Zen in English Literature and Oriental Classics,* a thick paperback by R. H. Blyth. An English scholar once tutor to an emperor's son, Blyth had published this compendium of quotes from Bashō, Wordsworth, Cervantes, and a hundred others, with his own commentary. I'd picked it up in Monterey out of curiosity, at a time when everyone around me was reading Alan Watts and going off for sitting retreats at the new Buddhist center in Tassajara.

I didn't understand Zen, but that was the point. It stopped me from brooding hopelessly on the confusion in my life; it snapped me into attention.

I opened the book's dog-eared pages at random and read:

> For long years a bird in a cage;
> Now, flying along with the clouds of heaven.

I arrived in London wearing a black felt hat and a long black coat, already threadbare, both purchased at a St. Vincent de Paul thrift store in Monterey. I had a blue vinyl suitcase and the outlines of a plan. A few months before, I'd heard from my father that a portion of my grandmother's small legacy of $4,000, held in trust until I was twenty-one, could be used for educational purposes. With this lure, my father hoped to persuade me to drop my hippie lifestyle and return to college.

But I had other ideas. To me, education was seeing the world, traveling and living in foreign countries. For six years I'd studied French, the last three under the judicious eye of Mr. Heidelberg, who taught us English grammar while escorting us through the writings of Voltaire and Montaigne. I'd discovered Colette last year as well as

Dostoyevsky, Knut Hamsun, Henry Miller, and Anaïs Nin. Almost every writer I admired was either European or had gone to Europe to become a writer, beginning with Betsy Ray of the Betsy-Tacy books. As a child, long before I was familiar with Henry James, I'd read *Betsy and the Great World* and could recite by heart Betsy's explanation of why she, as a young woman writer, had had to leave college and head to Europe in 1914:

> "Guided tours are all right for some people, but not for a writer. I ought to stay in just two or three places. Really live in them, learn them. Then if I want to mention London, for example, in a story, I would know the names of the streets and how they run and the buildings and the atmosphere of the city. I could move a character around in London just as though it were Minneapolis."

Last year, under the sway of Rilke's poetry and the notion that I wanted to read *Das Buch der Bilder* in the original German, I'd gotten myself to Düsseldorf, where my college roommate had relatives who'd promised to find me a job. I'd expected to work a couple of months and then travel to France and Spain on my wages; unfortunately, the job they found for me was as a maid in a women's residence run by Lutherans and filled with dental hygiene students. I did learn a great deal of German, but I never saved enough to get much beyond the Rhineland. This time, I resolved, I'd really see some of Europe. I'd visit museums and historical sites, polish up my French, learn Spanish, and, most importantly, get the *feel* of a place. The first month I'd explore London, Paris, and Barcelona. Then Laura would join me and we'd hitchhike our way around Spain. I'd bought a one-way ticket to London, since that was cheapest. I wasn't sure where I'd be returning from.

The first three days in London I stayed at a student hostel in working-class Kilburn, on a busy street of betting shops, launderettes, and Wimpy burger restaurants, where the fog reeked of coal and oily fish-and-chips, and the mornings tasted of strong, milky tea and bacon and beans. I caught a cold from my habit of walking from morning to night in the sleet and drizzle, returning only to feed shillings into the small heater after dark and to huddle up in my under-blanketed bed. One morning after a breakfast of lukewarm boiled egg and cold toast, I got talking with a French boy at the table. Pierre was also of an ecstatic turn of mind and noticed I was reading a book about William Blake.

Est-ce que vous aimez la poésie, mademoiselle?

Oui, oui. Rimbaud? Baudelaire?

I accompanied him to his tiny private room, where, amidst a jungle of wet underwear hanging from two lines stretched from window to bedpost, he read me the poems of Jacques Prévert, in French. In return I read him snatches of Bashō from *Zen in English Literature and Oriental Classics*. He suggested that we save money by rooming together and that when I was in Paris I stay with him for free. I agreed.

That evening, panicking, I took the tube out of Kilburn and moved into the YWCA on Great Russell Street, in Bloomsbury, just a few blocks away from the British Museum. I never thought to leave a note for the French poetry lover; in those days the only way I knew to say no was to flee.

Large black umbrellas crowded Charing Cross Road and Tottenham Court Road as people pushed politely past me, an urban crush I'd never seen before. Once, in my childhood, the downtown streets of Long Beach had been busy at all times of the day, women in hats and gloves, men in suits and shined shoes; but that had long given way to the vast, empty sidewalks and boulevards of suburbs designed for the automobile. London's tube stations had their own dirt-sweet underground smells, and the cars themselves, rumbling purposefully far below the accumulation of history above, were nose-rich with rubber boots, dripping umbrellas, and the newsprint plastered in front of every face.

The city was filthy with history, as if too busy with commerce and knowledge to tidy or organize itself; it simply accreted layers, like a fantastic metropolis of barnacles attached to the banks of the Thames. Between the postwar office and government buildings crept narrow alleys and courtyards where a pub from the eighteenth century might still hang out a wooden sign or a secondhand bookshop, the size of an American bathroom, displayed in its bow window books on travel or the theater. Off any busy thoroughfare you might find yourself in a crooked warren of cobbled lanes that smelled of newly baked currant buns or sausage rolls.

Friends had asked me why I would want to go to London in winter, but London in winter was thrillingly foggy and damp. Through the pervasive, throat-choking mist, shops decorated with holly and berries or with swags of ribbon and wreaths glimmered under ornate street lamps. Poulterers offered turkeys and geese; butchers, suckling pigs and lamb in frilled collars; bakers filled their windows with mince pies and plum puddings. Bells jingled when you opened shop doors. The mood in the theaters was festive, as people traveled into London, dressed up in velvet and satin, and whispered expectantly before the curtain rose. I saw pantomimes and puppet shows, Maggie Smith in a Restoration comedy, and two different productions of *Twelfth Night*. Every day in London, especially now that I was out of Kilburn and into Bloomsbury, I felt enveloped in a world that was familiar as it was completely foreign. I bought a brolly early on at a shop completely devoted to umbrellas, and a wool scarf and mittens at Covent Garden. I bought a flannel nightgown at Marks & Spencer and a large, black-bound notebook of blank pages from a crumpled old impatient clerk with half glasses at a law stationer's near Lincoln's Inn Court. It was a dusty, dim shop that seemed to go back centuries, an older inventory of inkwells, pens, deeds, diaries, and leather-bound ledgers in which to enter accounts by hand existing side-by-side with the latest-style adding machines and electric typewriters. After I bought the notebook I went immediately to a steamy-windowed café on Chancery Lane, ordered tea and a buttered Bath bun, and began to write. I now discarded the drugstore-bought, spiral-bound journal I'd brought with me and began again, in a more determinedly poetic and artistic way, to capture London. I attempted sketches and notations differently from the first journal attempts, which had consisted of a variety of excited run-on sentences and conversions from dollars to pounds.

In my descriptions of the city, in which "Dickensian" is used an alarming number of times, I can see now that I immediately edited out the fish-and-chips shops and launderettes of Kilburn, as well as the Chinese restaurants and girlie shows of Soho where I'd spent an evening wandering with my new friends from the YWCA, the teacher from Trinidad, and the Greek American girl from New Jersey. I edited out the Indian restaurant across the street from the Y and the comic-book shop and described only the secondhand bookshops along Great Russell Street and Coptic Street and the approach to the British Museum. I never walked down a main road if I could help it or visited anything so tacky as Madame Tussauds, the Tower of London, or even Abbey Road or Carnaby Street, preferring all that was "shabby" and "begrimed" and "obscure," or "drenched in history" and "history-laden," or "stately," "sumptuous," and "imposing."

I saw what I wanted to see and described only that, often in fragments: "White wigs like poodles at courtroom of Old Bailey"; "Coal soot blackens the brick. Smell of coal, slightly sweet"; "The Thames and its bridges, a harsh sleety wind makes me hang on to my hat." On my own, walking miles every day, I sought out glimpses of the past in order to describe them: "ragamuffin man selling hot chestnuts: 'here, luv,' he tells me. 'Only a shilling now'"; "Victoria Station swirled in fog as man in bowler hat goes past and bumps me with his long, furled umbrella: 'So sorry, miss.'" How I would have loved to see rats and sewage in the cobbled streets, pigs squealing, Cockneys cursing, costermongers, hot eel men, and street sweepers. How I would have liked the fog to be that ghastly yellow color under the gas lamps; how I would have liked to hear the rattle of broughams through Hyde Park.

Instead, I had to use my imagination to transform London's grimy dark brick buildings, its winding lanes that led to larger and more modern streets, its curious squares with names like Neal's Yard, lined with odd little shops, into the setting for a pilgrimage that could be both my own story (young woman heiress arrives in Europe to become writer) and one that had a Dickensian flavor. By which I meant, I think, a story rich with incident and character and imbued with that peculiar vividness of Charles Dickens that makes his fiction more real than reality. To remind me of what I was experiencing, I pasted postcards into my notebook and made small drawings. I drew people with umbrellas queuing outside the Strand Theatre; I sketched pub fronts, one with an enlivening sign for COURAGE, never realizing that Courage was an ale.

Although my descriptions were thin, I was sure that when the time came for me to write about London, to set a story there, I'd have no trouble at all evoking its atmosphere. "Snow fell lightly on the dark brick house in an old part of the city that had hardly changed since the days of Dickens. . . ." Such sentences were already in my mind: All that remained was to find a story to tell that would allow me to use as many of the following words and phrases as possible: fog, soot, Chancery Lane, coal fire, antiquity, haunts, bygone days, a stately old mansion forgotten by time, a quaint old bookshop on a lane unchanged by the passing of the years.

The London I discovered that December, the London I superimposed over the city, was familiar from all the Dickens novels I'd read the summer I was fourteen, staying with my grandmother, Faith Lane. My father and stepmother had shipped me and my younger brother off to Battle Creek, Michigan, in part because Grandma Lane wanted to see us and had bought the plane tickets, in part to give our stepmother, Bettye, a break from the strenuous task of disciplining us, a job she'd taken seriously over the last year and a half.

Although we hadn't been to Battle Creek for some years, since before our mother died, Grandma Lane's house had a known and secure feeling. The soapy scent of damp laundry seeped up from the cellar to mingle with the shades-drawn, lace-curtained, old-lady smell of the front parlor with its piano and doily-pinned horsehair furniture, with the humid breath of the Midwestern summer, only slightly moderated by breezes in the huge elms out front on North Broad Street. My grandmother rose at four, as she had her whole life. After she'd read the Christian Science Daily Lesson, and selections from the Bible and Mary Baker Eddy's *Science and Health,* she had breakfast and sometimes made bread or biscuits, or pie from the abundant cherries on the tree out back; she did this while the air was still cool, and while we slept, so that when we got up, always late, the old-fashioned kitchen smelled deliciously of warm sugar and butter and fruit.

My grandmother prayed for a living. She prayed for those who suffered in body and spirit, who had come to her to be healed. As a Christian Science practitioner, praying was her work, and she was good at it. Sometimes people, troubled in mien, downcast and worried, appeared at the screen door, asking for Faith or Mrs. Lane. Sometimes a man moving haltingly with a cane or a young woman carrying a colicky baby was ushered into her small study at the front of the house and spent an hour with her. I could hear the rise and fall of anguished voices gradually calming, juxtaposed with my grandmother's always firm, often bossy tone: "Now, Thomas, sit up straight. Do you think God has any interest in seeing you suffer? Do you think that our Father-Mother is that sort of a God? He's certainly not. As God is perfect, so we are perfect. We are the children of God; He made us perfect. You are in error when you believe there is anything wrong with you." I heard her on the phone too, alternatingly berating and calming in that strong, certain voice: "God is love. God will heal you. You *are* healed."

A few years before, when Grandma Lane was much at our house in Long Beach, I used to hate that firm voice bullying my mother and demanding that she heal herself. Although no one mentioned my mother's breast cancer or the suicide attempt that had left her lower face burned and scarred, it was plain she was suffering in body and mind. I always took my mother's part when my grandmother told her she needed to get hold of herself. I saw how the hectoring never helped, how it only undermined my mother's fitful emotional and physical strength in the face of cancer and mental distress.

But at fourteen, with my mother dead two years, the loss of her still unbearable, and unbearable too the new torments I'd come to know through my stepmother, I clung to my grandmother. Grandma Lane seemed the only trustworthy adult in my life. She was seventy-one, as strong as a horse, solid in her beliefs and solid in her person, with heavy shoes, a full bosom, a small hat with a veil for church, and a cameo brooch at her neck. When I was a baby she'd delighted in me, and all through my childhood presents came regularly, books and clothes from Marshall Field's in Chicago, and dolls that I didn't care for as a tomboy. Then, at ten and eleven, I'd resisted her authority in the house, and we'd quarreled daily. According to my father, Grandma Lane was the stubbornest woman he'd ever met. "She could wear down a stone," he said. It was commonly agreed I was a close second for stubbornness. For I would not be worn down.

The summer I was fourteen, my grandmother shouted at me from time to time, but for the most part she considered me a hopeless adolescent and left me alone. I was dreamy and lazy, never lifted a finger to help her or showed any interest in learning from her, not how to bake bread or make a cherry pie, not how to tat or crochet. Half the time I didn't even make the bed and left my clothes in a heap on the floor. I could never be persuaded to study the Daily Lesson, though I did go to the enormous Christian Science church on Church Street a few blocks away on Sunday mornings and Wednesday evenings.

At home in Long Beach the atmosphere was angry, tainted, furtive, and sad. Here it was calm and orderly. At home my stepmother monitored me feverishly and often confined me to my room for the least infraction; my grandmother, although she grumbled, never punished. If not entirely benevolent, she was always fair and often kind. Perhaps she felt she'd punished her own children too often, to no success. Her daughter was dead of cancer; her son lived most of the time in the VA hospital nearby, diagnosed schizophrenic.

My younger brother found friends his age in the neighborhood and was often at their houses or down the block at the park, and I sometimes went canoeing and swimming with a girl in the church who lived on a lake, but most of the time I was happiest doing nothing. It irritated my grandmother that I woke at noon, and slouched off to my art class, and lounged around the parlor reading constantly, but she let me be. When she got really irritated, she'd organize an expedition for us with friends, or she'd say sternly, "Get out of the house. Go to the library!"

This wasn't punishment, for I loved my slow, hot walk down Church Street, over the river, to Willard Library; I loved the delicious smell of books in rows and the fact that I was no longer confined to the children's section but was now that wonderful thing, as a reader if not in the world: An Adult. I was a voracious, undisciplined reader, though I'd started late, at seven. The sad times of my mother's long illness had sent me to the imaginary world of books; I looked less for answers than for another world to live in, if only for a few hours. I took no recommendations, and few were offered. I found all the books I liked to read myself, and that meant fairy tales, poetry, Ogden Nash along with Emily Dickinson, *Ballet Shoes* and *My Friend Flicka* mixed in with Hawthorne, Twain, and Alcott. At twelve I grew interested in history, at thirteen I started to read plays, at fourteen, long Victorian novels. If I had any guide, it was the list of Modern Classics on the inside back cover of the dust jackets of the books published by Random House. I was convinced that if I read *War and Peace,* I would understand everything there was to know about living, and tried that summer I was fourteen, but I couldn't make it through the first chapter, so packed with Russian names.

Instead I decided I would read all of Dickens. We'd studied *David Copperfield* in school a year earlier; my grandmother had a copy of that and *The Old Curiosity Shop* in small—smaller than a paperback— editions. They were bound in brown leather and the pages were thin and white as the wings of night moths. The copyright was 1912. I read them first and then moved on to the library editions of *Great Expectations, Little Dorrit, Nicholas Nickelby, Hard Times,* and *Bleak House.* On the simplest level I took heart in how the downtrodden eventually triumphed over those who oppressed them. In Dickens' novels cruel and grasping adults had absolute power over children, often abandoned or orphaned, only for a little while; eventually the children grew up. The evil adults who had tormented them almost always came to a bad end. The children found their true parents, or partners, and became, though sometimes in complex and subdued ways, content and happy, or at least adults in their own rights.

A few years before, the fairy tales of Hans Christian Andersen had told me the same story, had given me the same hope. Like Andersen, Dickens helped me understand, so much better than the Christian Science teachings, which constantly emphasized that the world *was* perfect—it was we who just didn't see it—that the world was a heartless, often unjust place but one in which goodness and justice prevailed in the end. Yet that summer of Dickens in Battle Creek was more than just a fictional reenactment of my yearning to see my stepmother crushed and my father repent of his hasty marriage. To read Dickens, to read novel after novel of Dickens, was to live in a world that seemed more real than my own. It didn't matter that I was lying on the horsehair sofa, or bent over the kitchen table, or sitting in a hard chair at Willard Library among the stacks. I was in a London so real it was as if I walked with Little Dorrit across the bridge to the Marchelsea to visit her father in debtor's prison, as if I followed the closemouthed solicitor Mr. Tulkinghorn through eerie gaslit lanes in search of Mr. Krook's rag-and-bottle shop. The novels of Dickens offered the same pleasures of favorite children's books: They enabled me to stop living my own life, to forget about my own life, and to live somewhere else.

One August afternoon toward the end of my stay, my grandmother came into the kitchen where I was reading. "Dickens again," she said and sat down, the soft bulk of her, in the wooden chair. She had thin white hair in a bun, a big nose, blue eyes; she wore a flowered cotton dress, neatly pressed, with a starched apron. She smelled of cold cream and ironing. To me, she had always looked and smelled exactly the same.

"When I was your age, I was a great reader, too," she said. "Even though my mother would never have let me sit around reading for fun. Oh, no, late summer was the time to start canning and making jam."

I nodded warily, certain this conversation was going to go down the usual path: how lazy I was and how industrious she had been; how pampered modern-day children were, how they didn't realize how good they had it, etc.

But instead she said, "Reading gave me dreams, too. Not of London but of the West. I wanted to go out West and be a pioneer like girls in the books. And I did. After I got my nursing degree, I lived with the Navajos for a year."

The Navajos? Usually her stories about her life held a moral. I waited for a tale of struggle overcome, of uplift and enlightenment.

"It was very hot there in Arizona, but a different kind of heat," she said, remembering. "There was poverty, but I liked the people very much. They were spiritual. It wasn't like the books said the West would be. It wasn't cowboys and Indians. It was people growing corn and riding horses and having a lot of different ceremonies. Even then, long before your grandpa and I joined the Christian Science Church, I had a great interest in the spiritual. I never liked the Methodists."

I'd heard from my father that my grandmother had trained as a nurse and worked as an RN, but it was usually put in a slightly pejorative sense, as in, "She makes a living as a practitioner, but she renews her RN license every year." I knew she and my Irish-born grandfather had lived in Brooklyn, where my mother was born, and that she and my grandfather had moved back to Battle Creek during the Depression. Some things I'd find out about her only years later, through research and conversations with her friends. She and my grandfather had become staunch Christian Scientists in the twenties, when the church was popular, and had studied to become practitioners and were successful at it.

That late-summer afternoon, I thought my grandmother might be going to try to talk me back into religion again. I was too nervous to tell her I'd lost my faith in God last year and that I'd thought of suicide because most of the time I found my new life intolerable. I knew for a fact now that the world was not only an imperfect place, but that there was no God at all. Because I had prayed so much for my mother to become well and instead she'd died.

But Grandma Lane asked, "Have you thought about what you want to do when you grow up? Maybe teaching?"

"I want to be a writer." I thought everyone in the family knew that. I had been saying it since I was eight, when I used to fold and staple paper to make my own little books, then illustrate and write them.

"Still that?" she sighed. "Well, you certainly read a lot."

"I want to travel. I want to learn languages. I want to live in London. And I want to go to France too, maybe live in Paris."

"Your mother studied French . . ."

I held my breath. We never talked about my mother, her darling daughter who had crumbled under the realization that she had a lump in her breast that no amount of praying would take away.

"I want to go everywhere in Europe," I said. "That's why I'm studying French, because everybody understands French in Europe. And writers need to go to Europe."

She snapped out of whatever painful reverie she'd fallen into. "Well, why shouldn't you go to Europe?" she said and pushed herself out of the chair. "You are certainly strong-willed enough to make your way in the world. Only time will tell if you have any talent as a writer. Talent is nothing without persistence," she added, and then frowned. "But as far as I can tell, you only think of yourself and what *you* want. When you get married and have children that will have to change."

"But I'm never getting married."

"That's what I said!" She walked away as the phone rang, and soon I heard her urging some hapless soul on the other end of the line, "Harold, now listen to me. There is absolutely nothing wrong with that leg. I have told you time and time again, if you want to walk, nothing is stopping you. Are you a perfect child of God or not? Well, then!"

By Christmas Eve, I'd been in London almost two weeks and was scheduled to leave for Paris in a few days. That night four of us girls in the dorm were tucked into our neat little white-painted wooden beds, with crisp white sheets and a couple of thin blankets. Radiators purred under the small-paned drafty windows; the heat would be shut off soon and all of us would pile our coats over the blankets, but for now it was peaceful and warm up in our fourth-floor room. I'd just returned from the green-and-white-tiled bathroom down the hall, had washed my long hair and wrapped it in a towel. I was in my flannel nightgown and smelled of soap. Dickens' *A Christmas Carol* was on my lap. I felt about nine years old. Nine was the last good Christmas I could recall.

The other girls—all women, really, somewhat older than me, with complicated reasons of their own why they were at the London YWCA on Christmas Eve—were also in nightgowns, with their hair in rollers, reading or writing letters. Outside, some flakes of snow drifted past. It never really seemed to snow in London, not as it must have in Victorian times when Dickens was writing; still, Valerie, the teacher from Trinidad, pointed at the window excitedly: "Look, maybe we'll have a white Christmas."

I'd received a Christmas card from Laura and had propped that up next to me on the small bedstead with the lamp. In her large, round handwriting she wrote how she was spending the holiday with her mother and sister but that Christmas Eve she'd be working at her second job, as a ticket seller at a porn theater in downtown Sacramento. She wished me Merry Christmas and Happy 1971 and added, "I might not get to Spain right exactly on January 15. I want to make sure I have enough money to travel. But I hope you'll wait for me. I want so much to see you and explore the world together!"

I pictured Laura, with her rippling golden brown mermaid's hair, her springy dancer's body, and her unwavering belief in me as a writer, even though all she'd ever read were letters. I wanted her here with me, in snowy, Dickensian London. I wanted to take the boat-train to Paris with her and walk the streets of the Left Bank arm in arm. Yet, at the same time I felt curiously content to be on my own in Europe.

No card came from Rob and I didn't expect one. Last Christmas he was rehearsing and forgot all about the holiday. He was apt to miss birthdays and Valentine's Days too. It was strange how little

I'd thought of him since arriving in London; I couldn't imagine him in the city with me. We would have gone to the theater every night, but he would have been opinionated instead of merely entranced. My father had my address c/o the American Express, but there was no Christmas card from him either. I usually tried not to think of him and how he'd changed. I forgave him much because I pitied him.

Looking around, I could imagine myself in boarding school and that in a moment the headmistress, Miss Wimpledown, might come to the door and tell us with kindly sternness to turn off the lights: "Christmas will come soon enough, young ladies!" I was suprised at how comforting I found this dorm room, this sleeping with three strange girls; it was far more comforting than sleeping with Rob in the narrow bed in the seaside apartment in Long Beach. Then, I often had to absent myself from my body; then, I often lay awake afterward, wishing he would talk to me. I'd once longed to grow up and to be independent; I'd longed to get away from the unhappy household of my adolescence. I'd rushed into a quasi-married life sooner than I should have. Much about me was still a child, still longing to be safe and taken care of by those older and wiser.

After the summer my brother and I spent with our grandmother, she and I kept in touch. She told me she couldn't intervene with my stepmother, but Grandma Lane began to send me small gifts of money and books, anything I asked for. She sent me Shakespeare and Carl Sandburg and Mark Twain and Jane Austen. The Christmas of 1966, when I was sixteen and had almost forgotten about my infatuation with Dickens, she sent me a copy of *A Christmas Carol*. It had been her own, she wrote, given to her when she was sixteen, in 1909. When I opened it, I found the flyleaf inscribed by a Genivieve Gillespie: "Here's wishing Miss Lipscomb a very pleasant Yuletide."

The following summer, my grandmother died. I'd been pestering her to let me come and stay the summer again. I promised I'd changed and would be helpful around the house. I planned, once there, to beg her to let me stay and finish out high school in Battle Creek. She'd sent my father money for a plane ticket and all was arranged; then suddenly in June she had a stroke and was gone a few days later.

I stayed home for another year, until my stepmother finally went too far and hit me in the face. When I left home that day, at seventeen, I didn't suspect that I was at the beginning of many years of homelessness. Restless and unanchored, I was now going to have to make my own way in the world, or depend on the kindness of people I was never sure I could trust.

In the YWCA on Christmas Eve, it seemed right to be reading *A Christmas Carol* because I'd been thinking of it so much as I walked around the city, everyone rushing by with wrapped packages and heavy shopping bags. The story of how a tightfisted man grew large-hearted when he looked at how he'd wasted his life made me want to be generous, made me grateful. I was in London because of my grandmother's generosity; perhaps, I hoped, she wouldn't mind that I was spending her hard-earned prayer money on myself and my own ambitions and longings.

Only time would tell if I had talent. But as for persistence, I was Faith's granddaughter, no longer the second stubbornest person in the world but the surviving stubbornest. My only problem now was what to write about, since any mention of the past—all that I had lived until the last two weeks—seemed to bring up emotions of bewildered loss and grief. I hoped that travel would give me my subject and that all the new experiences I planned to have would solve the problem of the pain of bygone days.

❧ TWO ❧

The Vagabond

FROST AND ICE in Paris turned the precisely pruned *jardins* into enchanted open spaces; to walk diagonally through the Luxembourg or the Tuilleries was to come across tiny children in matching blue and red coats and hats kicking balls along sparkling, crunchy pathways or to discover elegant ladies in furs walking their poodles, scattering the sparrows. Along the tree-lined, leafless boulevards, fashionable young women strode with long coats flapping to show off hot pants like boys' underwear, and suede boots up to their knees. And men actually sat in cafés and wore berets and smoked Gauloises and sipped alcohol from small glasses at zinc tables in the middle of the day.

The openness and clarity of Paris were a great contrast to London's fog and grime. The morning frost and pale blue sky, the metallic bright sheen of the river when the sun glanced over its surface made everything brighter. It was colder but never rainy, and no seas of black umbrellas surged through narrow streets; the French city seemed both more orderly and more leisurely. In the glass-enclosed cafés, people whiled away the hours, or they sat in the sun on benches along the Seine, smoking, studying, talking intensely. The children wore knee socks and uniforms, and everyone threw very long scarves around their necks and let them dangle over their coats.

Paris was foreign in the way that Düsseldorf had been foreign to me last year, and just as full of arcane formalities and inscrutable contradictions. No one could ever explain to me why you couldn't simply put money in the phone, why you had to purchase *jetons* from a woman at a *tabac*. Why a box to the United States could not be taped shut but must be wrapped in special thin brown paper, with the address written in exactly the right place, and string tied around the whole thing, before the man at the post office would deign to accept it. Or why there were so many copies of receipts, or why even the smallest purchase from a pharmacy had to be handled like a Christmas present, yet why the groceries never provided bags but simply left the cheese and yogurt sitting on the counter for you to stuff as well as you could into your coat pockets.

Yet the foreignness was not in the language as it had been in Germany. All those years of repeating dialogues in the classroom language lab *(Répétez, s'il vous plaît)* and taking *dictée* from Mr. Heidelberg now paid off. I could read the signs and I could speak (though I could not always be understood). Beyond the ordinary, useful expressions I'd mastered in school ran a concurrent river of poetry, mostly memorized from Rimbaud's *A Season in Hell*, and phrases from Montaigne and Voltaire. Mr. Heidelberg had given us extra credit to read books in translation by French authors, and because he favored *le mot juste*, the clarity and precision of the great essayists, so did I, though it would be half a lifetime before I truly came to appreciate Montaigne. More than the novels of Colette and Balzac, which I'd also read, it was the calm and measured voice of Montaigne, the bitter wit of Voltaire, that were *la vraie langue française* to me. To be in Paris was suddenly to have a context for the disembodied language I'd been studying since I was twelve.

My first night in Paris I stayed at a barracks-like student hostel in Pigalle. I had my almost-full tube of toothpaste stolen and went out with a Chinese girl to the film *Battle of Algiers*. The next day, December 31, I took the Métro to the Latin Quarter to look up Ben, a man I'd met on the airport bus from Stanstead to London, who was staying here with a friend. He'd said Nina was studying literature at the Sorbonne and to be sure to visit them. He'd kissed me lightly on the cheek when we parted in London and had added, meaningfully, that Nina was just a neighbor from the Village.

Ben and Nina had left town for the holidays, to Majorca, but the man next door, another young American from New York, took me in for coffee, after hearing me knock on Nina's apartment door. Charlie had a lot of frizzy hair; he was short, solid, and, as I soon discovered, bankrolled by an uncle who'd made a fortune in television—selling TVs, that is. The uncle, unlike Charlie's father, an accountant on Long Island, had encouraged Charlie first to get an English degree at Columbia and then to spend two years in Paris, writing.

"He said, 'Live all you can; it's a mistake not to,'" Charlie told me and looked expectant.

I smiled. "That sounds like good advice."

"It's from Henry James, *The Ambassadors*. The quote."

"Oh, of course."

Charlie's book-jammed studio was very writerly. On a wooden table piled with *Village Voice*s and *Herald Tribune*s, a black Royal typewriter sat with a page inserted. There was a bottle of wine next to the typewriter, a few unwashed dishes, and, most intriguing to me, a small pile of typescript.

"This is my second year in Paris, but I'll probably stay at least a year longer. It's a great place to write. I've had a couple of personal rejections from the *Paris Review*. Plimpton encouraged me to send more. I don't bother now to send my work anywhere else. I'm aiming high. I'm writing a novel. I have over fifty pages." He gestured at the pile of paper.

It looked more like twenty. "I'm writing a novel, too," I said, though this was not true. I hadn't even written a short story since I was seventeen. But there were certain kinds of men who brought out the competitive streak in me. Charlie, with his aggressive confidence, was one. "What's yours about?"

"It's very New York," he began, and went on for some time about a world that was more foreign to me than Dickens' London. Finally, when I stopped making encouraging noises, he asked, "And your novel?"

I thought quickly. "It's about a Hollywood stand-in. A stand-in for a famous male star. It's sort of Dostoyevskian—you know, the theme of the double." Rob had once been the stand-in for the main male character (not a famous actor) in a terrible film shot around Monterey and Big Sur. It was called *Thumbtripping,* and the last line was, "Have a nice life."

He looked at me with new interest and immediately asked me to a New Year's Eve party that night, to meet some other young American writers and artists in Paris. After a little more talk he decided that I had to get out of Pigalle—"Why come to Paris if you're not going to stay in the heart of the city?"—and walked me over the Pont Neuf to an inexpensive hotel he knew on the Place Dauphine, on the Île de la Cité.

My garret room in the narrow old hotel looked out on frosted chimney pots; it was four flights up, a small room with a big bed— every morning a knock announced a tray of coffee and hot milk with a fresh baguette, butter, and marmalade. I ate sitting up in the soft old bed as the steam heat puffed on and a sliver of winter light hit the sprigged wallpaper and threadbare rug. I placed my *Zen in English Literature and Oriental Classics* and *A Christmas Carol* on the deep windowsill and laid out my black-bound journal, a sketchbook, and watercolors on the wooden table.

Except for the flannel nightgown, I was as far away from the YWCA dorm room as I could be. Now the literary parallels that came to mind weren't those of a girls' boarding school but of a flat where one of Colette's heroines lived and wrote when she wasn't working at the music hall. At twenty I had one foot in childhood and another in adulthood; to go from the communal safety of the YWCA, with its prim rules and neat, narrow beds to the Hotel Dauphine, with its toilet down the stairs and sink and bidet in a corner of the room, was to experiment with shooting from protected youth to self-sustaining independence.

Although I wrote to Rob every few days, and as if he were my boyfriend, I couldn't imagine him here any more than I'd seen him in London. Yet in Paris, I could clearly envision Laura in this room with me: She would be wearing a black slip, like something from an old Simone Signoret film. Her long, curly golden brown hair would be piled on top of her head; my own long hair would be pulled back in a braid, dangling over my black turtleneck. We might be sitting opposite each other at the table, with a bottle of wine between us, smoking (though we didn't smoke), throwing around words like *auteur* (she was a film buff) and *existential* (I'd been a philosophy major). I would have bought a typewriter, and next to the black Royal would be a manuscript I'd read to her from.

Originally we *had* planned to meet here in Paris; that was in September when we were moving from a year of occasional flirting to something more. "Come to Paris with me," I'd invited, of course not telling Rob anything about this, and she'd agreed. Later the plan had changed to Spain. But now I wished for her here, imagined us in bed with our huge cups of café au lait and croissants in the morning, imagined long talks about literature, in which I would express all the things I felt about writing, everything I felt unsure of saying in the crowd I now moved in.

I'd gone to the party with Charlie and afterward saw quite a lot of his friends, all of whom were either staying indefinitely in Paris or were on their way to some place more adventurous: Morocco, India, Afghanistan. They were a little older than me, had graduated from college, and now, seemingly without having to work, were in Paris to find themselves, though they wouldn't have put it so simplistically. They wanted to be writers, artists, musicians; they wanted to see the world, study cooking, hide from the draft by enrolling in the Sorbonne, get high, buy clothes, make love. They were in Paris because Americans were always in Paris; they were under the spell of the city, which was still cheaper than the States then and which promised all the things that France had always promised Americans: more sex and better food.

They talked of subjects I hardly understood—of the *arrondissements* of Paris, the geography of Manhattan, the overland route to Afghanistan; of Monk and Coltrane, of Che Guevara and Mao; of Thomas Pynchon and Marguerite Duras. Money was never mentioned, and I never mentioned it either. At parties and informal dinners, in their hippie finery of spangled long skirts and sleeveless sheepskin vests, in their ornate silver jewelry, in their silk headscarves, in their berets and tight sweaters, they seemed glamorous but also egalitarian, even revolutionary. One or two had been in France during the strikes and demonstrations of '68 and referred knowledgeably to articles they'd read in *Libération*.

I was not like them, but I fooled myself into thinking they didn't know that. When asked, I said I was writing a novel, on my way to Barcelona. No one asked to see credentials, and they offered none, especially the writers. They had come here to play new roles and granted me the same favor. I spoke some French and could pay my way; that was enough.

For the first time in many years I didn't feel poor. Once, when I was a child, my parents had been modestly secure; then came the medical bills for my mother's illness. My father and stepmother had debts from the start of their marriage. My stepmother was often ill, from ulcers exacerbated by drinking; my father taught accounting at the community college and did taxes on the weekends. They fell into greater and greater debt and lost the house. I'd worked since I was eighteen, in offices, as a maid, at fast-food counters, on an assembly line placing plastic forks and knives on a conveyor belt as it went by. I'd had less money than many of the friends I'd grown up with.

I'd never stayed in a hotel by myself before, been addressed as mademoiselle by a desk clerk, cashed traveler's checks at the American Express, walked around with a wallet full of francs. The only luxury I'd permitted myself in London was theater tickets. In Paris it was almost impossible not to desire more: hard to pass a shop full of handmade watercolors and not come away with tubes of violet and burnt sienna; hard to resist onion soup at a café with art nouveau decor on the Place de l'Opéra; hard to walk by patisseries on the Rue de Rivoli, their windows full of pastel-iced éclairs, meringues, apricot tarts, and little cakes of chocolate cream and ground hazelnuts; hard not to take back to my hotel a slice of tarte tatin, a wedge of camembert, a blood orange from the south, or a book about Bonnard, a handful of postcards from the L'Orangerie's exhibit on Max Ernst.

I spent my days in museums and cafés, making notes and reading. As in London, my notes consisted of brief descriptions I expected to turn into something more someday. Years later all they are is words— few jottings about the outer world, none about the inner. Although I'd read Anaïs Nin with great fervor the year before, I couldn't imagine writing about myself as she did, disclosing all my secrets, baring my mysteries to the world. Anaïs Nin always seemed to be looking at herself from the outside; others were interesting to her only insofar as they reflected back who she hoped to be. Even her self-condemnations had a luscious, loving feel; look at me, she often seemed to be saying: I may be awful, but aren't I terribly fascinating? I didn't want to be that sort of writer; I'd left home to abandon my memories, and I certainly wasn't going to spoil my longed-for trip by writing about the past.

But I didn't have a reporter's eye either. I described nothing as it was; all was overlaid with a kind of scrim of self-conscious poetizing and again, long, disconnected lists of words, in French and English, as if by writing complete sentences, I would sully the beautiful expressions with more meaning than they could bear: *aller simple* (one-way), *papier à letters* (writing paper); *live all you can* (underlined twice).

More interesting to me now are impressions I gleaned from simply looking at paintings, building a vocabulary of style. Here and there is some flash of insight, scribbled next to art postcards into my notebook. I juxtaposed artists and compared them: "Chagall's women fly around the room, over the rooftops. They remind me of Blake's figures, ethereal, wrapped in clouds ascending to heaven." But for the most part my ability to describe what I was seeing lagged far behind my ability to intensely feel it.

One morning I took the Métro to the Musée d'Art Moderne. I'd been through it once and was standing in front of a large Maillol sculpture of a naked woman when a man, clean-shaven, blond and lightly balding, probably in his mid-thirties, wearing a jacket and jeans, clearly not French, approached me and, with a lopsided, engaging smile, began to speak to me in English. He couldn't help noticing my English-language floor plan; was I British or American?

He was American. Harry was his name. What was I doing in Paris?

"I'm traveling to educate myself, about art, about life."

"All by yourself then? That's brave. Are you a writer, by any chance?"

That was my dream, to be recognized as artistic and interesting, without lifting a finger. No one in California would ever ask a question like that. Paris was different.

"Yes."

"I wondered if you might be." Harry smiled his lopsided smile, which made him look like a boy. He was a writer, too, originally from outside Chicago. He'd lived in Paris for about five years and worked on the *Trib*, as a copy editor, part-time. "And—like everybody else here, I guess, I'm writing a novel. I've written a couple, actually." Offhand, not at all bragging, he added, "One was published a couple of years ago. That helped me get an advance for this one. Anything to stay in Paris."

Everything he said was intensely glamorous to me, especially "advance." I had seen that word in the *Writer's Digest* I'd subscribed to in high school but had never heard it uttered. I had, in fact, never met a published author. So much for Charlie with his rejection slips initialed by George Plimpton. Harry was the real thing.

We talked in the almost empty gallery for quite a while; then he asked if I'd like to get some lunch. He knew a wonderful little bistro; the owners were friends of his. Harry even had a car, and we drove to what indeed was a charming restaurant, family-run, with plates on the walls and flowers on the white tablecloths. The hefty *patron* kissed Harry on the cheeks when we came in, insisted I try his wife's coq au vin in its thick, winey sauce. He complimented me on my French, told Harry, "*Elle est très jolie!*"

"I know she's pretty," said Harry, winking at me.

He ordered for me, three courses with a bottle of wine. Although he drank most of it himself, I had enough to make me tipsy; I'd never had anything to drink so early in the day. I felt very grown-up but also at ease.

The more wine Harry drank, the more talkative he became. He told me all about his novel, the first one, and the one he was working on now. I was just as glad he didn't ask me about my writing; after telling Charlie I was working on a novel, I'd made a few notes on "The Stand-in," just to see if the idea went anywhere. It didn't. I couldn't really imagine myself writing a novel about Rob—or a novel from a male point of view. It's true that most of the novels I'd read were from a male point of view, but then, they were men who wrote them.

"I've been very influenced by Henry Miller. Do you know his work?" Harry asked.

"Oh, yes," I said, pleased to show off. "I've read lots of his books. About three or four." And that was true. When I was a maid in Düsseldorf the year before, I'd found Miller's *Rosy Crucifixion* trilogy in the Evergreen editions in the train station. Starved for English, needing something besides Rilke, I'd devoured first *Sexus,* then *Plexus* and *Nexus* in the uncritical way I read everything, searching only for what fed me, discarding the rest. I'd been greatly taken by the character Mona. After I'd returned home and read Nin's journal, I'd realized that Mona was June Miller, Henry's wife, whom Anaïs Nin had fallen for as well. I'd underlined this from Nin's journal:

The love between women is a refuge and an escape
into harmony. In the love between man and woman
there is resistance and conflict. Two women do
not judge each other, brutalize each other, or find
anything to ridicule.

I'd razored out the photograph of June from the library edition,
the one of pale June with the enormous, kohl-rimmed eyes, and had
taped it to my wall.

Of course, I had found some of the writing arousing, and
sometimes, when my roommate Edelgard was off visiting her parents
in Bonn, I had read with one hand. But there was something greater
than mere sex scenes that I took away from those Miller novels
read so greedily in Düsseldorf: It was his onrushing, exuberant,
crazy, loving-it-all, joyous sense of life. Miller had worked at awful
jobs, had known poverty and misery and obscurity, yet he described
everything with such verve that it was enchanting, not demoralizing.
He had given me courage to accept—even to laugh at—my dismal
situation scrubbing floors, surrounded by dental hygiene students.
On days that I'd read Miller, I used to walk around the dull,
businesslike city and see everything with new eyes, as vibrating
with life.

Harry's eyes glistened. He seemed surprised that a young woman
would be such a big fan of Miller's. In fact, there was only so much
of Miller that I'd been able to take, and he no longer interested me
much, but he had led me on to Dostoyevsky, Knut Hamsun, and Nin.
I said something about Anaïs Nin's diary to Harry.

"That self-absorbed idiot," he laughed. "She got famous on his
coattails." He looked directly at me. "They had an affair, you know."

"In her diary she says they're just friends. It was really his wife
she liked, June Miller."

"Mona. Mara," said Harry and then quoted, "We were 'conjugating the verb love like two maniacs trying to fuck through an iron grate.' From *Tropic of Capricorn*. Now, she was a piece of work. She ended up in a mental institution."

I didn't like to hear that. "Well, Anaïs Nin was in love with her, too. Everybody was in love with June. I would be, too, if I'd known her."

"Aren't you the innocent!" he laughed. "I don't know whether to believe you." He got up and paid cheerfully for lunch, kissed the *patron* on both cheeks, and opened the car door for me.

I hesitated. "Actually, I'm going to another museum now." I got out my map. "It's the Musée de l'Homme." I had no idea where we were.

"Hop in," he said. "I'll drive you." His face was flushed, and he took my arm to move me toward the little car.

Somewhat reluctantly, I got in. I was still impressed that Harry was a writer and grateful to have had such a nice meal. I didn't want him to think me timid and inexperienced in the ways of life in Europe.

We began driving and he started talking about Henry Miller again, about some of his favorite books, then some of his favorite scenes from the *Tropics*. "No one writes like Miller about sex." Said aloud, all those words, the *twats* and *cunts* and *hard-ons* and *peckers,* which meant little when I saw them on the page, seemed threatening and invasive.

I closed my ears. At a red light, he leaned over and kissed me with an open mouth. He smelled of wine and garlic.

"Stop that!"

"Haven't you played that game before? A kiss at every red light?"

"No."

"Come on, don't be like that. Let's go to my place. We'll have fun. Nothing serious, just some fun. You said you liked Henry Miller."

"No thanks. Just drop me at the museum."

"Is this the kind of thanks I get for taking you to lunch?"

Now I knew where I was—in danger. I had hitchhiked so much around Northern California that I knew how easily men who were friendly suddenly became demanding, how they could suddenly unzip themselves, or speed up past the stop you'd requested. I knew how boys and men who seemed like perfectly normal companions could turn into sex maniacs, no longer interested in having a conversation, only in jumping you.

I shrugged and didn't say anything to Harry. He wasn't worth talking to. He probably wasn't even a real writer. We were approaching another red light. With a quick movement I was out of the car, standing in traffic first, then running for the side of the boulevard. He had no choice but to drive on. I waved down a taxi and returned to the Place Dauphine, glad I hadn't told him where I was staying.

In the waning winter light of the late afternoon, I wrote a letter to Laura, joking about what had happened and emphasizing my quick wits. Both of us had evaded several dangerous situations hitchhiking in California. In reality I felt sobered, and obscurely furious with Henry Miller.

Ben and Nina returned from Majorca a few days before I was to leave for Barcelona. Charlie told him where I was, and Ben turned up one afternoon, a reedy guy with glasses and soft brown hair much longer than I remembered. In a short coat, with a long scarf tossed over his shoulder the French way, he'd mysteriously transformed himself into a foreign-looking person.

"Stay longer," Ben asked. He had a degree in business from NYU; his parents owned a jewelry store on the Upper West Side and had given him the gift of six months' travel before he returned to look for a job. He'd told me, en route to London, with the intensity spawned of a sleepless night across the Atlantic and the close proximity of bus seats, that he planned to get as far away from his parents as he could. "Someplace where they don't even *have* American Express, maybe not even a post office."

"I feel like I want to get to know you," he said. "It's Paris, after all!" Things had not gone well between him and Nina, whom he described as "needy." Later I met Nina, a chain-smoking, black-haired, bitterly thin woman who wore an Afghan vest over a black dress with black tights. She was twenty-seven, ancient. She looked at me through her large, horn-rimmed glasses and said, kindly, considering that Ben was spending all his time with me, "Are you enjoying Paris?"

"She's one of those super-intellectual women who live in their heads," Ben said. "Then suddenly they jump from the mental to the physical, like a starved puppy. They don't want to be separated, they're clingy. But at the same time, they don't like the way you are. They get bossy about where you throw your underwear. Then you're fighting, then they're crying. Who needs it?"

Ben spoke like a man of the world, though he was only twenty-two.

He wasn't going to move out of her apartment though—"What's the point? I'm flying to Tangiers in a couple of weeks. Why don't you come with me? Spain—what's Spain to you? It's touristy on the coast, I've heard, repressive in the countryside—the Guardia Civil, you know. You don't speak the language. In Morocco you could use your French. It's so cheap we could live for six months. If you're worried about money, don't be. We can sleep on the beach."

We were walking along the Seine, around the Quai de l'Horloge. As usual there was no snow, but it was cold, with a white mist coming up off the river, the stones slippery under our feet. Ben removed his glasses, rubbed his hazel eyes. He had a beautiful profile, a soft, sensitive mouth. He didn't speak a word of the language, but waitresses were kind to him, and the shawled, stern ladies in the *tabac* smiled at him the way they never did at me. I could kiss a mouth like that at a red light or anywhere.

I liked that he was not artistic, that he seemed to have a breezy, live-for-the-moment philosophy combined with a down-to-earth frugality (he could convert francs to dollars instantaneously in his head and could walk away from something he wanted, shrugging, "So who needs it at that price?"). It was that rapid-fire response to life that had drawn me to Zen and kept me reading Bashō, hoping to develop a talent for being present that didn't come naturally. Ben was pragmatic but also fun; not literary, but with a streak of true poetry. He hadn't read Henry James or Henry Miller, much less Duras and Sartre, and only one obligatory novel *(A Farewell to Arms)* by Hemingway, but today he threw back his head when the sun came out and said, in his strange New York accent, "I'm dazzled by you, California girl." Then he lifted me up slightly and spun me around, so my black coat flared. "Couldn't we fall in love, right here, just for the fun of it? Won't you come to the Casbah with me?"

"But I have plans," I laughed. "My friend Laura is joining me in Spain."

"Change your plans! She'll understand."

"My boyfriend . . ."

"Oh, screw him. He let you get away, didn't he? Do you ever get a letter? One letter, you told me. That's not much of a boyfriend. It's more of an excuse not to live in the here and now."

"No," I said. "I don't know why, but I'm set on Barcelona. It appeals to me, just like Morocco appeals to you." I couldn't help noticing that Ben didn't suggest, for all his apparent infatuation, that he follow me to Spain. I suspected sometimes the real reason he wanted me with him in North Africa was that I spoke French and could make his way easier.

Still, for a few days Ben and I were romantic. Paris seemed to require it. We walked the frost-slippery hills of Montparnasse, took an elevator up to the top of the Eiffel Tower, walked holding hands on the quays of the Seine, had an espresso in the Closerie des Lilas in homage to Hemingway. I stopped writing daily to Laura—she owed me many letters by now—and pretended to be a girl in one of the French films I'd loved in high school. When I removed Ben's glasses before we kissed, he looked a little like Jean-Louis Trintignant.

We ate *steak frites* in bistros, bought hot chestnuts in rustly little paper bags, listened to Mass at Notre-Dame, laughed with the children in the Jardins du Luxembourg and tossed their balls back to them. I lost track of Charlie, my companion of the first week in Paris, and stopped going to museums and sitting in cafés. I could feel my sweet privacy slipping away, the delicious anonymity of my first days, but I didn't mind, or perhaps only a little. I wasn't sleeping with Ben, not out of loyalty to Rob, who seemed to have vanished from my conscience as quickly as from my life, but because it was hard for me to imagine bringing a man to my hotel room. I still cherished those mornings waking alone to the tray outside my door.

Ben had no interest in Nina's friends. "Fakers, most of them," he decreed. "They'll tell you they're writers, but they never publish anything. Or they've got a studio somewhere filled with horrible paintings. *Nobody* comes to Europe to be a writer or a painter anymore. New York is where it's at."

I'd confided to Ben on the bus to London that I wanted to be a writer, but he seemed to have forgotten it, and I didn't have the nerve to remind him lest he count me among the fakers. I *would* start writing, once I got to Barcelona, I promised myself. I had such a vague notion of Spain that I imagined it almost like a bare room, lit by sunshine, that I would fill with myself and my dreams.

Ben and I planned to spend my last day in Paris together, after which we'd take a taxi to the Gare d'Austerlitz and he'd put me on the overnight train to Barcelona. The afternoon was very cold, and a little snow fell. He wanted me to come back to Nina's with him, while she was at classes, but that didn't seem right; instead, in a state of unsatisfied sexual tension, we walked around some of our favorite places in the Latin Quarter and found ourselves at Shakespeare and Company, where I wanted to buy a book for the train trip. I went immediately to a shelf of translations into English and pulled out Colette's *The Vagabond*.

Shakespeare and Company, a bit dusty and piled to the ceiling with new and secondhand books, reminded me of a much smaller version of Acres of Books, a sprawling secondhand store that took up half a block in downtown Long Beach and that had been one of my cultural refuges since I first discovered it in high school. Its murky warrens of moldering volumes were the closest thing to Dickensian offered by my city, whose heyday had been the twenties and whose shabby palm-tree, art deco charm had not yet been rediscovered.

Acres of Books had been where I'd first discovered *The Vagabond* last year, when Rob and I had driven down from Monterey to visit his mother. I had found myself in the fiction section, breathing in the mildewed, comforting exhale of half-forgotten authors. Colette I knew only vaguely—I had seen the film *Gigi*—but the word *vagabond* suited my mood. I pulled out the narrow volume and began reading. There was a dusty window, a shaft of light on the bookshelf, all the time in the world. Colette's tone of melancholy and regret enchanted me. How persuasive was her knowledge of life, how tender, fresh, and yet so worldly. Finally I came across this passage toward the end of the novel:

> For I shall flee. A premeditated escape is being organized far away, down in the depths of my being, without my taking so far any direct part in it. At the decisive moment, when all that remains will be to cry, as though in panic: "Quick, Blandine, my suitcase and a taxicab!" I shall perhaps be taken in by my own confusion, but O dear Max, whom I wanted to love, I confess here, with the most genuine sorrow, that from this moment all is resolved.

On my last day in Paris, at Shakespeare and Company, I bought *The Vagabond* and tucked it inside my bag, a talisman against the lure of romance. Ben and I had dinner, and he tried to persuade me once again to stay longer in Paris, to travel to North Africa with him.

But even at the last minute, at the door of the train that would take me south to the Spanish border, when Ben took off his glasses and suddenly looked like a boy in love (just like a scene in *The Umbrellas of Cherbourg*), when he kissed me and said, "I didn't think I could fall for someone so fast," I held fast to my resolve. "We'll write," was all I promised.

❦ THREE ❦

Mediterráneo

ONE DAY NEAR the end of January, exploring the hills near my apartment building on the Avenida República Argentina, I came over a ridge and found the city of Barcelona spread out below me. The Ramblas made a leafless, tree-lined passage from the cobalt of the Mediterranean through the tangled ochre and brown medieval quarters to the Plaza Cataluña. From that central plaza, boulevard-circled, sped large and small streets in many directions, through the blocky bourgeois district of the Eixample to the university and the Plaza España. From this viewpoint I could see my progress through the city over the past two weeks.

I'd spent my first days in Barcelona in a cheap *hostal* not far from the train station, where I'd steamed in from Paris two weeks ago and where my blue vinyl suitcase had been quickly snatched up by a porter paid to steer travelers to one of the nearby *pensiónes*. From that early toehold in the city, I'd investigated the skinny streets of the Gothic quarter, between the Ramblas and the port, where laundry ran like damp flags between the crumbling buildings and where everything reeked—in descending order, air to stone pavement—of wet black clothing on the line, olive oil, garlic, harsh tobacco, and piss. It was the oldest part of a city that Franco was still punishing, three decades after the civil war. No money from the coffers of Madrid flowed to improving Barcelona, and the Guardia Civil still patrolled the streets in their stiff black boots and hats, sternly Mickey Mouse–eared, at right angles to their profiles. The city was shabby, even derelict in sections, grimed with neglect; yet people still flocked to the opera in black tie and ball gown; businessmen, correct and frugal, walked to work with briefcases; and the birds still sang in their cages along the center promenade of the Ramblas.

From up here in the hills, on a wind-blown sunny day, the Barrio Gótico looked attractively jumbled, not dark and a little sinister as it did in the evenings. I'd been timid in those gloomy streets, timid yet voracious. I knelt awkwardly in the cold cathedral, where Catholicism smelled like tallow, incense, and confession, and statues of saints I'd never heard of drew small followings in shrines around the perimeter. I breathed in the sharp smells of citrus, iced fish, and onions in La Boqueria, a vast indoor market off the Ramblas. I wandered past curtains of skinned rabbits and plucked yellow chickens, asked, *por favor,* for a sample of manchego cheese, goat-sharp on my eager tongue, and bought green olives stuffed with garlic or pimento and dry soft figs that I carried back to my room with a long loaf of bread. I fingered mantillas in shops hardly bigger than a closet, ate cold potato omelet sandwiches with a glass of fizzy water *(con gaz),* stayed out later than I would have at home by myself, perching in smoke-filled bars at ten at night with an espresso, a blue aerogram filling with description under my fingers. I avoided the Plaza Real after dark, wary of the prostitutes and drug dealers I'd been told about by other tourists in my *hostal,* and never went into the Barrio Chino. But even so, I was sometimes followed in the damp, dark twisting lanes; my long, dark blond hair made men hiss at me like teakettles: *Rubia, rubia, hsst, hsst.*

Gradually I moved into the more open squares and regular blocks of the nineteenth-century buildings in the Eixample. I strolled past Modernista architecture on the Paseo de Gracia up to Diagonal and came back via Rambla de Cataluña, admiring the elegant shops, even if the facades above were brown with dirt. I signed up for classes in Spanish at the Berlitz School across from the Plaza Cataluña and memorized verbs while lounging at an outdoor table at the Café Zurich, my face upturned to the Mediterranean winter sun. I went every day, sometimes twice, to the American Express on the Paseo de Gracia, where I waited for a letter from Laura or, better yet, her appearance.

Every day I explored more of the city, and my excursions began to take me away from the port, up into the hills. After London and Paris, I longed for a vista. One day, talking with a waiter in a café in my new, broken Spanish, I said that it would be nice to live up here. He said he knew a widow with two daughters who took in lodgers in a nearby apartment building, and before I knew it he'd arranged everything. I arrived by taxi the next day and moved into a room with two beds and a desk, in an apartment on the Avenida República Argentina.

From my ridge, I suddenly spied in the near distance two curious towers belonging to two bulbous munchkin houses; from here their roofs seemed like white frosting slathered in waves and curlicues over gingerbread cupcakes. Descending quickly through residential streets, closing in on the buildings, I discovered that in fact the frosting was an elaborate pattern of mosaics. Each undulating cupcake was topped by a Moorish-looking dome, and from one of the pale brown houses a blue and white mosaic spire with a cross shot up.

I searched on my map until I found an entrance to this Parque Güell. I walked in to find an astonishing world, not so different from paintings by Max Ernst, full of brown concrete caverns, dipped and plastered like the surface of a sand castle, and walkways terraced into a hillside of palms and yuccas, lined by concrete pillars formed like tree trunks. The two small buildings with towers were gatehouses, behind which two sets of stairs, split by a fountain in the shape of a mosaic lizard, led up to a plaza supported by pillars. I wandered through the park for hours, gradually understanding that this landscape was the magical and mildly deranged vision of Antoni Gaudí, the same strange man whose cathedral with its unfinished spires, La Sagrada Familia, protruded from the regular streets of the Eixample like a huge broken molar.

In 1971 it was still possible to travel to Barcelona and not know in advance about the architect Antoni Gaudí. He was still something of a local phenomenon, not much celebrated except as a symbol of the proud eccentricity of a city that had never bowed to Franco. But in Barcelona itself, the city authorities had debated tearing down the uncompleted cathedral, which many thought an eyesore. Even if Gaudí had been world famous then, I might not have known about him. At twenty, I had many things I was against, and one of them was a guidebook of any sort. I preferred to arrive in a place and to discover it. All I really knew of Barcelona was what I'd heard a bearded poet saying some months before at a reading in San Francisco, that the city had once been a hotbed of anarchism and poetry. Anarchists, I came to know later, had loathed the devout Gaudí, and during the civil war they'd dragged plans and models out of the cathedral and burned them, which is why no one knew for sure how Gaudí himself would have finished La Sagrada Familia.

I spent much of that day and others in the Parque Güell, usually with my tiny painting box and finger-length brushes, my 2B and

4H pencils, my London notebook and a square sketchbook bought in Paris, up on the wide plaza supported by a forest of pillars like dripped-wax candles. The plaza was rimmed with undulating benches of concrete, set with brightly patterned bits of broken ceramics. I drew the munchkin houses and wrote in my notebook about Gaudí. I wrote a letter to Laura about Barcelona, now my favorite of cities, and about the life I was living, so much better, so much more full of happiness and wonder than I could ever have dreamed possible. The winter sun warmed me, and I took off my black hat and long black coat; in the distance the blue Mediterranean lapped at the shores of Barceloneta and its rickety seaside restaurants.

Sometimes, attempting to describe my life here in Barcelona to Laura, I fell into Anaïs Nin moments, when I looked at myself from the outside, breathlessly investigating my existence, like an animal grooming itself:

> I sit here at the Parque Güell, created by that mad master of mosaic, Gaudí. I can't really describe it; it's like a surreal Disneyland, as if Disneyland had been covered by a mud slide. A man came up to me a while ago and said I had *"una cara de ángel."* An angel face. I know I look younger than I am. But I feel quite strong, quite ready for life's adventures. I'm waiting for you to arrive so we can begin our travels around Spain, but I've lost the impatience I had in Paris. Is it the Spanish state of mind? I feel only curiosity and peace. In Paris I thought that when I got to Spain I'd begin writing fiction; but I now understand a few things about writing I didn't before. One, you can't force it. Two, living is more important for a writer, at least at the beginning. If I sat in my room writing a novel, I wouldn't be experiencing Barcelona. It's a choice I make daily, and I always come down on the side of *living*.

Although my journal descriptions were sparse and I complained often that I didn't know how to write about what I saw, my surroundings worked on me powerfully. I was committing Barcelona to memory, just as I'd absorbed and remembered London and Paris. It's also clear I was on to one of the major problems of being a writer. To sit at a desk typing for hours every day is not to live in the physical body. It's to live in the mind, with the doors to the outside world shut and the lights on bright inside. Because I believed my vocation as a writer was fiction, I saw describing where I was as secondary to imagining the characters who would move through this landscape. But I couldn't then quite imagine a plot other than my own life, and I knew that in order to create that plot, I'd have to live it first.

Drawing in my sketchbook, I was content to simply record what the eye saw, but when it came to writing, I always tried to make something happen—and then was invariably dissatisfied. I tried writing about the strange experience with Harry in Paris but crumpled it up. That was *not* the kind of experience I'd come to Europe to have; I could have that any day of the week at home. I tried to write something about Laura and our hitchhiking adventures last summer but discovered I didn't seem to know her well enough to really describe her: I kept falling back on her long, rippling hair. "She is like a madonna from Northern Europe," I wrote, "with an oval face, blue eyes, a receding chin, and long, rippling hair." But "receding chin" did not seem very romantic, or kind, and besides, all that wasn't really *Laura*. Laura was her bubbling laugh, and her lively way of walking, as if she moved on rubber floors, almost bouncing, and her long, intricate Jungian dreams of oceans and unicorns. When I wrote down some of the conversations we'd had, even the ones that had interested me most, all I felt was a sense of dismay, at the woodenness of the details and the talk. *When she gets here*, I thought,

*I'll really look at her. I'll write down what she says. What I say. I'll
write the story of our travels and turn them into short stories.*

"No, no, not *cojón. Cajón*," Lola laughed as I tried to explain
that one of my desk drawers—*un cajón*—was broken. "*Cojón—
cojones*—that's a very bad word," she said in Spanish. But she looked
delighted when I repeated it—"*cojón, cojón*"—while paging through
my dictionary. Lola was my age, the widow's younger daughter, a
hair stylist whose own short dark hair was frosted like a zebra's. She
wore false eyelashes and thick makeup, artfully applied; she smelled
of shampoo and chemicals, sweet and bitter.

Her laughter brought her sister into my bedroom. Maria was
some years older, prematurely aged, a thin, dark version of her white-
haired mother, dressed in a gray cardigan, shapeless gray wool skirt,
and clunky brogues, the gray only a lighter shade of the widow's
black her mother wore.

Maria flushed when she heard me say *cojones*—balls—and she
reprimanded, "Never, never say that. A girl should not say that."
But she couldn't help laughing herself, in a thrilled, nervous sort of
way. I couldn't find *cojones* in my blue *Inglés-español-Español-inglés
diccionario*. Maria grabbed it from me and flipped furiously back
and forth; finally she settled on page 417. "*El sexo!*"

The apartment had cold linoleum floors and was sparsely furnished
with a few pieces of dark secondhand furniture and the requisite
crucifixes. The three had arrived, Lola told me, husbandless and
fatherless, some years before. They were economic refugees from the
south of Spain who didn't particularly like Barcelona or the Catalans;
"*Son tan orgullosos,*" Maria said dismissively, "so stuck-up."

"When they don't want you to know what they're saying," Lola
added, "they start speaking Catalan."

She said it as if it were a secret language, but in fact, I had recently been told by my Spanish teacher at Berlitz, a university student, that Catalan was something different, the true, suppressed language of the Catalan people. Once, in medieval times, Cataluña had been a country of its own, with a literature of its own. They did not teach Catalan at Berlitz.

"The south of Spain, where we come from—there the language is soft and beautiful." Lola showed me on my map: Granada. "That's where you should go when your friend gets here. Then you'll see the true Spain, a land of heart and soul. All they are here is business: work, work, work!"

But all of them worked hard; they had to. They rose earlier than I did and headed out to their jobs. Maria was a bookkeeper; her mother, a janitor. I was not permitted to use the tiny spotless kitchen, not even to boil water; the widowed mother explained with hand gestures that I might blow up the building by lighting the gas.

Instead, I took the metro down to the Plaza de Cataluña and, standing at a zinc counter, dipped my croissant into a white cup of *café con leche* at the café next to the Berlitz School. The rest of the day was free; I had nothing to do but wait for Laura, who, day after day, did not appear.

It was almost February when a white envelope postmarked Sacramento arrived. Laura wrote that she was going to delay her arrival in Europe by a month or more; she hadn't saved up enough money yet—because she'd decided that she wanted to be gone six months and to visit Italy and Greece.

> I should get to Barcelona by the end of February. I hope you'll wait for me. Your letters are so fantastic, they make me feel like I'm really there with you. I really want to travel with you. Maybe it's even

better to travel around Spain in March. Maybe you
can come with me to Italy?

In those days, transatlantic calls seemed out of the question; it never
occurred to me to phone her, to discuss the changed plans, to explain
that I had a limited amount of cash, which I was going through more
rapidly than expected. I took Laura's letter to a bar nearby, where I
often whiled away an hour or two, studying Spanish grammar and
practicing on one of the waiters, who had a soft spot for me. He and
I had a joke dating from my first visit, when he'd asked me where I
came from and why I was in Barcelona:

¿Por qué eres en Barcelona?

Porque—¿por qué no?

"Because—why not?" became my standard answer to him.

It enchanted me that *why, because,* and *why not* were all
practically the same: a Zen koan where question and answer were
contained in the same sharp, rhythmic words.

He would always smile and agree: "*Si, señorita, ¿por qué no?*"

The bar was almost empty on this late morning; a pale sunlight
streamed through the ornate windows, onto my wooden table with
the sketchbook and pencils arranged just so. I ordered a *café con
leche* and tried out some of my new phrases on the waiter when he
brought over the cup of espresso and poured warm milk into the cup
from a great height.

"*Hace frío,*" I said, shivering and pointing outdoors, and he
shivered and winked in response before going back behind the bar to
his cigarette and newspaper.

I reread Laura's letter and considered. I was now six weeks
into my two-month European trip. Perhaps I could write to Mr.
Butterworth at the Bank of Battle Creek and explain how much I

was learning by living abroad. Europe was more expensive than I'd thought, I could tell him, so expensive that I'd had to use my return fare to live on. I didn't know Mr. Butterworth, but I had a kindly feeling toward him, because of his Dickensian name and because he had accepted the idea that travel to Europe fell under the education clause of the trust. Whether my grandmother would have agreed that the Berlitz School in Barcelona and a plan to hitchhike around the country were in any way the equivalent of a college education was highly debatable.

I practiced several approaches to Mr. Butterworth in my notebook and copied the most earnest and adult-sounding request for another $200 into an aerogram. I asked that the money be sent to me care of the American Express in Madrid at the end of March. I would fly home from there. I then wrote to Rob and gave Laura's delayed arrival as an excuse for my own delay. This was crucial, because I'd just received a letter from him saying that he was looking forward to my return soon. He wanted to move out of Jeff's seaside apartment in Long Beach and down to Costa Mesa into an apartment we'd share together. He was sure I could get some sort of job there, or I could go to the UC Irvine campus and study. He'd been offered the title role in the musical *Tommy,* scheduled for August. It was his first major role—the West Coast premiere—and he really needed me to be there for him.

In the past, these were the kinds of pleas that had always sent me running back to him. That he needed me, that I was his muse, that we were kindred spirits, that no other girl was like me, no one understood him so well. And that was true. But it was also true that the more I understood him, the less I understood myself. In high school, he'd pursued me and I'd gradually come to accept him in my life, even though I sometimes felt, in spite of his straight blond hair and his soulful green eyes, that his prominent upper lip made him look a little like a frog. Later, I'd fallen in love with him, because he said so often he was in love with me and it made me happy when he said it. Even when his enthusiasm for my acting and writing disappeared, and he began to pick away at my self-confidence and to sneak around my back with girls in the drama department, I was always susceptible to his blandishments.

Now I wrote him a long letter, explaining that Laura was getting here a little later than she'd expected, a month later, in fact, and that most likely I wouldn't be home until sometime in March. I'd dreamed for a long time of traveling with Laura; I couldn't give that up. I'd promised Laura, and she was working herself to the bone to make the money to travel.

But what I really didn't want to give up was the possibility of being with Laura outside the constraints of home. I didn't want to give up the self I felt I was becoming here in Europe. I didn't want to give up the possibility of turning my trip with Laura into fiction.

I dug out a postcard of the Parque Güell from my bag and scribbled a note to Laura: "I'll wait as long as it takes for you to join me."

"No, you hold the knife like this," Monzo explained, picking up an orange from his metal tray and beginning the familiar ritual. "You take off the top and then just slip the knife into a fast curl around the fruit, until the peel's off!" He held up a single spiral of orange peel in one hand and a denuded fruit in the other and laughed as my own efforts resulted in juice dripping down my arm and spraying across the cafeteria table.

"It's just a matter of practice," said Lluís comfortingly to me in French. "Monzo is as usual showing off. He wants to be a surgeon, so he likes to cut up everything in sight."

Lluís and his best friend, Ramón, or Monzo, were from Palma, on the island of Majorca; second-year medical students, they were a few years older than me, yet they seemed younger in many ways with their innocent faces, practical jokes, and devotion to pinball and soccer. Lluís had a round head, full cheeks, a cap of black hair, button-black eyes, a neatness of person. He always wore a sweater over a long-sleeved shirt, and pressed trousers. He was eager and decent, a romantic in life and in love. He was the one who'd asked me to dance at the disco where Lola had taken me the other night, who'd walked me home afterward, who'd invited me to have lunch with them the next day, and the day after and the day after that.

Monzo had thick, longish hair, he wore jeans, he smoked, he was fiery on the subject of Franco and the Fascists. "You can't just come here and think that Barcelona is the way it is because that is the way it is," he lectured me one afternoon, soon after we met, at their favorite bar (favorite because of its two pinball machines) in a combination of French and Castilian. "You're looking at a city that only seems to be quiet—underneath it is ready to explode."

Lluís looked nervous. "Lower your voice, you idiot," he said. "Don't you know anyone here could be spying?" And then they burst into mutters of what seemed to be Catalan but was in fact the dialect spoken in Majorca, a further dangerous step away from Castilian.

All this cloak-and-dagger business was both amusing and thrilling to me. I had no way of assessing the risks they took criticizing Franco, of speaking Catalan in public. Before I came to Barcelona, I'd never heard of Cataluña, its rich history, its periods of autonomy. My Berlitz teacher, who was himself Catalan, said that there was no chance the province would ever rise again and that people who thought otherwise were just deluding themselves and bound to end up in jail. He couldn't help talking about it, though, even though we were supposed to be studying tenses.

"Franco is almost dead—I give him one year, two years at most," Monzo said later as we were out on the street walking.

"Franco is going to live forever," Lluís joked. "They'll just put some wax on his face and in his veins and prop him up in a chair."

The two had of course spent their entire lives under Francoism; they didn't remember anything else and weren't sure what would come next. There was a large gap in their knowledge of Spanish history: There were the Romans, the Visigoths, the Moors, Isabella and Ferdinand and the Reconquest, the Hapsburgs, Napoleon—and then Franco. Only anecdotally did they know the events leading up to the civil war, the struggles among the Socialists, the Communists, the Anarchists, the Fascists; they knew these stories not from history books but from their parents and grandparents. Monzo's family was originally from Barcelona; his father's two older brothers were students when the city voted for the Popular Front in January 1936. They had joined the Republican Army to fight the Nationalists under General Franco during the civil war.

"One of my uncles was killed in a battle around Gerona," Monzo told me. "The other one was captured and put in a concentration camp, and then shot during the war tribunals." The rest of the family had fled to France when Barcelona fell in 1939. They lost everything. Eventually they went to Majorca, where they had some land and a summer place. "My father had been too young to fight. He was the only boy left in the family."

Lluís's family had been spared death and reprisals over on Majorca; his father was apolitical, "afraid to express his opinions," more interested in making money. But Lluís had an aunt in Barcelona, a wealthy widow once married to someone with ties to Franco. Lluís had lived with her his first year in Barcelona; then he couldn't stand her politics. "We always fought. She never wanted me to speak Catalan—she said it was ugly, like Castilian without the consonants."

When I first knew Lluís and Monzo, we often spoke in French with Spanish thrown in, but over a relatively short period of time, we switched more and more to Castilian, though they also taught me a few words of Catalan. Neither knew more of English than song lyrics and phrases they'd practiced on foreign girls in Palma—*Hello, you want dance with me?*—phrases I preferred they not use because they sounded like such hapless Latin lovers. I was diligent with my verbs, eager to pick up new vocabulary. I wanted to have a working knowledge of Spanish before Laura and I set off on our trip. I also wanted to be able to explain to Lluís and Monzo who I was and where I came from: why women were different from men, why Americans were different from Spaniards, why America shouldn't be in Vietnam. I also wanted to understand their world: why Franco had come to power, why Cataluña was different from—far better than—Spain; why the Balearic Islands were different from—far better than—Cataluña.

Much of my Spanish came via songs. Like all Catalans, they loved music, and they often sang when we walked along the streets at night, both pop songs and traditional music. They introduced me to Lluís Llach and Maria del Mar Bonet, and of course their hero Joan Manuel Serrat, a popular folk singer who composed his own songs and sang them, many—in a spirit of defiance—in Catalan. In 1968 Serrat was to represent Spain in the Eurovision contest, but when he announced he'd sing in Catalan, Spain had pulled the plug on the broadcast. His concerts, Lluís and Monzo told me, were heavily policed by the Guardia Civil; to have all those young people in one place, singing along in Catalan, their chests swelling with indignant patriotism, was combustible.

Years later, nothing brings back the memory of those weeks in Barcelona like the melancholy love ballads and the danceable anthems of Serrat; I have only to play the songs from his album *Mediterráneo* or *Material Sensible* to recall myself and my two Catalan friends, eating free olives and drinking a glass of wine at the pinball bar, with its sawdust on the floor, its harsh cigarette smoke, singing along with "Lucía" or "Aquellas Pequeñas Cosas" or, my favorite, "Mediterráneo."

"Fed up with being fed up," one of the stanzas went, to a cheerful beat, "I'm sick and tired of asking the world, *¿Por qué, por qué?*"

¿Por qué, por qué? Why, oh, why? No song for us better caught the mood of those times, that longing for personal and political revolution. I had Nixon, they had Franco; we were sick to the teeth of our governments. The rhythm and the words in English and in Spanish were completely different; the emotion was the same.

My first week at the apartment on the Avenida República Argentina, I'd often spent evenings practicing my Spanish on Lola, but now that I knew Lluís and Monzo, I was less often there. I would meet my friends for lunch, and sometimes those lunches and the pinball games that followed lasted all afternoon. In the evenings we sometimes went to the movies or to the cheap bars in the Barrio Gótico and ate tapas for dinner. They had little money, so we never did anything expensive. Much of the time we just seemed to walk around, endlessly up and down the Ramblas and the Paseo de Gracia, around the streets of the university. Now, no strange men followed me, hissing, "*Rubia, rubia.*" When I was with Lluís and Monzo, we stayed out as late as we wished, and often it was long after midnight before Lluís put me on the metro back to the Avenida República Argentina. There was something about hanging out with a couple of boys that brought me back to childhood, when I was one of the few girls—and the only adventurous girl—on the block.

It took me some time to realize that few other girls my age were out that late at night. Even though women in Cataluña were said to be more liberated than those in the rest of Spain, they still went home to their families in the evening. Girls from Andalusia were treated even more strictly. Lola got off work at eight; she returned to the apartment to have dinner with her mother and sister. She never went out on dates; the excursion to the disco where we met Monzo and Lluís had been a rare event in her life. Now she seemed both avid to know what I was up to, and alarmed. Did I go the place where the boys lived? she wondered.

I confessed that I didn't even know where they lived. We made our arrangements from day to day, and now that I knew their main hangout, I could always find them at the pinball bar during the siesta.

That was good, Lola told me. "Because if you have sex with one of them, they won't respect you. Sex is for marriage."

"Oh, we're just friends," I said, though things had taken a more serious turn with Lluís. Gradually, between Monzo and Lluís, and between Lluís and me, a kind of consensus had grown: I was with him. This meant hand-holding, kissing on a park bench, sweet gestures on his part that seemed gentlemanly, almost old-fashioned. He bought me a small silk scarf, flowers from the sellers on the Ramblas, a book of the troubadours' love poetry in Catalan.

I had not mentioned anything about Laura and my crush on her. I *had* mentioned Rob, briefly, as someone in the long-ago past. When pressed, I said I'd lived with him "for a short while." Now Lluís knew I'd had sex. His courtliness did not fail, but it seemed to have a deeper intention. He broached the idea that I stay on in Barcelona or that, when my friend came, we travel and then return to Barcelona.

I could come to Palma and work during the summer. There would be jobs available in tourism. Perhaps I would think of going to the university in Barcelona in the fall.

"*¿Por qué no?*" I said. I'd never liked a place as much as I liked Barcelona. Why did I feel so at home here compared to in London and Paris? It was partly because I had friends that the city was accessible to me, and it was tempting to think how I could enter more and more fully into the experience of Spain with a boyfriend and a commitment to stay. I didn't love Lluís, but I loved the feeling of being special to another person, and that fought with my desire for independence. Was it impossible to have both?

One afternoon, Lluís and Monzo asked if I'd like to go with them to the university, where a big demonstration was scheduled. "*¡Claro que sí!*" Of course! I'd never been to the new university, which was built away from the center, precisely so that the police could keep control of it. We arrived by bus; there were hundreds and hundreds of students milling and marching and shouting. I had no idea whether they were protesting something in particular, something to do with classes or professors, or just the whole dirty rotten regime, but I shouted along with everyone else.

I naively thought I knew everything there was to know about demonstrations, having attending them since I was in high school with my friend Ruthie and her mother, Jane, who was fervently anti-war. The year I'd finished high school, 1968, was the year of the assassinations of Martin Luther King and Bobby Kennedy, the rioting in Chicago at the Democratic National Convention, the election of Nixon. I had arrived at the University of Washington in the fall to a campus roiling with Black Panthers, Yippies, Young Socialists, and masses of people linking arms around the Administration Building to protest the war. In Monterey the next year, it was more of the same: Vets back from Vietnam at nearby Fort Ord hanging out at the G.I. coffeehouse, hoping for a visit from Jane Fonda; conscientious objectors working in laundries; disaffected boys with adult beards and their barefoot girlfriends going "back to the land" in Carmel Valley because they believed the end of civilization was at hand; newly fledged Zen Buddhists baking bread in the mountains of Big Sur; outspoken activists bonding with the farm workers in Salinas—I knew them all. Ruthie and Laura transferred to UC Berkeley from UCLA, and I went there several times to run around the Berkeley campus as the police threw tear gas canisters at us. When the Cambodia bombings began in the spring of 1970, I was in solidarity with my college friends in the UC system who went on strike and dropped out.

I thought I knew everything about protest marches and tear gas, about raising my fist high and shouting, "The People, United, Will Never Be Defeated," about taunting cops with names like "Fascist Pigs."

I didn't know anything.

Lines of tanks began moving through the wide boulevards of the campus and trucks arrived, filled with Guardia Civil carrying guns with bayonets. More Guardia Civil on horseback, seeming phalanxes of them, appeared to block off other exits. The students began running, some attempting to taunt the Guardia, others just trying to get away. Students were clubbed in the head or knees, dragged off; at least one was trampled by horses. In the confusion, Lluís and I were separated from Monzo. The last I saw of him he was drenched and flailing from a water cannon aimed in his direction.

Lluís grabbed my arm and hauled me with him, both of us running as hard as we could. When a bus appeared, already packed, the driver stopped, and a couple dozen more of us crammed inside, some wet from the cannons, many sweating, gesturing, and talking Catalan at the top of their lungs.

"We shouldn't have left Monzo," I kept saying. "What if he goes to jail again?" I knew he'd already done some time last fall, and that his medical education was in jeopardy if he were to be arrested again. "What if he's *killed?*"

"He can take care of himself," said Lluís. "We'll go to our room to wait for him."

It was the first time I'd been to their place, and I could see now why they hadn't invited me there. It was a single large room in a flat owned by a doctor's family, in one of the huge old apartment buildings on Provenza, not far from the Faculty of Medicine. We'd walked past it many times. It was easy to guess which was Lluís's side of the room; the bed was made, and posters of soccer stars lined the walls. Over the desk were anatomical charts. We sat side by side on the bed, awkward. I felt as if I were with a stranger, in some boy's room in junior high. To disguise our awkwardness, we began kissing and I let him touch my breasts. From time to time I'd say something about Monzo being killed, and Lluís would say, "Don't worry, he's fine."

Finally Lluís said, firmly, "Look, I wasn't going to mention this, but Monzo agreed not to come back here this afternoon."

The implication was clear.

"We won't do anything you don't want to," said Lluís, adding shyly, "This would be my first time."

He reached over, not for me but for a book on his desk. It was the *Kama Sutra,* in Spanish. He had clearly been studying up. I felt like a medical subject suddenly, completely uninspired. But I didn't really know how to leave gracefully. One of the problems of the sexual revolution is that it seemed to dispense with the possibility of saying no. I'd been on birth control pills since I was eighteen; I was experienced. Why not help Lluís out?

He opened the book to some positions I didn't think anatomically possible. "These might be for later," he said doubtfully.

"Yes, it's probably best to begin at the beginning," I said, finding it strange, for the first time in my life, that I seemed to know more about sex than someone else.

Later, back in my room at the apartment, I sat in my room, depressed and uncertain. It wasn't so much the experience of making love with someone who referred to a diagram from time to time; it was that, as always, a sort of despair engulfed me as I realized how little excitement I seemed to feel compared to my male partner. My sole objective around sex with Rob, and now Lluís, seemed to be to get it over so we could get back to what was so much more enjoyable: kissing, holding hands, being romantic.

Lola came in and I told her about the demonstration, trying to find words for water cannon, horseback, bayonet, and falling back on clutching my neck and repeating, "*Tenía tan miedo!*" I was so afraid! Lola tapped one of her long, polished red fingernails on her temple, a gesture that meant either I was crazy or Monzo and Lluís were not using their wits to drag me along to such a battle. She tried to tell me I would be kicked out of Spain if I was arrested. "Those Catalans," she said. "Always making trouble."

I shrugged. Any political discussion with Lola seemed to end with her calling the Catalans *idiotas.* Although we were the same age, nothing else about us was alike, or seemed to be. A year later she would write me a letter and tell me that all the time I'd known her, she'd had an older male *amigo,* who was married.

She opened my desk drawer, which Maria had fixed with some wood glue. "It's working now?" she asked, and then, because secretly she loved to say it aloud, and because my being an experienced foreign girl gave her permission, she whispered, "*El cojón* is no longer broken?"

"Don't say *cojones,* señorita." I pretended to frown. "Say *el sexo,*" and, as usual, we went into gales of laughter.

❧ FOUR ☙

George Sand's Cigar

THE WOMAN ON SCREEN wore trousers and a man's short jacket. Her long, dark hair was bundled up under a sort of Oriental fez. She strode around a monk-like cell, smoking a cigar, as mournful piano music began, broke off, began again, to the accompaniment of incessant rain. She sat at her desk until dawn, writing and writing, by the light of candles, with a quill pen. The pages of foolscap grew by inches. She lit a cigar, then another one; her brow was furrowed. A nursemaid brought in children to say good morning. After a brief kiss, they were dismissed. In the background, there was coughing. A man in a heavy silk dressing gown, incongruous in the shabby circumstances, a pale man, with blood on his handkerchief, appeared in the doorway. They embraced; she put him to bed; she returned to her desk.

The film was *Un Hiver à Majorque,* "Winter in Majorca." Its language was French, with Spanish subtitles, and it told the story of the writer George Sand and her lover, Frédéric Chopin, and the winter they spent in Majorca in 1838–1839. They'd gone there, with Sand's two children, within months after beginning their relationship, ostensibly to give Chopin, who had a persistent cough, a warmer winter, and had first settled in Palma. But after a doctor diagnosed Chopin with consumption, the visitors were made to leave their lodgings, and few Majorcans wished to have anything to do with them. They instead rented former cells in the abandoned monastery of Valledemosa, outside Palma. At first the weather, in November, was still warm, and Chopin exulted in the eagles soaring overhead. Then the rains began. The cells were damp and cold; nothing could have been worse for a man in the early stages of tuberculosis. Still, the two of them were remarkably productive over the three months of their stay. Sand wrote a novel; Chopin composed some preludes. When the travelers returned to Paris (Chopin spitting blood), George Sand wrote a scathing two-volume attack on the Majorcans as well as a description of the winter, in which Chopin's name never comes up once.

Needless to say, George Sand wasn't well liked in Majorca after *Winter in Majorca* appeared, and a formal rebuttal appeared in a Palma newspaper of the many falsehoods she'd perpetrated about the island. It wasn't to see George Sand that Monzo and Lluís had suggested we see this film, although they informed me that "*George Sand era una escritora, como tú.*" A writer, like you. We went instead so that they could recall a much-loved landscape and so that I could see the spectacular beauty of their home across the Mediterranean.

My French wasn't good enough to catch everything that was said, nor my Spanish adequate to read the subtitles; nevertheless, I was riveted by the film. It was, perhaps, the first time I'd seen—on screen or anywhere else for that matter—a portrayal of a woman who was stronger than her male lover. It was the first time, too, I'd seen any depiction of a woman writing. Certainly I'd seen movies with men typing or scribbling in apartments and garrets. I remembered Omar Sharif as Dr. Zhivago, wrapped in wool and fur in the middle of the night, writing lines of poetry in longhand, in a freezing cold villa in the Russian countryside, while Lara slept. But here was George Sand, dressed in trousers and jacket and scarves against the cold. She was stronger, bolder, more productive than her ailing lover Chopin, who huddled under a blanket in his freezing room at the convent, while rain poured down outside. He coughed and wheezed and complained that he was cold and sick. She alternately succored and ignored him. All night George Sand wrote by the light of the candles in her big, drafty room: pages and pages. Smoke from her cigar was tawny in the light; her profile was intensely focused, preoccupied.

She was a writer at work.

The late afternoon was damp with sea fog when we came out of the cinema in the Eixample, and the city, from street to sky, wore that particular, dispiriting shade of gray that many called *Barcelona gris*. It put my friends in a melancholy mood; they longed to return to Palma. In the late spring, as soon as they could get away from the medical college, they'd be sailing. Of course I must come with them.

The three of us had coffee and sandwiches in a nearby café; then Lluís and Monzo went off to study for an exam the next day. Fired up by caffeine, I began walking around the long, regular blocks of the district as the streetlights went on and the shops opened again after siesta. With a grinding noise the heavy metal doors rolled up, the buckets of flowers came out at the florists, and well-dressed women in fur coats and stylish hats made an appearance with small dogs. The stones that had constructed these nineteenth-century apartment blocks were brown with exhaust and soot; the Modernista touches—curvy, wrought-iron gratings and balconies; serpentine-carved wooden window and door frames; here and there mosaics spelling out a name or date—were often battered and also cloaked in layers of dirt. The buildings had massive wooden front doors that opened into unlit foyers with cracked marble floors, enormous stairways with banisters of polished wood, and a cubicle for a woman all in black who washed the floors and attended to the mail.

Underneath the gray and grime of this district it was possible to see how beautiful, how wealthy it had been at the turn of the century. The shops were still quietly opulent, nicer than anything in my neighborhood. They displayed chocolates, liqueurs, and books in their art nouveau windows; even the small grocers and butchers took pains to present their wares attractively. Here you could find imports from France and Italy, cheeses and pâtés and wines; here it was easy to accept the claim that Lluís was always trying to make to me, that Cataluña belonged more to Europe than to Spain. "We have been industrialists, artists and architects, and scientists while the rest of the country has only been building castles and trying to drive out the Moors for centuries. We have been democratic and progressive citizens while they have been landowners and peasants."

But even as Lluís lectured me proudly, I was always aware, from even my brief time in Germany and France, how much Barcelona was *not* like Europe, not yet. It was poorer economically, and while that was excellent for me as a tourist, and one of the reasons why I'd come here, it created an imbalance between me and my friends. What to me was cheap to them was out of reach, even as the children of the bourgeoisie. They'd never been out of Spain, not even to France—it was too expensive—and that insularity of theirs gave them an inflated sense of Catalan virtue. *Everything* in Cataluña, especially Majorca, was better than elsewhere, or why would so many tourists come to Palma and the Costa Brava? They couldn't imagine my country other than through the few American films they'd seen, but they didn't think they would like it, because of all the guns. England was where people drank tea and wore sweaters; Scandinavia had snow all year round. The charming fact was that my Catalan friends saw their province as the center of the universe.

But I, too, felt strongly about Barcelona; it seemed the right size and shape for a city, walkable all times of the day and night. Paris was more beautiful and London more obviously historic, but Barcelona had the Latin spark that England lacked and was cheaper and more agreeable than France. Spanish was a joy in my mouth, easier than French, more fun than German. Perhaps, I thought, as I walked around the streets of the Eixample that evening, I *could* live here. I could, as Lluís was always urging, enroll at the university in the fall. I could study Spanish literature and write.

I felt a great expansiveness that evening. A certainty about things. Laura and I would travel around Spain for a month, and then I'd return to Barcelona. I'd get a job in Palma for the summer. Maybe Laura would like it here, too, enough to want to stay on as well. In my mind's eye, as I walked quickly up and down the broad, lamplit sidewalks of bourgeois Barcelona, I kept seeing George Sand in the film, striding around her room, scribbling at her desk, and I was seized by the feeling that I had to begin writing myself, writing far more and far differently than I'd managed on the trip so far.

I went into one of the little shops selling books and stationery and bought a new notebook. This had begun to be a habit with me, to buy a new notebook every time I wanted to change the way I wrote, the way I was in the world. This one had tiny squares instead of lines. I now decided I wouldn't be so parsimonious with my words. I would let them flow out; I would write and describe everything I saw, and everything that happened to me, and I would begin tonight.

A letter had finally come from Laura announcing the date of her arrival. She was flying to Amsterdam and taking the train to Barcelona, and she'd be here sometime around the end of February.

"What's she like?" Lluís and Monzo, especially Monzo, wanted to know. "*¿Es guapa?*" Is she pretty?

"*¡Guapísma!* She has the most beautiful hair, much longer than mine, like a mermaid. She has blue eyes, a wonderful laugh. Like a little river. She's taller than me. She's a dancer." I used my hands as I spoke, the way I often did to try to give shape to my insufficient vocabulary, and they laughed, because in the absence of a word for mermaid, I'd used *mujer pescado,* or fish woman.

"She sells fish? Or she is a fish?" they asked.

"Neither. She has a tail like a fish. I mean her hair has a tail like a fish," I tried to explain and laughed too. I didn't have the words for Laura: Adventurous, vital, dreamy, independent, daring was how I thought of her, but those words weren't yet available to me in Spanish.

"*Bueno,*" said Monzo. "I love fish. Does she have a *novio?*"

"Not now. She used to, but not now." That was Warren, and they'd parted, in a friendly way, Laura had written, sometime before Christmas.

I tried to tell Lluís and Monzo about Laura, all too aware that she came, as I had, from a world they could hardly imagine: the souped-up, sexed-up world of California teenagers in the late sixties. If I said she was wilder than I'd been, they would have completely gotten the wrong idea. Spanish girls didn't act like I had growing up, and Laura had been even more liberated.

Laura had been popular in high school, a song girl with a flaring short skirt and pom-poms, kicking her legs up at football games. Laura had had an older sister and a mother who worked; she'd grown up early and with little supervision. Laura had been to wild parties in high school with drugs and drinking and sex in the bedrooms, with no adults present, whereas I'd merely gone up to Los Angeles to plays with friends from the drama class or over to Ruthie's house, where we listened to Dylan and Baez and made papier-mâché buttons that said PEACE to sell at rallies against the war. While we'd been tentatively smoking a little pot at parties in Long Beach, Laura had been driving to Golden Gate Park to drop acid at be-ins and love-ins.

When I sketched her in the air for Monzo and Lluís, what I was trying to suggest was her aliveness, not her curves, for in fact she had small breasts and was far from an hourglass. Laura seemed to be in her body in a way I envied. I, too, had been an active girl, roller-skating, riding my bike, playing softball in the neighborhood with the boys, swimming in the ocean, and surfing as a teenager. I, too, had taken ballet as a child and modern dance in high school. But I never felt as at ease as Laura seemed to be; there was something hunched, modest, and protective about me compared to her. Perhaps that came from being raised in a religion that disavowed the physical world and in particular the body. Laura had some wonderful wild vitality under her skin. She had a way of being female that attracted me immensely, and that I'd felt the first time I met her, when I was eighteen.

I was visiting Ruthie just before I set off for Germany in the spring of 1969. Laura was her roommate at UCLA, and Ruthie had been telling me how wonderful she was. I'd heard from Rob how wonderful Laura was too. He'd managed to sleep with her while I was up in Seattle. I was prepared to dislike her, but as she came into the dorm room, my heart leapt up. She had very long, flowing golden brown hair and was wearing a black leotard, smooth and scoop-necked, with jeans, a wide leather belt, and leather boots. The three of us chatted for a while; then Ruthie shooed us out because she had to study, and Laura and I walked around the campus for many hours.

I told her I was going to Germany because I loved Rilke's poetry so much that I wanted to read it in the original. Without really knowing her, I found myself pouring out my dreams. "I want to be a writer. I want to know languages. I want to travel!"

She talked about wanting to study German, too, because of Jung. She was taking a psych class that focused heavily on myth and archetypes, on quest literature, and the main authors they were reading were Jung and Joseph Campbell. "We're required to keep a dream journal," she said in a low voice that bubbled with laughter. "I'm a great sleeper," she said, "and now I feel I have permission to sleep and dream. It's my homework, to remember my dreams."

She was majoring in psychology, minoring in film studies. "Watching films all the time is kind of like dreaming. Again, it's having permission, getting credit to do what I love best."

I was swiftly smitten, enchanted by some quality of magic about her, enthralled too by how she seemed to accept me as a writer, merely on my own say-so.

"I have a feeling," she announced, holding me in her blue eyes, "You *will* write a lot of books. Wonderful, marvelous books. Just the way you're talking about Rilke—I can *tell*."

Writing books—a *lot* of books—was something I'd hardly dared to imagine, and her confidence bolstered me at a time when the two people closest to me, Ruthie and Rob, seemed increasingly doubtful of my future in literature.

After several hours of wandering around, Laura asked me about Rob, not only if I felt okay about her having slept with him ("It was only once, and not that great frankly—he's kind of self-focused, isn't he?") but about why I was going to Germany just after having returned from Seattle if I wanted to be in a relationship with Rob.

I didn't know how to answer that; I never knew how to answer questions about my relationship with Rob. Everyone wondered about us, and no one, from my father to Ruthie, thought it was any good. Perhaps because they could see what I couldn't admit: I was unhappy.

"We're going to move in together in fall, I think," I said after a moment. "We're going up to Monterey to live for a while. We both want to get out of Southern California."

"Oh, I'm going back north next fall, too. I'm transferring to Berkeley, and so's Ruthie. There's so much more happening up there. If you're there, too—we'll see each other often!" Spontaneously, she took me in her arms and hugged me. She smelled of sandlewood incense. I felt faint with elation.

For the next year, every time I saw Laura, though it wasn't as often as we'd hoped, I felt that same sense of elation and promise. I didn't know what to call it. It wasn't the love mixed with despair and yearning I felt for Rob. There was a lightness and dreaminess about Laura that was hard to pin down; I only knew that when I was around her, I felt happier. I seemed able to believe in myself and to feel energized, not defeated. It was only the following summer, when I began to visit her in Sacramento, that the feelings began to have a name.

One evening at the end of February, around eleven at night, she turned up at the Avenida República Argentina. The bell rang and I rushed to answer. A boyish stranger stood at the door expectantly. It was Laura, with all her long, mermaid-wavy hair chopped off. She was plumper, more freckled than I remembered. More American too, with her big backpack and hiking boots.

"I didn't know Barcelona would be such a *city*," she said, following me into the flat. "All these apartment buildings! You, living in an *apartment* building." She gestured to my small bedroom, with its two twin beds, its crucifix, the window that faced a dank airshaft. "I imagined you in a whitewashed adobe house, on a hillside overlooking the Mediterranean," she laughed, but I could see she was quite shocked.

She was starving, not having eaten anything on the train but some peanuts that someone had given her. I took her to a bar down the street and ordered *raciones* of shrimp in garlic and *pan con tomate,* bread rubbed with tomato, as well as olives, anchovies, and some wine. These were the things that Lluís and Monzo had taught me to eat. She wondered where the enchiladas and tacos were. Like me, Laura hadn't bothered to do any research or reading on Spain, or to learn Spanish. In spite of all my letters, she'd persisted in thinking of it as something like a European Mexico.

She'd thought Spain would be hot, so she hadn't brought anything but a thin sweater and a jean jacket, both of which she was wearing. But in Amsterdam there was snow, and snow all across France. She had a sore throat, she said after we'd eaten, and jet lag; she needed a good night's sleep. I gave her a hug before she got into bed, but I could tell she felt as awkward as I did. We hadn't seen each other since last September, under very different circumstances, and had talked on the phone only once, in December just before I left home. Now it seemed to hit both of us at once that we were alone together here in Europe. The very thing we said we'd longed for had happened.

The next morning she was dull and confused, still complaining of a sore throat. We met Monzo and Lluís at the cafeteria of the medical school. They'd been so eager to get to know her; Monzo had been half-primed to fall in love with her on the spot. But we'd reckoned without the fact that Laura couldn't talk to them. "I can't believe you know Spanish as well as you do," she said to me. "In just six weeks?" It almost seemed as if she were accusing me of something, rather than admiring me, as she usually did.

I kept staring at her, trying to reconcile this new boyish-looking girl in the jean jacket with my memory of Laura. I could tell that neither Monzo nor Lluís found her terribly *guapa,* and not so *simpática* either. She barely touched her food and looked drugged and drowsy.

Afterward, she wanted to go back to the apartment and rest. I went with her, swallowing disappointment. I'd so looked forward to showing her my Barcelona when she arrived, from the Ramblas to Parque Güell. I'd looked forward to eating seafood at one of the beachfront restaurants at Barceloneta, to taking the funicular up to Montjuïc, to sharing my pinball expertise, but I could see she was tired and wasn't up to sightseeing.

Back at the apartment, I sat next to her on the bed and spread out the map of Spain. I outlined a comprehensive plan for visiting some of Spain's major towns and cities: Tarragona, Valencia, Granada, Seville, Córdoba, Toledo, Madrid.

"But I thought we'd be camping in the countryside," she said. She had the covers up to her neck, her sleeping bag spread out on top. "I brought this sleeping bag and everything. That's how I thought we'd save money—hitchhiking and camping."

"Hitchhiking, fine," I said. "But when *hostales* are so cheap, there's no reason to camp. It's the *cities* that are the interesting part of Spain."

"But I don't like cities," she muttered before falling asleep.

I visited with Lola a little in the sitting room, then returned to my bedroom now shared with Laura, studying Spanish grammar, looking at the map. She wanted to get out of the city as soon as possible; we'd leave the day after tomorrow. For the first time I thought about what it meant that my independence was at an end, that I now had to take into consideration another's expectations and needs. The lamplight was thin, the unheated room freezing. It was the first evening I'd spent in the apartment in a long time.

I looked over at the curly head on the pillow. Laura had been offhand last night when I'd asked why she cut it so short. "There was so *much* of it. I knew that it would be a complete hassle traveling."

I remembered her brushing it dry in the sun one day after we'd gone swimming in the American River outside Sacramento, how the wet brown kinks fell over her face as she leaned over and let it hang to her knees. As she brushed, she told me and Warren her dreams from the night before, long, elaborate, mythic dreams, recalled in great detail. That was last year, when Laura left Berkeley and returned to Sacramento for the summer. She and Warren, her best friend from high school, had become lovers, and she'd moved in with him.

I liked Warren. Unlike Rob and Doug, Ruthie's main boyfriend— a musician and conscientious objector who bore an unsettling resemblance to Frank Zappa—Warren didn't take himself too seriously. He had a bright yellow VW bug and never wore shoes and rarely a shirt in summer. His hairless chest was warm gold brown, his long hair black and tied in a ponytail, and he always had strings of colorful beads around his neck. He was half Japanese, but there was, I imagined then, more of the South Seas about him, because of the beads and golden skin.

I visited them several times that summer of 1970, the last time in September for a week. The three of us drove around Sacramento in Warren's yellow Bug. Laura wasn't working and Warren was working part-time, so there were plenty of days to swim in the cold American River and lie around on rocks in the heat. We barreled around to flea markets and old gold-mining towns in the foothills. They taught me to drive stick and only laughed as I ended us up in a ditch in the rice fields that stretched out shimmering, pale green all around the city in the Sacramento delta. We went to films in the evening, and when we came out of the air-conditioned theaters, the air was still hot and dry, but no longer burning; the night was filled with the sounds of sprinklers and screen doors banging and music pouring out of open windows and convertibles.

I knew Warren and Laura had an open relationship, though it wasn't like mine and Rob's. Warren slept occasionally with other people, but they were men, and Laura was never jealous. Warren wasn't jealous of me and Laura either. The three of us had fun together, and that was something different for me. Because Rob and I so rarely had any fun. He was serious and intense except when he smoked dope, and then he was mellow, philosophic, and always interested in sex. Laura and Warren seemed to have the relationship I could only dream of—one that seemed to be between equals. Neither loved more than the other; neither loved the other with pain in their heart; neither seemed always to be trying to get away from the other.

I looked at Laura sleeping and remembered that warm, delicious, exciting week in September, all we'd talked about, all we'd done, all we'd imagined for the future. Once she got settled here in Spain, I was sure we'd find our giddy laughter and our deep connection again.

Through the night Laura's sore throat grew worse; there were chills, a fever. By the next day she couldn't get out of bed. "I want some peppermint tea," she pleaded. "Some soup." But the kitchen was still off limits. "It's so cold here. How do you stand it?" She grew silent, except for sneezes and, soon, hacking coughs.

I brought her tea and bouillon from a café, went out to report to Lluís that Laura was sick and getting sicker. He gave me small canisters of sample medications: large pills that fizzed in water. They were aspirin and vitamin C; one also mentioned, on the outside of the canister that it was good for "epilepsy and mental disorder." Laura laughed at that, but for the most part, she was still weak, coughing and in bed under piles of blankets and her sleeping bag that first week. What was a provisional arrangement in the apartment turned into our bleak daily reality. I felt guilty when I went out, "just for an hour or so," to write in a café or meet Lluís and Monzo for a meal. Barcelona's long evenings, which had once been so exciting to me, were now dreary.

I studied my grammar and practiced with Lola. Sometimes, while Laura slept, I tried to write in the spiral journal I'd bought on the evening I discovered George Sand, but that went nowhere, and when I looked at the pages I'd already written, at white-hot speed that first night, and then with diminishing confidence and interest, the nights afterward, I was disgusted. I had not lived *enough*. I had nothing to write. I couldn't write about what I had known and seen in my childhood; I didn't have words for anything of it, found most of it too shameful even to recall, much less explore. Oh, yes, I could make things up, but if I didn't write about myself, whom should I write about, in a way that could possibly be credible?

More, I hated the way I wrote, alternately poetic and gushing or fragmented and incoherent. There was no story most of the time; I couldn't figure out how to get the essential information into an ongoing narrative without backtracking and finding myself hopelessly tangled. I didn't know where to start anymore, and the endings were sentimental or never really ended at all. My descriptions were dull and the dialogue seemed forced, even when I wrote down exactly what people said. How was that possible? Once, when I was much younger, writing had seemed so straightforward. You simply picked up a pencil and made words on a page. I'd written poems all through junior high and high school, some short stories and a play. I wrote papers that got As, and I always raised my hand in class to offer opinions about books assigned. It was a point of pride with me that I'd read so much more than anybody else. I had not just read Dickens, I had read *all* of Dickens. I shuddered to think of the numbers of people who had written in my yearbook, "Here's to the writer" or "Someday I'll say I knew you when."

For, right around the time I turned eighteen, during my freshman quarter, something had happened. I stopped reading in the old way, for sheer enjoyment, or to impress others, or to obliterate my reality, and began to read as a writer. I began to see that writing was not easy at all, and that writers were not simply writing to tell a good story; they were working with language, they were working with structure, they were working with style. As soon as I began to read as a writer, I saw the enormous gulf that existed between me and the authors I so intensely admired. As soon as I began comparing myself, I grew paralyzed and lost my previous innocent hubris. As soon as I realized that writing was a craft and that all writers had different styles, I grew frightened. What was my style? How did you get one? How was it possible not just to write bad imitations of other writers and instead discover the true voice that lay within? How was it possible to write truly when you didn't want to write the truth?

I still called myself a writer for a long time after I stopped writing. Without that longing forged in childhood I was nothing. But, increasingly, the act of putting words on a page, unless I was writing a letter, grew to be a burden that I would just as soon avoid. I blamed it on not having something to write about but feared it was a deeper problem: not knowing what it was I wanted to say. Not knowing how to say it.

It was Laura who'd given me some hope again, merely by her continual interest. When she'd asked me, over the last two years, about my writing, it wasn't because she wanted to make me feel bad. "Don't worry," she'd said last summer, when I confessed that it was so much harder than I'd thought—not just to write, but to write anything worthwhile. "All great writers go through hard patches, they say."

Monzo and Lluís, packing their leather doctor's bags, came to visit us one morning, even though I wasn't allowed to have visitors. I let them in and we tiptoed to the bedroom. Very professionally, they both listened to Laura's chest with their stethoscopes; they stuck a thermometer under her arm; they looked down her throat and into her ears. They went out of the room and conferred. Bronchitis, they pronounced when they came back. They wanted to bring a friend of theirs, a real doctor, to confirm that it was not turning into pneumonia. He arrived the same day, in the early evening, after the widow and her daughters had gone out again after siesta. He instructed Laura to take off her nightgown. We all turned away and she removed it but clutched it to her breasts. After a week or more of eating almost nothing, she'd lost the slight plumpness she'd arrived with. Her short hair was greasy and matted. She seemed vulnerable and freckled in this strange country, surrounded by dark Spanish men, with a thermometer in her armpit. Her defenselessness was my responsibility, and I tried to reassure her.

"Don't worry, Laura. I'm sure nothing's really wrong. But if you need some medication or something, then they can give it to you."

The real doctor spoke some English and also tried to reassure her. "We give you antibiotics and something for the coughing. Be calm. Do not preoccupy yourself."

It was just that moment, as we four stood around the bed of the half-naked Laura, that Maria, in her eternal gray cardigan, appeared in the doorway. Had she been alerted by someone in the building that strange men were coming and going from the apartment? She'd thought to surprise us, no doubt, to demand an answer, to put an end to such goings-on, but the sight of what was possibly an orgy among three men and two girls so frightened her that she couldn't speak. The doctor rushed to explain, but Maria simply closed the door and disappeared out the front door of the apartment.

We all began laughing nervously, until Laura's laugh turned into violent coughing. The doctor confirmed the diagnosis of acute bronchitis and gave us more canisters of fizzy vitamin pills and some antibiotics and cough medicine. They were all free samples, so we didn't have to buy anything. He recommended that we not go anywhere for a while but stay in Barcelona until Laura improved and the weather got warmer.

"But the cold here is making it worse for me, tell them that," Laura said to me.

I explained as best I could. The doctor shook his head. "She needs rest for a week or so. The worst thing in the world would be for you to start hitchhiking. What if she got worse, what would you do? Here you have us, you have the clinic, medicines." Like many Catalans, he considered the rest of Spain a barbaric wasteland.

I explained that to Laura. "I want to be in the countryside," she moaned. "In a smaller place, with trees."

We settled on waiting two more days. After Monzo and Lluís and the doctor left, we suddenly began to talk about our situation in a way we hadn't before.

"I feel so helpless," Laura said. "Nothing's the way I imagined it. You seem different than I remember too. You're so . . . European," she said, for lack of a better word to describe what had happened to me.

"I'm the same," I tried to reassure her, but that wasn't true. Mysteriously I had taken on the coloration of Barcelona. "Don't worry; everything will be different when we get on the road."

But even as I said that, I wondered about the month to come. How would we negotiate what to see and where to go? How would we treat each other? I'd always deferred to her in the past, in part because we'd almost always been in her world, in Berkeley or Sacramento. Now we were in Spain, *my* world, and I seemed to be the one in charge.

What had happened to the magical sense of understanding, that physical spark between us? We had hardly even hugged since the day she arrived.

"Good night. Sleep well," we said that night, as we had said all the other nights.

And then, just as all the other nights, the coughing began, that constant, uncomplaining, reproachful coughing.

The day before Laura and I were scheduled to leave on our trip, I met Lluís a last time in the Parque Güell. It was the second week of March, a warm day with spring dazzlingly at the ready. Trees were in flower, bushes were in bud, bulbs were poking up from the red brown earth, and birds were everywhere singing.

Lluís was dressed as usual in pressed slacks and a crisp long-sleeved shirt, but now he wore a pullover, a thin wool yellow one, around his shoulders, like a short cape, with the sleeves loosely tied at the neck. He had on dark glasses, and his black hair shone. I felt like a frumpy hippy next to him in my corduroy jeans and Mexican blouse, my long hair braided back. I had been wearing the same clothes for some weeks now and didn't want to spend money to buy new, more Spanish outfits.

We held hands, kissed a little; then he wrapped his arms around me. Around us, on the suspended plaza, boys in short pants kicked a soccer ball as Lluís kept an eye on them and encouraged them with a shout now and then. In the distance, the Mediterranean was blue as a new beach towel, the breeze fresh and promising.

"I wish you didn't have to go."

"I do, too. But I promised Laura."

Sad as I was, I was also relieved to be leaving town for a while. Ever since that afternoon in Lluís's room, I'd felt a little compromised, and when he'd suggested another round with the *Kama Sutra,* I'd found excuses. Laura had told me she thought Lluís looked like a monkey, and I'd vigorously disagreed. Yet he was on the short side, and his head was round, round as a bowling ball. And there was the fact that his family was well-off, though in the frugal Catalan way that didn't permit him to spend anything, and conservative, which made him more timid than Monzo. Whenever we went to a certain part of Barcelona where his aunt lived and shopped, he put on his dark glasses, apparently thinking that was a disguise, and made me go ahead of him, so we wouldn't be seen together in case Tía Antonia suddenly appeared.

"Promise me something too," he said, holding me tight.

"What?"

"That you'll come back to Barcelona when you have seen Spain. I want to hear about your experiences. Even if you don't stay this summer, I want to see you before you go home."

I nodded. I certainly intended to return to Barcelona. But of course by the time I did come back, I had changed, and it would have been useless to look him up and try to recapture what we once had had, singing together in the pinball bar "*¿Por qué, por qué?*"

❦ FIVE ❦

Saffron

LAURA AND I left Barcelona on a warm morning in early March by taking a bus to the city limits, which turned out to be much further from the center than I'd ever imagined and were far less picturesque, a glimpse of the many industrial suburbs we'd eventually traverse. The day before, we'd gone to a sporting goods store, where I had bought a basic sleeping bag and a gray canvas-and-leather rucksack and Laura had bought a small Camping Gaz stove and a canister of fuel.

"Think how much money we'll save by being able to make soup and tea and to boil eggs in the morning. Especially when we start camping," she said happily, and I didn't try to dissuade her, even though I hoped, once we began to travel and she saw how inexpensive *hostales* and *pensiónes* were, that she'd abandon the idea of sleeping outdoors. For the first time since she'd arrived, Laura was showing some of the independence and spark I remembered.

We finally caught a ride to Tarragona, where we sat exhaustedly on the steps of a Roman amphitheater and had a picnic and our first argument. I wanted to stop for the day. She was still coughing, and I was tired. "What's the hurry?" I said. "It's three o'clock and we don't have a plan for where to go next. It's beautiful here. Let's stay."

The amphitheater was built into the side of a bluff that overlooked a rocky beach and the fresh blue sea. Above us was the town's medieval quarter, with a cathedral and an archaeological museum. By train Tarragona was ninety minutes from the center of Barcelona. It had taken us six hours to get here.

Laura felt we were still too close to Barcelona, which for her was a hated place now, evoking only miserable memories of a dark, cold room. A cloud settled over her face. "Just because you know your way around Spain, are we going to do everything your way?"

"This is all new to me, too, you know." I didn't like the newness. I was struggling with my longing to be back in Barcelona—home. What wouldn't I have given right then to have walked away from her and taken the next train back to that beloved city, to an easy life of doing whatever I wanted without having to answer to anyone. "I'm going to walk around the ruins," I announced. "They're historically interesting. I want to write in my journal, draw a picture. This was the most important city of Roman Spain, Laura!"

"Go ahead," she muttered, and started coughing again.

"Do you want some water?"

She shook her head and waved me off. I glanced back at her several times as I made my way around the ruins. She looked small and forlorn sitting on the amphitheater steps. I felt like a brute. But why wasn't she doing anything? How could a person just sit there and not be interested in the Roman conquest of Spain?

I found myself longing for the company of Monzo and Lluís. With them, in spite of the language barriers at times, I felt I knew where I was. I might not have known how to avoid having sex when I didn't want it, but psychologically I knew all the places to hide, all the ways to flee, and where the edges were. I didn't really understand girls, I sometimes felt, and was afraid of losing myself in a churning, boundaryless space of emotion. My stepmother, back in the days when she'd still spoken to me, had often seemed to be telling me something different from what she was saying. I felt, uneasily, that Laura was doing the same.

We compromised that day; we'd stay in Tarragona, and the next night we'd look for a small village in the countryside. That night we ate in a cheerful *casa de comidas* and had fish with an almond sauce and a half carafe of red wine, after which we both felt so good, so relaxed, that we ordered another. As the wine flowed, we opened up.

"We're on our big adventure finally!" Laura said. Flushed with wine, she looked healthier. She wore a light blue sweater over her blouse that matched her eyes.

We toasted each other. "We actually made it out of the city!" And then we apologized for the sharp exchange earlier.

"It's just that I'm a younger sister," said Laura. "Sometimes I feel like I have to dig in my heels. My sister was really bossy, you know—as well as being so talented. Every time I came to a class where she'd been four years before, the teachers waited for me to shine. They were always disappointed."

I knew about Laura's sister, who after dazzling everyone in musical comedies in Sacramento had moved to New York and was now working as a waitress and going to auditions.

"I never think of you as a younger sister," I said, and it was true. She was ten months older than me and had always seemed quite assured and decisive.

"But you know Spanish, you know what's going on—I'm only now starting to walk upright. And in *your* family, don't forget, *you're* the older sister. It's the personality of the older to tell the younger what to do," she said with a half smile. "Just don't be mad if I sometimes won't do it."

"I'll always listen to what you want," I said. "I'll try." I wanted us to get back to the way we'd been in California, when we had never seemed to quarrel over what to do and how to do it.

After our first Spanish dinner, pleasantly tipsy, we walked through the cool spring night, under a moon, around the town to an overlook. There was the Mediterranean, sea of a hundred dark centuries of history, with the moon spilling its sheen in a line straight to us. We held each other around the waist, as Spanish girls did each other, before returning to our *hostal*. For a moment, looking at the two single beds, we hesitated, but neither of us suggested pushing them together.

Back on the road the next day, traveling along the Mediterranean coast, we passed miles and miles of almond trees in flower and thick, green groves of oranges and lemons. The breeze through the open car windows was a heady mix of citrus and saltwater, and our slight hangovers burned off like the sea fog. The Mediterranean was a deep marine blue today, the beaches narrow and spangled with glinting stones and the dark green of kelp. One of our drivers pulled off the highway to a stand where he bought us ten oranges, arranged like a string of croquet balls in a long net bag. We passed Castellon and a driver took us to the village of Almenara, where he lived. There was a *pensión* and restaurant in the same building, and Laura suggested that this was where we should stay. We wandered in the orange groves, bought some figs and cheese in a small store.

"It's so wonderful to be out in the country," Laura kept saying. "This feels like the *real* Spain."

I was bored.

We could hardly wait for dinner and were the first ones in the restaurant when it opened at nine. We had the tourist menu, but the steak was thin, the potatoes greasy. In Spain the main condiment was olive oil. Again we drank a half liter of red wine, and then another. The restaurant was still empty when we finished; it felt less romantic and more desolate to wander around the village of whitewashed houses with women in black dresses sweeping and gossiping in front of their houses. It was hard to tell their ages; they could have been anything from twenty to eighty. They stopped their chatter and stared at us with harsh black eyes as we walked by. A talkative boy of about ten attached himself to us, and then his persistent older brother, who kept drawing an imaginary gun and making *rat-a-tat* sounds when he heard we were Americans. We could lose them only by returning to the bar inside the *pensión*'s restaurant. The bartender suggested a liqueur and served us small glasses of liquid sun: Cuarenta y Tres, or 43. We liked it so much we had two shots each.

Now our conversation turned to Barcelona and how strange it had been to re-encounter each other under those circumstances. I told Laura that I wished she'd been with me in Paris, that it was easy to imagine us there. She thought I was criticizing her for taking so long to catch up with me. No, I only meant I had longed for her there. Before you met Lluís, she joked.

"That was nothing."

"Good."

We were flirting now, skirting around what we wanted to say, what we wondered. We spoke in English, but in low voices, hoping that none of the local men edging up to us at the bar would understand. They were rough working men who offered us cigarettes, another drink, asked us our names. Laura laughed and shrugged them off. Her face was rosy and animated. I was getting used to the short curly hair.

We began talking about Sacramento and my visits there last summer, including the last one in September, when we'd first acted on an attraction that had simmered for a long time.

We'd gone to hear Betty Friedan speak in a large auditorium. Friedan was passionate, angry, righteous—a somewhat dumpy woman through whom a stream of new ideas poured out into our receptive ears. We heard her views on making abortion legal, on equal pay for equal work, about getting rid of words like *stewardess*. The audience cheered, galvanized, ready to sign up to a one in the new organization, NOW. Then, during the questions at the end, a young woman in jeans and a T-shirt, with short blond hair, stood up. Her clear voice rang out: "What about the rights of lesbians? You haven't said anything about women who love other women. Everything you say is about women and men."

Betty Friedan said, "My focus is equality for women, equality between women and men. I don't want to be drawn into—that's not something I'm interested in discussing—the special rights of women who . . ." There was reluctance, almost distaste in her voice. ". . . Are lesbians." I'd never heard the word *lesbian* spoken in public before. Now I'd heard it twice. I was red with embarrassment.

Before that young woman stood up, my notion of a lesbian had been almost purely theoretical, even literary. I thought that I had known a lesbian or two—in Germany and in Long Beach, where Rob had a theater friend who was "that way." All the same, I didn't quite think of lesbians as real people who could stand up and talk openly about it, much less demand their rights. Love between women had the tinge of something hothouse, tormented, and foreign about it: furtive assignations in the Bois de Boulogne;

opium pipes and Japanese silk dressing gowns in pillow-padded, lantern-lit rooms in Montmartre; Turkish baths, scented notes, the merging of two soft, rounded bodies in pink rooms with full-length mirrors to reflect back multiple versions of same-sex adoration. These images came via Colette and Anaïs Nin; I'd never heard of Ann Bannon and probably wouldn't have picked up a lesbian pulp novel if I'd seen one.

Instead I read *The Second Sex* by Simone de Beauvoir, which I'd come to by way of Sartre and existentialism, with its disturbing chapter "The Lesbian," which opened, "We commonly think of the lesbian as a woman wearing a plain felt hat, short hair and a necktie . . ." and its later pronouncement: "She is unfulfilled as a woman, impotent as a man, and her disorder may lead to psychosis."

But not all of de Beauvoir's thoughts on why women chose "forbidden ways" were so grim. I'd read a section to Laura that actually seemed quite reasonable:

> Among women artists and writers there are many lesbians. The point is not that their sexual peculiarity is the source of the creative energy or that it indicates the existence of this superior type of energy; it is rather that, being absorbed in serious work, they do not propose to waste time in playing a feminine role or in struggling. Not admitting male superiority, they do not wish to make a pretense of recognizing it or to weary themselves in contesting it.

These lines struck me with their truth, and with a kind of promise: for, in spite of my unfocused life, which seemed like laziness at times but was more a sort of anxious indolence, I longed to be absorbed in serious work of my own—to be a scholar, a nun, or a lesbian, not just a homeless waif at the beck and call of Rob. I did not wish to weary myself in contesting his ability to make a living from his art, and my inability even to finish a short story.

Laura and I had had our discussion about de Beauvoir on a weekend a year and a half ago, in August of 1969, just after I'd returned from Germany. I'd gone to Westwood to visit Ruthie and Laura, and we all traipsed off to see Bergman's *Persona,* which was in revival at the local movie house. With its painfully beautiful close-ups of Liv Ullman as the mute actress and Bibi Andersson as the increasingly deranged nurse, the film charted the women's slow unraveling of their facades, an excruciating merging of their personas. After the film, Ruthie had said it reminded her of her relationship with her younger sister; and Laura had laughed: "Which one are you—Liv or Bibi?"

"It's that feeling that Rachel's watching me, wanting to be me," said Ruthie. "It creeps me out."

"Yes, but of course she wants to be you," said Laura. "It's natural. You probably seem to have everything she wants."

I said little. When I was ten I'd seen the real face of a woman's madness, my mother's, and though I could never speak of it, I could never forget it either. I had separated from her emotionally then; the notion of losing my independence and merging with another person was nightmarish, yet at the same time oddly compelling.

We lounged around their apartment with the windows open on the hot August night, drinking iced tea, talking about the film, and playing Beatles albums. After Ruthie went to bed, Laura and I stayed up late talking about the differences between men and women. She said she found women attractive because they were so similar; I found them attractive because they were so different. I told her about two girls at the women's residence in Düsseldorf who had acted like a couple and been punished for it. One of them had been very mannish, and I'd found that disturbingly erotic. I had *The Second Sex* with me and read Laura some of the section on lesbians, including the part about the felt hat and necktie. The mannish girl in Düsseldorf had occasionally worn a fedora.

I looked at Laura across the room, lying on the beat-up old sofa covered with an Indian bedspread, in her tie-dyed undershirt and cut-off jeans, her hair flowing like a shawl around her freckled shoulders. Yes, I'd found the mannish girl sexy, though I never would have admitted it. But Laura had no male qualities, didn't look anything like a man, and I found *her* sexy too. It was for the strange quality of her femaleness, her tenderness, her openness to me. With Laura I felt I could say anything and be understood. Was that just deep friendship or something more?

"I don't think I could ever be a lesbian," Laura said. "I'm just curious. What would it be like? Would one of you take the male role, and the other the female? Or would you just sort of blend together like two kinds of ice cream, melting into each other?"

Clearly she'd thought more about the physical aspect of all this than I had. Quickly I said, "Oh, I wouldn't want to be a lesbian either, but . . . maybe I could be bisexual," I said, and then a little nervously, "I probably *am* bisexual. I just haven't acted on the . . . woman part of it."

"Well, according to some things I've read in psych classes," said Laura, "everyone is probably bisexual. In some proportion or percentage."

We looked at each other, wondering, perhaps, at each other's percentage.

"What would Rob say if you had an affair with a woman?" asked Laura.

"We have an open relationship. And anyway, Simone de Beauvoir and Sartre were always having affairs with other people, men and women. That didn't change their commitment."

"That's because they're French."

"Probably. If you and I wanted to have an affair, we'd probably have to go to France," I said daringly.

"I'll keep that in mind."

A year later, in the ordinary city of Sacramento, an ordinary American girl, not French at all, stood up in a packed auditorium and asked again, firmly, "What about the rights of lesbians?"

"Next question," said Betty Friedan.

After that talk, Laura and I went back to the apartment she shared with Warren. It was one of those dry, hot September evenings in Sacramento, without a breeze in the oak trees that lined the streets outside. We opened all the windows, put on Janis Joplin's *Pearl* and smoked a little dope.

"Did you know that girl?" I asked, as if conversationally. "At the talk?"

Laura lifted up her heavy mass of wavy long hair for coolness. "I can't imagine standing up in a crowd like that. Saying it aloud."

"Me either. And did you notice, nobody said anything? They just looked at her."

We smoked more dope. "Warren told me he thinks he might be gay," she said.

"Wow." But of course I knew that Warren sometimes slept with men. It was as much a part of him as the beads around his neck and the high, bright laugh.

"He loves me, and I love him. But I think he gets more from being with other guys," Laura said with a sophistication I envied.

"I can understand that," I said, in an attempt to be as wise as she was. "Love and sex are different."

"He's thinking of moving to San Francisco in the fall. He asked if I wanted to come with him, but I sort of think no. Not if he's going to be exploring the gay thing."

"Why don't you come to Europe with me?" I burst out, to my own surprise. I had only just heard about the possibility of using the trust money for travel. "We could live in Paris."

"You really mean it? I'd have to get a job instead of going back to school. Two jobs probably." She got up from the sofa and put on an old Aretha record.

"I won't probably go until November or December. Rob hates the idea. He says I'm always going away."

"Well, you are. Why don't you take him with you to Europe this time?"

"I want to write. And I can't write around him."

"Maybe you wouldn't write around me either!"

But suddenly, the idea of traveling together took shape. It gave a focus to the future that neither of us had; it promised something that we could hardly imagine happening here at home.

She turned up the music. "Hey, Aretha's calling! Let's dance."

I always loved to dance with Laura. Her long hair flew out around her shoulders, and she used her whole self inside the music. Her shoulders shook, her hips swung, her footwork was fast and rhythmic. Sometimes she kicked up her legs, like the song girl she'd once been, for the joy of it. After we'd been dancing for a while, we collapsed in a heap on the sofa, and as naturally as if we'd been doing it for years, and without discussing it at all, we began to kiss.

The men in the bar in Almenara were no longer far away but standing next to us, smoking, talking loudly. We let them buy us a drink— "*Oiga, hombre*, another 43 for the *señoritas*"—and then Laura dealt with the situation in what would come to be a common ploy. "I don't speak Spanish. Good night!" said with an inoffensive, utterly charming laugh.

We returned to our bare room, one of the many bare rooms to come, with two beds, a crucifix, a sink, and a freestanding wooden closet, which Laura often used as a kitchen, when she against all rules boiled water and scrambled eggs on her Camping Gaz. I fell into one bed, and Laura fell on top of me. In a decisive voice she said, "It's now or never."

We took off our clothes, tried to find something to do with our limbs, kissed and stroked each other's faces. My head was reeling from all the drink. I felt as if a large, hot freckled peach with a sweaty, pungent, womanly, disturbing smell had opened and pressed itself all over me. I didn't know how to be absent, but I couldn't be present either. I closed my eyes and hoped for the best. There was no lesbian *Kama Sutra* to refer to.

It didn't matter to Rob if I didn't respond much, but Laura wasn't Rob. Gradually our kisses grew more timid, our grappling more self-conscious.

"Well, this isn't working," said Laura, retreating.

We sat on the bed, side by side. "I am *so* drunk," I said. "Sorry."

"We should take an aspirin," said Laura. "Or else we'll have terrible hangovers tomorrow."

We didn't have any regular aspirin, but we did have the many small canisters of fizzy pills pressed on us by Monzo and Lluís, and we got them out. I read from the tiny instructions on the canisters, looking for the word *aspirina*. "Here's the one that says it's good for epilepsy and mental disorder," I said.

"Let's take it! Mental disorder is close to drunkenness."

We filled our water glasses and each popped in a large disk that fizzed. The taste was unpleasantly metallic, with a gritty aftertaste in our throats.

"Do you feel anything?"

"Nope."

"Let's take another."

We popped in more disks, not only from that canister but from others. Then we ate one of the oranges and some chocolate we'd bought in the store earlier. I was the one to throw up, down the hall in the bathroom; Laura handled it somehow. She would always have a stronger head than me.

Laura and I ate our first paella at an outdoor table of a restaurant on the main square in Valencia. At two in the afternoon, it was bright enough for sunglasses, but Laura sat without them or any other protection, bare-armed and bare-legged, like a piece of toast soaking up butter. Around us, at other restaurant tables on the Plaza del Ayuntamiento, were other tourists wearing sundresses and sandals and hats, shaded by umbrellas, drinking pitchers of cold sangria. It was a touristy place we'd chosen, in direct contravention of earlier vows to eat on the cheap and with the real Spaniards. Exhausted and starving, we'd simply fallen into chairs on the plaza and, like everyone else, ordered paella and a pitcher of sangria, which quickly went to our heads.

The paella was a thick blend of dark yellow rice mixed with chorizo, chicken, ham, pork, onion, garlic, and parsley, decorated with shrimps, clams, mussels, and lemon wedges, all in a shallow pan with handles. We ate as if we could never get enough, yet the saffron taste was strange to both of us, more bitter than expected, in spite of the golden color that was so beautiful on the plate. Saffron came from the crocus stamens; picked by hand and roasted slightly, it was the most expensive herb on earth, I read in the brochure I'd picked up from the tourist office.

We drank more sangria, and with that our hangovers from the night before began to mellow. We'd hardly spoken this morning other than directional grunts and queries; now we began to loosen up. Yes, we'd stay here tonight, and for several days, so that we could rest up a little. "Finally I feel far enough from Barcelona," said Laura. "And I can't bear the idea of trying to get through the outskirts of Valencia again so soon."

I was glad to be in Valencia, away from the sinister village amid the orange groves and disconcerting memories of the night before. Valencia reminded me a little of Barcelona, but the buildings were more baroque than Modernista. On our trudge through the city, I'd noticed museums and bookstores; here we might be able to put into practice a plan I wished to present to Laura: of separating for a few hours every day. I would write in my journal and explore on my own, find my way back to my own center. But for right now I had no desire to separate from her; we sat in the sun, drinking the afternoon away, starting to smile at each other again, to feel the warmth of affection flood back.

I wanted to ask her why she'd said "now or never." Did the fact that she'd gotten up and gone over to her own bed meant that it would never happen again? I looked to Laura as the experienced one; it didn't occur to me that her assertiveness last night had come out of a fear as deep as my own.

We stayed three days in Valencia, and every night we drank too much. Every night we flirted with each other, edging around our attraction and the difficulty of doing anything about it. We always had these discussions in the most public of places, a crowded Spanish bar where the men around us, whom we were also flirting with, didn't speak English. Laura had been accustomed to drinking beer from high school, but I never had. I'd grown up in a teetotal house; Christian Science frowned on all sorts of intoxication. My stepmother was alcoholic and that disgusted me; pot was the drug of choice in the circles I moved in with Rob.

Now wine fueled my conversations with Laura and made them possible in a way we couldn't manage sober, especially when it got on to the subject of making love, which we spoke of as if it were a piece of difficult choreography that we could master if we put our minds to it. Both of us had come of age sexually at a time when there seemed to be no such thing as foreplay. All the teenage boys Laura had been with went straight to the point, as quickly as they could. Rob was just the same, and so, in spite of his gayness, was Warren. But of course that direct approach didn't work for us; there was no external stiffening to semaphore the onset of what we both thought of as the sexual act. For both of us sex had never been connected with love and was not its expression. It was a physical problem to be solved; how could women make love in a satisfying way?

Every night after one of these discussions, we stumbled back to our *pensión* room, and I threw up, and we fell into our separate beds under Jesus on his cross, without doing anything sexual that might end in failure again or, worse, lead to expectations that that's what we were now: lesbians.

Every night in Valencia we ate paella, tasting its bitter warmth, marveling that the minuscule crocus filaments could color a pot of rice bright yellow, like a single obsessive thought that could color your mind.

"Something so golden should not be so bitter," Laura said. "It's a surprise every time."

Since we didn't travel by guidebook, we suggested destinations to each other by the size of the dots on the maps: Something larger than Almenara, smaller than Valencia was what we were looking for the afternoon we were dropped off in Benidorm. But this was a vision of hell neither of us was prepared for. Lines of towering apartment blocks stood up along the beaches where plump red and tan people, mainly English and German, lay on towels and beach chairs. We were immediately approached by swarthy young men in tight Speedos who invited us to have a drink.

We waded disconsolately in the dirty-looking waves and then walked back out to the highway and stuck out our thumbs. Was Spain going to be like Southern California? We took a ride to Alicante, now uncertain what we would find, and were dropped off at the train station, where an aggressive widow took hold of us and herded us to a room in her apartment not far from the sea.

"¿*Matrimonio?*" she asked, gesturing to the lumpy double bed. We laughed nervously, and I tried to clarify our relationship. It's true Laura had short hair now, but she wore a sleeveless shirt that showed the clear outline of her small breasts. "*Somos—dos chicas,*" I explained. Two girls.

She shook her head, more confused than before, gave us a key, and left. It took a number of days before I came to understand that *cama de matrimonio* referred to a double bed.

We went out in the evening, for a walk along the esplanade. It was a beautiful evening, with a full moon, and Alicante seemed to us the perfect size. We wandered around the barrio of the old part of the town, had a glass of wine or two in a bar while eating from small plates of manzanilla olives and chorizo, went into a small restaurant, ordered the *menú del día,* had wine with our dinner, and then more wine because we were so pleased to be in Alicante, and then more, before hitting the bars for some liqueurs. It wasn't long before we had a retinue of young Spaniards around us, creating a thick cloud of smoke from their Ducado cigarettes and practicing their terrible English on Laura as I practiced my hardly better Spanish on them. At some point I switched over into French and then began to quote Rimbaud.

Rimbaud was a bad sign. Laura began to look at me worriedly, though I reconstructed that only later. I was talking very loudly about the poet's theory of the "systematic derangement of the senses" and how alcohol was the path to poetry. I continued emptying glasses of 43.

It was the drunkest I'd ever been; it went beyond drunk, to a place where I was temporarily out of my mind and where I didn't know what I was saying or what language I was speaking in. There were men in the bar, men leaning into my hair, with their hands on my arm, faces in my face. There was a lot of discussion about me, but it came from outer space, and I didn't pay any attention. Poetry was the only thing that mattered. From Rimbaud I moved to Rilke: "'Strange violin, are you following me?'" I began in German and quoted the whole poem and many of his other poems.

Sometime later I realized Laura was half-carrying me, half-dragging me along the dark, cobbled street, stopping only to let me throw up once in the gutter. We got back to the *pensión* and sank onto the bed. The word *matrimonio* hung in the air. We kissed, tasting only alcohol. My head was spinning; it was like a small spider on a web that was jiggling in a stiff breeze. Thoughts were broken into fragments; through the window I saw the moon.

We rolled around the bed hardly able to focus. She was the same, but other, and I was repelled by that sameness while I had the frightening desire to merge into her. No one here was the man or woman; no one was older or younger. The edges were gone; I was falling, and my stomach heaved and I got up and was sick in the sink.

Laura was asleep and snoring, half dressed and spread across the double bed. How long had she been asleep? Would she remember any of this? I leaned over her, looked at her closely. She had on a white undershirt and bikini briefs, printed in a polka-dot pattern. I felt like Henry Miller in one of his books, clinical in his observation of the female body. Laura had firm skin, pale and freckled; her thighs were soft, her calves muscled. Her feet were bony and strong. Her hands were bigger than mine. With her eyes closed, and her mouth slightly open, her weak chin was more apparent. I wished she hadn't cut her long hair; I had loved it so. I stared at her with longing and revulsion. I wanted to know her, to plumb her depths, but as my eyes bored into her, she grew less and less transparent, more opaque.

What did it mean to be a lesbian? What did it mean to love a woman?

Was it a felt hat and necktie? Was it an escape from male egotism? Was it freedom? Was it a matter of rights? Could it possibly be love?

And if it were love and not curiosity or sexual choreography, then what would that mean for me? I thought back to the young woman who'd stood up in the Sacramento audience and asked the question of Betty Friedan. No one had stood up with her; no one else had demanded that Friedan answer the question. She was alone. Being alone like that, being looked at by everyone, frightened me. I'd had to hand a note to the school nurse when I was six, saying I couldn't be vaccinated for polio because I was a Christian Scientist.

I'd had to leave classes whenever we studied science because it might give me forbidden information about the reality of the body. I'd had to stand with my mother and her ruined face and see people unable to stop staring at her. I didn't have the nerve to be a lesbian, if it meant being isolated and stared at. I needed a movement behind me, and there was no movement.

That night in Alicante I stood by the open window with the sea breeze strengthening, bringing me salt and shame, and I made my decision. It didn't matter that no one we knew could see us here; something about all this wasn't right. It shouldn't be this complicated and this hard. Desire wasn't strong enough in me that it couldn't be diverted. For Laura it seemed only to be about curiosity; for me it seemed more dangerous. Because to really be in love with a woman would change my life. To love a woman would require an honesty I didn't have yet. I was too busy with the project I'd begun in my teens: hiding my story, reinventing myself.

I turned away from the salt breeze and was sick again in the sink, then carefully moved Laura's leg and lay down in the double bed beside her. Laura and I had been fooling ourselves. We had mistaken friendship for something else, something that just wasn't there. We weren't lesbians, never had been, never would be. I didn't even (hearing her snore openmouthed next to me) find her all that attractive. I wouldn't have the courage to stand up, like that woman in Sacramento, and demand any special rights.

The next day, my head as heavy as if the *pensión* roof had collapsed on me the night before, I put it to Laura: We might as well stop trying, and just continue to be good friends. She agreed, in what seemed to be relief.

And from then on, we never drank as much.

❧ SIX ❧

Iberia

In Lola's closet in Barcelona I'd temporarily left behind the blue vinyl suitcase, some books, and most of my clothes when Laura and I set off on our hitchhiking trip. I also left behind two notebooks. The large one from London, whose black cloth cover always recalled a wet umbrella, was full of feverish exhortations to myself about choosing independence and not settling for love. The George Sand notebook began with a gush of descriptive writing that dwindled to a trickle of terse remarks about Laura's coughing keeping me awake.

To describe my travels with Laura around Spain I chose a square, soft-covered journal, with ruled lines as wide as those from elementary school. This journal is all that remains of that trip, along with the Michelin map and some faded tourist brochures. There are no photographs; Laura and I both maintained then that cameras got in the way of "truly seeing." The journal isn't full, and there are gaps of days with no entries. Our mode of travel made it difficult to write consistently, and in any case, I was conflicted as to what to write. Should I describe the world around me, the cities and villages of Spain, the sea, the mountains, and the high plateau, or should I describe Laura and traveling with Laura? And if I described Laura, should I describe her as she really was, sometimes cheerful, often grumpy, occasionally wonderful, very often annoying, so that I could put her in a short story sometime in the future, or should I fictionalize her immediately, so that I could get the practice?

I compromised: I sometimes wrote about a woman I called the Mermaid or, occasionally, Mujer Pescado, the Fish Woman. This was Laura but not-Laura, a Laura transformed by imagination. In these short, plotless paragraphs, I related the underwater life of the Mermaid and how she slept and swam through her dreams ("She slept and while she slept, she swam, and while she swam, she dreamed, and she carried her dreams to the surface and gave me one and then she disappeared").

In reality, the amount of time that Laura spent sleeping was highly irritating to me. I liked to get up in the morning, have my *café con leche,* and get moving; she liked to sleep in, often until ten or eleven, then write down her dreams. When I wasn't writing about the fictional Mermaid, I would allow myself the luxury of complaining, "Another morning hanging around waiting for Laura to get up. And then she wants to boil an egg and have a cup of tea, and the day's practically *over.*" Sometimes as I sat writing in my journal waiting for her to pull herself out of bed in the morning, a rumpled, yawning Laura would look over at me and say, "I hope you're not writing about me."

"The love between women is a refuge and an escape into harmony. In the love between man and woman there is resistance and conflict. Two women do not judge each other, brutalize each other, or find anything to ridicule." Anaïs Nin had written that, about June Miller, and I had faithfully copied it down, sure that she was right. Now I was positive Nin didn't know what she was talking about, and if she'd ever gone hitchhiking around Spain with June Miller, she would have written something else entirely.

In addition to the sleeping issue, there were other conflicts. Laura's yearning for the countryside clashed with mine for city streets. I was a spendthrift, she a penny-pincher. She'd decided on a budget and planned to stick with it, even if that meant eating bread and cheese for meals. I couldn't do without my coffee and croissant in the morning and a hot dinner at night; eating out cheaply and well was part of the pleasure of being in Spain. I wanted to buy poetry books and go to museums; she wanted to sit in a park and read the used Penguin copy of *Don Quixote* she'd brought with her. I was feverish about art, language, history, and culture. She sometimes seemed only to want a vacation.

For purposes of literature, I wanted our travels to be the stuff of magic, as, in fact, my own travels in London, Paris, and Barcelona had been. At the same time I wanted to teach myself to see more clearly and describe more accurately the texture and flavor of the places we passed through. I wanted to set down what happened to us as we traveled, and that meant delineating the many differences between me and Laura, and the complications and irritations of daily life. Years later, while the passages about the Mermaid are fascinating to me, in a tenderly embarrassing way, it's instead the unpoetic voice, what I then dismissed as dull and matter-of-fact *reporting,* that brings that month of travel in Spain to life.

The more factual voice isn't that of an overwrought girl of twenty, so given to fits of exaltation and despair, but that of the writer I was becoming. In the anecdotes of people who picked us up as we hitchhiked, in the scraps of conversation, in the descriptions of the olive groves of Andalusia, the gardens of Córdoba, the paintings of El Greco in Toledo, I see sentences I could have written many years later: simple, clear prose.

What I also see, with no real surprise, is all that the notebooks don't touch on and that memory must now reconstruct. There are a few passing references to drinking too much, a burst of anger at Laura over something or other. The word *lesbian* doesn't come up; in fact, there's nothing about sex at all. Hangovers are rarely mentioned; instead, there are poems in Spanish, by Lorca and Machado, recollections of dreams, responses to paintings, and questions, perhaps written to the person I'd one day become:

> Suddenly I remembered that most all my dreams are about traveling—taking boats or trains or cars or planes . . . I asked myself, *What are you running away from?*

After Alicante, we hitched along the coast and eventually ended up in Granada, an enchanting enough place that even Laura thought was worth spending a few days exploring. In the cold March sunlight, the high mountains of the Sierra Nevada cut white triangles in the soft blue sky. The Muslim caliphs had chosen the city's site because of the views but also, of course, because of the proximity of water from those mountains. Although the Muslims had been in Spain for hundreds of years, they still carried with them the memory of the deserts of the Middle East and Africa, and one of their delights was to turn southern Spain, arid but watered by rivers, into irrigated orchards and gardens. Two rivers ran through Granada, the Darro and the Genil, and the palace of the Alhambra, on the hill overlooking the city, was famous for its pools and fountains.

In Granada Laura and I agreed to go our own ways for a few days. She slept in as long as she wanted, while I went out walking in the city, sitting in cafés, and standing in bookstores reading guidebooks without buying them. I wanted to know the history of the places we passed through, but only enough to get my bearings. I was afraid of being influenced in my perceptions. I didn't want another writer to tell me what to look for. I was less likely to see a travel writer as a fellow pilgrim than as a kind of dictator intent on only one thing: robbing me of surprise. I didn't yet understand that to read a traveler's tale might be part of a conversation about a country and its meanings.

For myself, I couldn't imagine writing a travel book about Spain, or a travel book about anywhere. How could you convey the complexities of place? How could you write about a country without turning into a know-it-all? How much better to use place as a launching pad for fiction, to create characters who moved through a landscape. I could imagine the character of a girl—call her Melissa or Stephanie—walking through the palace of the Alhambra; I could imagine *her* observing her surroundings, but it would be poetic, without dates, without the endless facts that travel books seemed far too jammed with.

All one afternoon I sat in the gardens of the Generalife, next to the Alhambra, in a bower of foliage perfumed with orange and jasmine, writing in my journal about the Moors, the gardens, the fountains, and Stephanie. The Mermaid was somewhere far away, sleeping or reading *Don Quixote*. After an hour or so a young man asked me in English if he could sit with me; he had noticed I was writing. Was I a poet perhaps? Did I speak Spanish? A little? He was a university student and also a poet; we had a talk in broken language about dreams and how to use them in our writing. He quoted part of a beautiful poem by Antonio Machado to me:

> Anoche cuando dormía,
> soñé, ¡bendita ilusión!
> que una fontana fluía
> dentro de mi corazón.
> Di, ¿por qué acequia escondida,

> *agua, vienes hasta mí,*
> *manantial de nueva vida*
> *de donde nunca bebí?*

Laboriously, he tried to translate it for me. I could understand very little but loved the sound of his voice. It was another Spanish than I'd known in Barcelona; softer, with many of the words half-swallowed. The poet was quite different from Monzo and Lluís; he was darker-skinned, moodier, more romantic, my first introduction to the men of the South, so many of whom seemed to be poets and who said they had Gypsy blood. "If you knew more Spanish," said the poet, "you could translate Machado's poetry to English. Or perhaps my poetry if I become famous." He told me about a special year-long course at the University of Granada that enabled foreigners to become proficient in Spanish and to learn about literature, art, and history.

After a while, we walked back through the Alhambra, cool in the shadows, the fountains playing in the courtyard, the walls covered with indecipherable writing—Arabic—down into the city to a bookstore, and he encouraged me to buy a copy of one of Machado's books, containing this marvelous poem, which came to mean so much to me.

> Last night when I was sleeping
> I dreamed—Oh blessed vision!—
> that a fountain flowed
> deep within my heart.
> Tell me, water,
> By what secret channel
> have you come to me,
> A spring of new life
> I've never drunk before?

The poet wanted to take me and Laura up to the caves of Sacromonte that night to hear and see flamenco. Flamenco? Was it dancing or singing or music? It was everything, he told me. It was the language of the heart. We agreed to meet later, at a bar near the *pensión* where Laura and I were staying, but perhaps we got the time wrong, for he never turned up. Instead Laura and I made our way through the old Moorish quarter of the Albacín to the whitewashed caves where Granada's Gypsies played guitars for the tourists and women in flounced, polka-dot dresses took dramatic poses before clacking their heels and castanets. It was touristy but thrilling to us, in part because it was so unexpected. Not having read anything about Gypsy culture or flamenco, we carried away the magical impression that this was a little-known art form of Spain, something we'd discovered on our own. Descending back to the city center, along the rushing Darro River with the palace of the Alhambra floating above us, we were arm in arm, in a festive, dancing mood, and I thought it was just as well the poet hadn't been with us, for it would have only created complications.

From Granada we hitchhiked to Seville, where we finally stayed in a campground outside the city. It had been colder than we expected in Andalusia in March, especially in the evenings, but after a warm day in Seville, Laura decided it was time to move into the countryside, and after having put her off so many times, I had to agree.

When we arrived at the campground it was midafternoon. We paid for a spot and carefully laid out our sleeping bags and the Camping Gaz. We walked in a small forest of birch trees planted by a stream. Laura was enchanted—"Finally! Nature!"—and even I, obscurely worried about the fact that everyone else had a tent or a camper, found it very beautiful and restful to hear water running through the earth and to be among European couples and families, away from the eagle eyes of the elderly widows who ran our *pensiónes* and the boys and men who followed us around the towns like crows hoping for roadkill.

As the sun lowered in the sky, it began to get colder. We put on our sweaters and extra pairs of socks. Laura boiled up some water for tea to warm us. Our dinner was to be sardines, cheese, and bread, and she suddenly wondered if we shouldn't eat now, while there was light, since, belatedly, we realized we had neither flashlight nor lantern. All around us now we smelled chicken and steaks grilling at other campsites.

While we were washing up in the twilight, a boy with wild blond hair came over and asked if we'd like to have a beer with him and his friend in their tent. They were nineteen and Dutch. One of them was quiet, but the other, Hans, who'd approached us, had an opinion on everything. A student from a small town in Holland, he liked boxing and judo, he told us, and brawling with the police on Saturday nights. "I admire strength more than anything," Hans said after a couple of beers (he'd clearly had a few before we arrived). "That's why I don't like girls."

"Why is that?" said Laura, irritated.

"Because they're too weak."

His friend said, "Now, Hans, they're our guests."

"They're weak, and they can't defend themselves. We've been traveling in Spain for two weeks and we've heard stories about foreign girls being raped. They have tears and cries for mama, but against the stiletto, they can't do anything."

"Okay, we're going now," said Laura. "Thanks for putting the idea of the stiletto in our minds."

The friend said, "Just shout if anything happens. We'll be here and save you."

Hans jumped up and did some judo, awkwardly, outside the tent. "I can take on a man with a knife, easy." He kicked his long leg up.

Laura and I went back to our sleeping bags. It was about nine o'clock now, and freezing. "The stars are so beautiful," said Laura. We lay close together for comfort. She fell asleep before I did.

I recalled the comfortable bed in the *pensión* in Seville, with *rejas* over the windows, and a courtyard draped with burgundy and orange bougainvillea. In the center of the patio was a small fountain and more pots, blue and white, of geraniums. Flat, riverside Seville, more than anyplace else we'd been in Spain, recalled Southern California to me, with its arched openings, red tile roofs, and ironed grilled doorways, its patios, and palm trees. Here it was possible to think back through history, from the Spanish-style architecture of California to colonial Mexico to Seville itself, once queen of the Indies trade and one of the greatest ports in the world before the Guadalquivir silted up.

All night both of us dreamed of stilettos and violence, when we slept at all, that is, for the ground was hard and the sleeping bags merely flannel. After that, Laura never mentioned camping again.

Córdoba was suffering under a cold spell that frosted its orange trees with snow; one day, Laura chose to stay inside the *pensión*, just reading. She was still tired and coughing some, and a night outside hadn't helped. I went to the Grand Mosque and marveled at the forest of red and white striped arches in its interior and then went looking for a bookshop. I read a little in one of the guidebooks about the city and found out that Córdoba had been, from 756 to 1031, the pearl of al-Andalus, the queen of Western Islam, second only to Constantinople. It had been founded by the Umayyad dynasty, a breakaway family from Damascus who had established a caliphate. I gravitated toward a rack of English books. Laura despaired of my buying expensive imported books, but it was hard to resist. I kept waiting for her to finish *Don Quixote* so I could start it, but at nine hundred pages, it seemed as though it would take her forever.

I picked up a paperback by a writer I'd never heard of, Jorge Luis Borges, called *Labyrinths,* and was immediately certain I had to have it. Books very frequently seemed to have that oracular power over me, as if the voice on the page reached out and took me by the hand and pulled me inside, commanding me to listen. I grew up in a religion where words were revered—if they were written in the King James Version of the Bible, that is, or by Mary Baker Eddy. We had one supreme text, *Science and Health,* which was consulted as if it were the *I Ching.* The Christian Science Church provided small sticks of blue chalk, and once a week I saw my mother doing what she called "Mental Work," underlining sentences and paragraphs in her Bible for the Daily Lesson. She studied these cryptic phrases every morning and quoted them in times of need. It's no wonder I looked to words as divine messengers bearing wisdom and inspiration.

I read the narratives in *Labyrinths* while sitting in the Patio of the Orange Trees outside the mosque. I wanted very much at that moment to be a writer like Borges, hinting at vast erudition while not being required to produce any scholarship, never having to create characters or plots, and all the while pointing to the huge, inexplicable mysteries of time and alternate realities. In my notebook I transcribed a passage from my favorite tale, "Tlön, Uqbar, Orbis Tertius":

> One of the schools in Tlön has reached the point of denying time. It reasons that the present is undefined, that the future has no other reality than as present hope, that the past is no more than present memory. Another school declares that the *whole of time* has already happened and that our

> life is a vague memory or dim reflection, doubtless
> false and fragmented, of an irrevocable process.

I'd been accustomed to metaphysical thinking from childhood, since Christian Science maintained that the physical world did not exist, nor did evil or unhappiness; they were only our misapprehension of the true state of God's mind. Of course, I no longer believed in Mary Baker Eddy's teachings, but my early training in the power of belief had left me with an understanding of the human capacity to make up systems to suit one's temperament. Borges created possible systems out of curiosity and playfulness; still, this passage of his corresponded to what I believed might be the truth. For what could be closer to my *lived experience* than "that the present is undefined, that the future has no other reality than as present hope, that the past is no more than present memory"?

While I was reading, I was approached by a tall, sloe-eyed young man, Fernando, who spoke some English, albeit with an odd Scandinavian accent. This was because he had a girlfriend from Sweden, whom he'd met in Málaga. She was helping to support him while he studied. He had been to Stockholm, he said. It was very cold. Did I want to walk around Córdoba and he'd tell me its history?

I was hesitant at first. I'd found the south of Spain very different, and part of that difference lay in its conservative view of women—they were Madonnas or whores, *novias* or *putas*—a view reinforced by the legions of Northern European girls who came to the Costa del Sol apparently looking for only one thing: a handsome Latin lover to spend a week with. You couldn't talk long with a man from the South without hearing about the Scandinavians, often lumped together as *las Suecas* (the Swedes). As light-haired North Americans we were included in that willing breed. Our mere appearance on the street in corduroy jeans or with backpacks seemed enough to show how shameless, or *sin vergüenza*, we were.

But I decided that it couldn't do any harm to spend some time with Fernando, for at least it kept the others who'd been bothering me at bay. Fernando and I walked around the whole town, past patios with dozens of pots strapped to the white walls and tiled entryways. "A thousand years ago," said Fernando, "Córdoba was a seat of learning and poetry, with universities and libraries holding thousands of volumes, hundreds of mosques and synagogues, and as many hammans, with a thousand pools for bathing. The great scientific studies of the Greeks and the philosophy of early Western civilization were kept alive. The manuscripts were copied and recopied. Averroës, the great scholar, lived here, and so did Maimonides, the Jewish philosopher."

We had sherry and *raciones* of shrimp in garlic, meatballs, and *patatas bravas*. Fernando ate hungrily. I paid, since he seemed short of cash. In the bar, dark and smoky, with sawdust on the floor, two old men sat in a corner with *cañas* of beer. Fernando said that they were singers, masters of the *cante jondo,* a form of singing that went back to the time of the Moors. He suggested that he could ask them to join us for tapas and perhaps they'd sing a little. I was thrilled when they came over and, with very little prompting, began to clap their hands and break into a wild, aching song. Fernando taught me the rhythmic clapping, and we had more to drink and the hours went by. He asked me to stay longer in Córdoba, and I was very tempted. I felt, for the first time, that I was in touch with something deep within the Spanish soul. But when I returned to the *hostal* and found Laura waiting patiently for me, having boiled some chicken noodle soup for her dinner on the Camping Gaz, I felt guilty.

Besides, I couldn't afford Fernando. I was nearly at the end of my pesetas.

The Fowlers were just the kind of tourists Laura and I loved to hate: Americans, first of all, traveling in a new tan and white VW bus, bought in Germany; a nuclear family, with the father driving, the children quarreling, and the mother reading aloud from James Michener's *Iberia*, a book we felt free to despise without having read, first, because it was a bloated doorstop written for a popular audience and, second, because it caused people—like the Fowlers, a dull, self-satisfied academic family from Arkansas on sabbatical—not to really look at what they were seeing, the landscape they were moving through, the country they were supposedly visiting.

So even though we were secretly grateful that they had picked us up and were taking us many miles up the highway through Castile to Toledo, grateful in spite of ourselves that the car was clean, that they offered us snacks, that they showed a parental concern for us, we also felt free to look down upon them, from our lofty perch of travelers who knew Spain, because we'd walked its streets and highways and met its people instead of merely driving through the country reading from guidebooks.

We'd left the green-fringed rivers and dusty olive groves of Andalusia behind, and now the dry Castilian plateau, magnificent and barren, rolled past: gorges and tableland, hills topped by ruined Moorish fortresses, castles in the distance, all of it pale ochre, bleached by sun and wind. This land had a grandeur unlike that of Andalusia and the Mediterranean coastline. It was La Mancha, home to the errant knight, his nag, and his servant. Laura looked out the window with interest; and I realized this was one of the rare times in two weeks that we'd been *together*, sitting on the same seat, in a vehicle, where we weren't having to fend off a truck driver or make conversation. Usually she made me sit in the front seat, talking with the driver and dealing with wandering hands, while she sat in the back and snoozed. Now I saw that she had actually become interested in Spain; she was thinking about Sancho Panza and his don riding over the high plateau.

In high school I'd played Dulcinea in a production of *Don Quixote*: I'd had little to do but keep a skeptical expression on my face and run barefoot across the stage, robust in my bodice and skirt. With a raucous laugh ("Try to sound bawdy," said the seventeen-year-old director), I mocked the knight who believed I was a lady and not a dirty peasant girl. Rob had been a minor character in that play, a villager, and at the thought of Rob, my stomach tightened, but not with anticipation. I might be home in a week. That was far too soon.

"Aren't you two a little nervous just traveling around by yourselves, hitchhiking?" asked Marge.

"It's really the best way to get to know the Spanish," I said, in the voice I used to speak to adults. "We've met lots of interesting people on the road."

That was only half true. The kind of people who picked up two girls hitching were sometimes Good Samaritans, and sometimes slightly crazy. Earlier this morning, we had walked out of Córdoba along a wet, muddy road, followed by an American guy who wanted to "thumb" with us. We hadn't been encouraging but let him stand with us for a while in a cold wind, while he told us how hard it had been to get rides. A semi stopped, and the driver said, "Just two of you. Just the girls."

A little nervously Laura and I got in, and the door slammed on the guy with the oversize backpack. Our driver was young and vehement. When he found out we were Americans, he went on a rant against our country's wealth and imperialism, the Vietnam War, the American military bases in Spain. A couple of times he became so angry it seemed he might kick us out of the cab.

"We've had some strange experiences," Laura chimed in. "But nothing dangerous. And we've had fantastic times too. We were waiting outside a village called Carmona, when a car in a caravan of students stopped. They were on their way to Córdoba, and they planned to stop at every bar they could along the route. It was sort of a moving pub crawl. And they just picked us up along with them, and we had a great time."

"That's very dangerous," said Mr. Fowler from the front seat. "Drinking and driving. I suspect from some of the accidents we've narrowly avoided that there's far too much of that going on."

Laura and I stifled a laugh. "You're right, sir," said Laura, and winked at me. "But the Spaniards don't really drink that much compared to the foreigners." She'd noticed, as I had, some crumpled beer cans in a bag.

Marge wanted to know if Laura and I were students. I started to explain about dropping out and the school strikes, but I could see from her husband's haircut that Vietnam wasn't up for discussion. Instead I began telling her about Granada and how I was thinking of returning there to spend a year at the university studying Spanish. No sooner had I said it than I realized this was something I very much wanted to do. Maybe I could even start this fall. That was only six months away. If only I had my birthday earlier in the year, like Laura; then I could have been finished with the Bank of Battle Creek in January.

"What about you, Laura?" asked Marge.

"I'm going on to Italy and Greece," she said, but her voice sounded uncertain. "I'll be traveling on my own after Spain. Then, in the fall, I guess I'll probably return to college."

"I'm glad to hear that," said Mr. Fowler. "There's far too much of this dropping in and out of college going on, in my opinion. Young people need to be encouraged to stick with one thing. And they shouldn't be in college just to get out of the draft either. I have far too many students like that."

I resisted the temptation to stick out my tongue at his crewcut, and Laura nudged me. After a while, Marge turned back to James Michener; she skipped forward to read about Madrid, for the Fowlers were heading there next. Laura began to doze, with her head on my shoulder, and I listened with half an ear:

". . . Catholicism . . . Golden Age . . . pride . . . arrogance . . . Philip II . . . bankers from Genoa . . . expulsion of the Jews . . . Inquisition . . . auto-da-fé . . ." until suddenly I heard a passage that seemed to speak to me:

> How utterly lovely the Puerta del Sol was in those days, how exciting for a foreign tourist! This word has come into ill repute in recent years, because so many tourists have gone abroad with no preparation which would enable them to appreciate what they were about to see and no humility to make them approach the country on its own terms. In Spain I have always been a tourist and have been rather proud of that fact. This is the book of a tourist and the experiences herein are those which are open to any intelligent traveler. If, as I once heard an Englishman say, 'to be a tourist is to stand gape-eyed with love,' I have been one, and never more so than in my first days in the Puerta del Sol.

Perhaps James Michener did know a thing or two about travel after all, I thought. He was not ashamed to be a tourist, not ashamed to stand gape-eyed with love and to write a book about it. A very long book. ". . . Carlos V . . . Holy Roman Empire . . . gout . . . keg of anchovies . . . Juana la Loca . . ."

In spite of Michener's paean to Madrid—probably because of my friendship with Lluís and Monza—I'd expected the capital city to be nothing more than a cold, faceless metropolis, whose sole purpose was to issue edicts and regulations aimed at curtailing the rights and freedoms of the far superior Catalans. Madrid was the lair of the beast, Franco, and his puppet prince, Juan Carlos, whom he was said to be grooming for the succession. Madrid was the evil center of the spider web of the Falange. I thought that our time there would be short, just enough for me to cash my wire from the Bank of Battle Creek at the American Express and head back to Barcelona with Laura to collect my suitcase and notebooks, before taking the train to London and finding a flight back to Los Angeles.

But, surprisingly, I was gape-eyed with love as soon as our ride dropped us off at the Tourist Information office and we made our way to a *pensión* on the Plaza Mayor. Laura felt it too. Madrid had an easygoing quality in spite of its bustle and sophistication. We both noticed immediately that no boys had followed us through the streets, no men had hissed.

"It's a big city, but it doesn't somehow feel like it," she said when we'd dropped our packs in the room and sat at the table looking out the window on the massive square. The Plaza Mayor was a vast, stone-paved expanse, enclosed on all sides by what seemed to be one continuous building, several stories high, with colonnades running under the whole thing. The buildings were broken by small towers with thin spires, many of them with clocks, and the windows had iron balconies. Built in the seventeenth century, the Plaza Mayor had once been used for coronations, bullfights, and public executions.

Now it was a bit shabby, in a pleasant way. Nuns in long black habits crossed the square in pairs, on their way to and from one of the many convents nearby; sometimes a crocodile of uniformed schoolgirls followed them; they were also in pairs, dark-haired, impeccable, giggling. The Guardia Civil also walked in pairs; sometimes they rode horses through the square, and the flag of Spain, along with the flag of the Falange, hung from several official-looking buildings.

In the colonnades and in the small squiggly streets off the plaza were dozens of tiny shops, selling hats, corsets, toys, books, umbrellas—a shop for every object— and behind the counter a well-dressed man or woman who would sell it to you. I often walked in the colonnades and noticed that the shade in Madrid had a different smell than the sun. For it was now almost April and heating up on the high plateau where the city had been built. The light in the plaza was bold, and the heat smelled of horses and ancient blood and gold and glory. But in the colonnades the scent was poor and dusty, with the dry scent of passing nuns and priests, the cheap black tobacco smoked by all the men.

My favorite shop was one that sold fans of every size, mantillas and mantilla combs, and enormous Manila shawls. These were the kinds of shawls that Goya's women wore, and I wanted one intensely, a soft silk or thin wool shawl, with brilliant colors of red and yellow, to wrap around me and help me be Spanish inside, long after I'd left this country.

But, of course, I didn't want to leave now, and neither did Laura.

We went to the Prado and I returned several times, and the Retiro Park, and the flea market of the Rastro, and even out to Escorial, an enormous structure of buildings around a central courtyard that made even the Plaza Mayor look modest. Most of all we liked just to walk through the streets, in the morning, in early afternoon, in the hours after siesta and long into the night. We were used, by now, to the Spanish habit of eating at ten and staying up until two, but always before, from Valencia to Córdoba, we'd felt a little unsafe being out at night. In Madrid no one bothered us, and that turned us into citizens of the street, too, just like all the others.

We'd planned to stay two days; then it was three, then five, then a week. I'd gone to the American Express and found a wire from Mr. Butterworth, cashed it into traveler's checks, and felt rich again. I no longer had to ration myself to one *café con leche* a day. If I wanted to sit in a café in the afternoon and have two, along with a small *bocadillo* of ham or a pastry, in addition to my morning coffee, that was fine. I bought some books in Spanish and a few more in English for the journey homeward, so that I could carry some of Spain with me back to California. I wasn't rich—or spendthrift enough—to buy a large silk Manila shawl, hand-embroidered with flowers and birds, but I did buy a soft red shawl of light wool that I wrapped around my shoulders in the evenings or when I sat at the window of our *pensión*, looking out at the Plaza Mayor and writing.

I bought a new notebook, too, one that I used to describe the paintings of the Prado and the streets of the city and that I believed would be my homeward journal, bridging the gap from a life of imagination and independence to one of narrowed hopes and doomed love back home.

"I can't imagine us parting so soon," said Laura one evening. "I can't imagine trying to travel without you." We were in the midst of what had become our daily ritual, visiting the *tabernas* and *tascas* in the streets around Plaza Santa Ana for the tapas that made up our dinner. Each evening we hit a particular street, and moved from bar to bar in what Madrileños called the *tapeo,* or tapa crawl. In a *tasca* with beautiful hand-painted tiles around the inner door and behind the bar, we tried octopus and squid; in another, loud with flamenco music, we sampled *callos a la madrileño,* or tripe, with onions, tomato, some chorizo, and some parts of a pig better left undescribed. The atmosphere was always friendly in these places; the waiters, in white shirts with bow ties, poured us one small glass of wine and brought out small plates for us to try. We stood at the bars and like the people around us threw our used napkins, toothpicks, olive pits on the floor into the mix of detritus. Strangely it didn't seem unsanitary; it just seemed fun.

"I know," I said, leaning into her as newcomers pushed up to the bar. "Suddenly the time seems to have rushed by." I meant the month since she'd been here, but also my three and a half months in Europe. Standing in a Madrid *tasca,* mildly intoxicated, with Spanish in my ears, and a plate of *patatas bravas* and another of black olives, and a third of tiny meatballs in front of me, with Laura's eyes upon me, it seemed terribly unfair that I should ever have to leave any of this.

Something had shifted between us; something was now open again, after being closed at the beginning of our trip around Spain. It had begun to shift in Seville, perhaps, as we huddled together on the bare, cold earth, ready to jump up to defend ourselves if men with stilettos appeared. It had begun to shift outside Carmona, when we'd sat for hours waiting for a ride, but not impatiently. I'd drawn a picture of the village, and Laura had read her book. We'd heard a hum in the distance, as if locusts were approaching, and had stood up to see what was coming down the road. It was a bicycle race; fifty cyclists whizzed past us, and then they were gone. Afterward we'd been picked up by the caravan of students en route from Seville to Córdoba who included us in their car *tapeo.*

It had shifted in the Fowlers' van, when we'd stifled our laughter at them, when Laura had dozed on my shoulder, and again in Toledo, when, without saying much about it, we'd visited the museum and cathedral together instead of going our separate ways as we had in Andalusia. In Toledo, we had kissed before we went to sleep in our double bed, not a sexual kiss but a loving one. Now, in Madrid, with only a short time left, it seemed as though we'd finally figured out how to travel together, what each of us needed to feel good.

"Why don't we just stay here? Here in Madrid." I put my hand on her arm, but I could feel her draw away a little, hesitate over her words.

"How could we live?" Laura shook her head.

"We could teach English! I could . . . support you with my money until we get settled."

"What about Italy? What about Greece? I know you love Spain, and I've really come to love it, too. But all this time—I've wanted to see Italy. Neither of us would know the language there. Really. I want you with me."

She'd said before she wanted me to come to Italy with her, but now it seemed stronger than a wish. It was what I wanted, too. I couldn't bear to be parted from her, not yet.

We left the bar and began walking down the street, in the direction of the Puerto del Sol. All around us—it was about nine—were the people of Madrid: elegant women in suits, with bouffant hairdos; men with briefcases; schoolkids with satchels; tiny old ladies in black carrying string bags of food. The Puerta del Sol, the heart of the city, was all neon and street lamps, motor scooters and honking cars, young couples walking hand in hand, crowds of students, tourists like us.

"Do you want some dinner?" I asked. We had left the busy square and were suddenly in quieter streets.

"No, I'm full from the tapas. Let's stop somewhere and get another drink close to home."

Home, she'd said, and it sounded natural. We put our arms around each other and matched our steps, walking in perfect harmony. Her springy step had come back over the last week, and I felt buoyed up by her.

"I don't see why I couldn't at least go to Italy with you," I said. "What does it matter to anyone if I'm gone another month?"

"What about your return fare?"

"I can write to the bank again. Why not?"

The next day, when Laura went out to buy some food, I sat at the table overlooking the Plaza Mayor, writing to Mr. Butterworth with what I thought was impeccable logic, that when I'd asked for money to be sent to Madrid, what I really should have asked for was *more* money and for that money to be sent to London at a slightly later date. I apologized for any inconvenience, thanked him profusely, said that I was learning a great deal of Spanish and thinking about enrolling in the University of Granada in the fall. I wrote too that I had an opportunity to go to Italy, home of some of the greatest museums in the world. I couldn't pass it up. In another month, right around May 1, I'd be back in England and ready to go home.

Afterward I wrote a postcard to Rob. I should have written him a letter, but I thought my news might be better conveyed in tiny script on an art postcard of one of Hieronymous Bosch's paintings from the Prado. "Laura has suggested that we continue traveling for a few more weeks together, to France and Italy. I don't feel like I can say no because she's only now starting to feel better (I told you she had bronchitis! for almost three weeks!). But really it won't be that much longer. I'll be back in May. I miss you!"

I added as I always did, "I love you."

Laura came in, smiling, with her string bag full of cheese, bread, and a bottle of red wine. We sat eating lunch at the table looking out at the square and drinking out of the bottle since we had no glasses.

"Won't you miss Spain?"

"I'll be back," I said. "No country has ever meant as much to me—all of it, Barcelona, Granada, Madrid. I love it all and I can't decide which place I love best."

"Someday do you think you'll write about all this?" Laura gestured out the window at the nuns and schoolchildren and Guardia Civil on their horses.

"I'm writing it all down now. Everything that's happened on this trip."

She looked a little nervous suddenly.

"Don't worry," I said. "I never write anything much about you. In case somebody might read it." I meant Rob. "But I'm remembering it as hard as I can. Maybe someday I'll put us in a story."

"Then they'll read the story. Don't say I slept too much. I *know* that's what you think. Don't say we got drunk all the time. Don't say . . ."

"I'll wait at least twenty-five years, how's that? We'll be really old then, and who will care?"

"Maybe we won't even know each other."

"Of course we will."

"Maybe you'll marry Rob and have five children."

"I'm never getting married. Especially to him."

"Me either. And definitely not to him."

"It's a pact then."

She laughed. "Don't write that we drank a whole bottle of wine in the middle of the afternoon."

"I'll say we spent our time in Madrid improving our minds by going to the Prado, and then one day, giddy with spring, we packed up our rucksacks and stuck out our fingers and headed to France and Italy. Better?"

"I like the sound of that."

Outside the window, on the Plaza Mayor, life went on, as it had for centuries, and we were content to watch it, to eat our lunch and drink our wine, and to rest easy in the fact that, unlike everyone else who'd come and gone from this square, we would live forever, or at least for a very long time, without ever getting old.

SEVEN

The Garden of Forking Paths

I DRAGGED MY blue vinyl suitcase, now packed with books by Borges, Cervantes, and Lorca, Vasari's *Lives of the Artists,* and a history of the Medici family, into my new room at the Great Russell Street YWCA in London. In my gray rucksack was a Spanish matador's jacket, slightly stained with blood, which I'd found in a Madrid flea market and which I planned to give to Rob. I also carried my journals and sketchbook in the rucksack, along with a few shabby clothes. I had abandoned my black hat and long black coat in Barcelona. Laura I'd parted from at the train station in Rome. Tomorrow I planned to pick up the money Mr. Butterworth would have wired from Battle Creek and to buy a cheap ticket to Los Angeles.

The double room spilled over with feminine clothing and toiletries and smelled like a woman, not a girl, the kind of woman I didn't know—one who wore a thin red nightgown and matching peignoir and bedroom scuffs with a fluff of white at the toes, one who smoked Carltons. I removed some of my roommate's extra clothing from my bed and lay down. Just as I was falling asleep, the door opened, and a waft of perfume entered and introduced herself in an faintly Southern accent: "Leanne Lorimer."

She held out a soft, manicured hand, and I took it limply. She was about five eight, twenty-three or twenty-four, dressed in a bright coral sleeveless shift, stockings, and sandals that showed toenails enameled to match her shift. She had a coral and blue scarf through her dark pageboy, and though she was beautifully made up and absolutely stunning, she looked—not that I knew much about fashion—a few years out of date. Or so I thought, just before I fell back onto my pillow with a giant yawn. Didn't scarves go out with Jackie Kennedy?

The next morning I set off confidently on foot for the American Express on Haymarket. I marveled at the change in the city streets now that warmer weather had come. I'd been living in a perpetual spring since March, and now London, too, had trees leafed out and birds singing, even if they were just sparrows in Leicester Square. I asked for my mail at the desk and found letters from Rob and Ruthie, giving me news of home and much love. But from Battle Creek came only a curt letter from Mr. Butterworth explaining that the first "disbursement" for travel had been a onetime exception; that the second "disbursement" to Madrid had been in the nature of emergency funds; that I had clearly mismanaged my grandmother's money and had misrepresented what I was doing with it—that, in short, I had made my bed and could lie in it. I wouldn't be getting anything further from the Bank of Battle Creek until I turned twenty-one in October.

I left the American Express and walked the few blocks to Trafalgar Square, which in the sunshine and crowded with as many picture-snapping tourists as pigeons looked completely unlike the

London I recalled from the winter, when I used to make my way so happily up the steps of the National Gallery. Today I had no heart for the museums I'd planned to revisit. In my pocket, changed from lire, was about £15. Since I'd been in London last, Great Britain had shifted over to the decimal system; now there were no more shillings and half shillings. But costs were the same: Each night at the YWCA was £3.50. I walked over to the post office near the church of St. Martin-in-the-Fields and telegraphed to Mr. Butterworth: "Arrived London. No money. Desperate." And to my father I wired the same message, with the request he call Mr. Butterworth right away.

This done, I felt better. They surely wouldn't ignore pleading telegrams like that. In fact, just sending telegrams with the word "desperate" made me feel interestingly dramatic. I walked over to one of the cheap travel shops upstairs in one of the shabby lanes near Charing Cross Station and made a reservation for a flight from London to Los Angeles in three days. I said I'd be back tomorrow with the money.

"Iceland," Leanne declared that evening, during dinner at the Indian restaurant across the street from the Y, "isn't just a large rock in the middle of the sea, a place to refuel. Iceland is one of the oldest democracies in the world, a thousand years old."

She waved her Carlton with red-tipped fingernails over a plate of half-finished curry and painted vivid scenes of geysers and lava fields, of storm-tossed waves crashing against high, inhospitable cliffs, of a people self-reliant and proud. She spoke of the sagas and the fact that though they were written in Old Norse, contemporary Icelanders could still read them, because they'd preserved their language and still spoke in just the same way as their ancestors, the Norsemen and women who'd settled the island in the ninth century.

Eventually she came around to the story of how she'd ended up there for a month earlier this spring. It began with a car accident in Raleigh and a settlement of some thousands of dollars that had made it possible to walk away from her boring job in data processing and her boyfriend, Ralph. She had decided to stop off in Iceland for a day, had been invited to a cocktail party at the SAS hotel, and had met an Icelandic man named Gunnar.

"I was wearing a black cocktail dress. He knew I wasn't Icelandic. We started talking and couldn't stop. He was so different from the crass, stupid men I knew in Raleigh, the college boys, the men I worked with. He wasn't a *bit* like Ralph at home. Gunnar is very tall, and blond. Of course, he spoke perfect English; he was well read, well traveled. He stayed with me that first night, and the next day I moved into his bachelor apartment. It was everything I'd dreamed of. . . ."

Gunnar turned out to be married, however, and although Gunnar claimed that he wanted a divorce, his wife hoped to work things out. The wife was furious when friends told her about Leanne. So, in spite of the delicious plans for Gunnar to teach Leanne to ski, and to go horseback riding, and to drive the entire ring road around the island once the snow melted, Gunnar, an honorable man, began to urge Leanne to fly onward to Europe while he sorted out his feelings about his marriage.

Leanne lit another cigarette. Her dark hair was shiny, held in place by a red bandeau. "He told me, 'You've dreamed about Europe for years. You can't miss this opportunity. Travel to all those places you've wanted to go—France, Italy, England—then we'll see how you feel. And how I feel.'"

"At first," she said sadly, "I thought Gunnar was right. But I dreamed of him the whole time I was in Paris. I just couldn't enjoy it without him. We talked on the phone, we wrote, but I could feel him slipping away. He asked for more time, kept urging me to go on with my travels. But the days were empty. I couldn't speak French. All I could do was shop."

So she'd come to London, in part because Gunnar had given her the name of a good friend, a fellow medical student from the Royal College of Surgeons, a Persian called Manny, who'd been wonderful to her. "He takes me out as often as he can, to theaters and concerts and for dinner, and we talk about Gunnar. But I can't really confide in him—not like *this*."

Then, perhaps mindful she'd been talking straight for over an hour, she asked me where I'd been. I told her about my most recent travels, the last three weeks in Italy. It was strange to realize that the time with Laura was now over and that all our adventures, so vivid and real, were beginning the long and convoluted process that would turn them into amusing anecdotes.

I described to Leanne how Laura and I had arrived in Genoa from the south of France, which had been a wet week of Fiats and Peugeots speeding past us and spattering us with mud. We'd had potato gnocchi the first night, one of many delicious meals to come at neighborhood trattorias. After Genoa, we'd gone to Milan, where a widow who rented us a room caught us cooking an omelet with gorgonzola cheese on the burner of the Camping Gaz on top of an antique table with a glass top. In our surprise and horror at her sudden appearance, Laura spilled the egg mixture all over the glass, where it dripped off onto the rug.

I told Leanne about the peculiar brother and sister who'd picked us up en route to Bergamo, offering to take us to a hotel where we could "wash our hands." They had then asked us if we had passports and wanted to *fare amore*. Laura and I had stared at them in horror.

Make love?! With them? We'd persuaded them to let us out but then had had to hike several miles back to the highway where they'd first picked us up.

We'd stayed in Lugano in Switzerland, then dipped down to Verona and Assisi. We'd spent Easter Week in Orvieto, where we'd hung around the small circus that was giving performances, daring each other to join up: Laura as a bareback rider, me as a juggler.

Leanne listened and was shocked and intrigued. "I can't believe you were hitchhiking. The two of you must be very brave, or very foolish. Didn't anything bad ever happen to you?"

Some stories were probably better left untold. "Oh, just the usual," I said cheerfully. "Constant harassment, especially further south. Near rape. I had to punch a guy once. Several very tricky situations in cars. We were followed all the time—once, we ran to a cop for help; he put us in his police car and said he'd take us to our hotel, and then he started driving out of town. We had to scream and shout and threaten."

Leanne shuddered. "I wouldn't enjoy that kind of traveling. What happened to your friend Laura?"

"She went on to Greece. And I'm heading home to California in the next few days."

"I bet you're glad to be back in a safe country. Iceland is *very* safe."

Back in the Y, in our room, Gunnar dominated the conversation, as Leanne, now in her red nightgown and peignoir, bought at the Galeries Lafayette in Paris and clearly purchased with an Icelandic lover in mind, told me every detail of their relationship and its bittersweet end, when Gunnar decided perhaps he really should try harder with his wife.

I kept my story of parting from Laura to myself. We had walked around Rome all afternoon, arm in arm, eating ice cream and reminiscing.

"I feel," said Laura, "that we finally figured out how to travel with each other. Oh, I *wish* you'd asked your Mr. Butterworth to send your money here so we could have gone on to Greece together. I can't imagine it without you." She had the bounce back in her step; she was nothing like the cranky and confused cougher of Barcelona. She was my Laura again, and my heart ached to leave her.

"We'll travel again," I promised, but my eyes filled with tears. "I'll never forget these two months."

"Me either. I love you. We'll see each other soon, at home." We kissed and pressed our bodies close. Now it was Laura who felt like the family member I was parting from. "I love you, too," I told her.

"Be careful," we admonished each other, in a last clutch, before I stepped back into the moving train. "Be safe. Don't talk to strange men!" were the last words we hurled at each other as the train pulled out of the station.

The next day at the American Express I found no letter and no wire. I returned to the bucket shop and was told I'd lost my reservation but could be on another flight next week. I waited until 4 PM, when it would be 8 o'clock in the morning in Los Angeles, and placed a collect call from one of the red phone booths near the British Museum. Through the crackling of the phone lines, I heard my stepmother's irritated voice refusing to accept the call.

Even with this bad news, I refused to lose hope. My father had left for the office already; I'd try again. Probably Mr. Butterworth just had to fill out some papers, because transferring money out of a trust fund wasn't quick and easy. I still had £6, enough to pay for another night tomorrow, and since Leanne didn't seem to be going anywhere and had *offered,* there was no reason to think she wouldn't loan me some money temporarily. I'd told her about the bank, and there being a misunderstanding about when I'd be leaving for California.

It was a clear, heartbreakingly soft late afternoon, with a scent of flowering hawthorns and lilacs. I bought a copy of *Time Out,* thinking of going to a half-price play. I sat on the steps of the British Museum and opened it, and my eye fell upon a photograph of Borges. He was in London, all the way from Buenos Aires, and he was scheduled to give several talks over the next couple of weeks. The first talk was tonight.

The room where he was speaking at the ICA wasn't terribly large (the next lectures would be moved to Westminster Hall to accommodate the crowds), and I was surprised to see that many in the audience were as young as me, boys with very long hair and girls in skirts to their ankles and mounds of silver jewelry. Borges came slowly into the room on the arm of a beautiful young woman. He was about seventy and dressed impeccably in a suit with a vest, a tie, and a handkerchief in his pocket. His hair was thinning, dark gray and brilliantined back from his forehead. I wasn't sure why he moved his head so stiffly or why his heavy-lidded eyes had such a fixed look. He was helped into a straight-backed chair and sat very upright. His English accent was British, hardly Spanish at all, and that surprised me, as did his fluency. Yet his manner of speech, laced with long silences and odd, old-fashioned words, was formal, at times as if he were reading, or reciting from a memorized text.

By the end of the evening, of course, I realized, from things he told us and from questions from the audience, that he was both blind and bilingual. He'd grown up with an English grandmother and had had an English governess; many of his favorite books as a child were by British authors, Robert Louis Stevenson, H. G. Wells, Sir Walter

Scott—authors it surprised me that a recondite Argentine author would have read. His blindness was hereditary and had come on slowly. Even now, he told us, the blindness was more yellow than black.

He spoke for some time about his own "essay-fictions," in which reading was as important as writing; about his interest in the labyrinth, "the maze that amazes"; his fascination with Poe and Chesterton and all detective fiction, which was the most classic of literary forms, because it always had a beginning, middle, and end. He spoke of his translation work in the past, how he had translated many works of English literature into Spanish, including Virginia Woolf's *A Room of One's Own* and *Orlando*. He told us that he'd recently been in Iceland and how that journey had fulfilled a longing he'd always had to experience the country of the great sagas. He had long been a student and teacher of Anglo-Saxon, and now he was planning to learn Old Norse.

As he spoke about the sagas, I called upon all that Leanne had told me about Iceland last night: the great lava plateaus, the horses, the wind-torn cliffs. I recognized Borges as a fellow reader, with a passionate erudition I aspired to, able to cross-reference texts with nimbleness, able to hint at worlds beyond our worlds. Old Norse was somehow linked with *Don Quixote* and with Japanese and Arab scholars, and with detective fiction, and with the tango, and with the *Encyclopedia Britannica,* the 11th edition.

When I came out of the lecture I felt awake and alive, and completely unconcerned about money and other worries. Borges gave me the same feeling that Henry Miller once had—that riches awaited in life—and I walked back to the YWCA, breathing in the hawthorn-and-lilac-scented evening air, loving the faces of those I passed, eager to read, to write, to translate, and to travel. I felt that my life had changed by hearing and seeing him, and also that every choice I'd made that had brought me to London the very week he was to speak was fated, in a very Borgesian way.

In one of the stories I'd read in Córdoba, "The Garden of Forking Paths," Borges had written, "In all fiction, when a man is faced with alternatives, he chooses one at the expense of others. . . . He thus *creates* various futures, various times which start others that will in their turn branch out and bifurcate in other times."

Borges aroused my curiosity about detective fiction and made me appreciate its classical structure and its possibilities. He spoke of translation as an art form. He enthused about Virginia Woolf as not only a writer but a publisher, which led me to learn about the Hogarth Press. And his praise of the sagas of the Icelanders watered a seed that Leanne had planted the night before. In due course I would become a writer of detective fiction, a feminist author claiming Woolf as a foremother, a printer and publisher, a Norwegian translator, and a frequent traveler to the lands of the far North.

Chance or perhaps fate brought Leanne into my life, and Borges as well; my future was created, and I began to create my future, without yet knowing that I'd taken one path and not another, that sweet May evening of 1971 as I walked home from the ICA to save the price of a tube trip.

Several days went by. I stopped faithfully by the American Express and was disappointed every time. I called Rob's mother; she sent a wire for $50 the next day. I knew Janet didn't have much money, and I was ashamed and resolved not to ask again. Although I'd often felt during the trip that Rob and I were not actually together any longer, being closer to home here in London brought back my old need to depend on him. He and his family still cared for me, I knew. I'd forgotten the many times he'd stolen my self-confidence and remembered only his loving looks. I was moved by his letter, by his assertion that he was still, even after my inexplicable delays and excuses, waiting for me.

I wanted to call my father again, but I grew oddly afraid. What if he'd really been there when Bettye refused the collect call? I could imagine that, could imagine her telling him that it was for the best, that I needed to learn to take care of myself, could imagine him weakly agreeing. What if I called and he himself answered and refused the call? Could I bear to hear his voice on the other end of the line saying no?

My father was unreliable in his love for me, and I'd had evidence before that he would never choose me over Bettye. He had been terribly upset the day that Bettye had slapped me hard in the face; he'd gone so far as to separate from her. But by the time I returned from Seattle for Christmas after one quarter away at university, they were seeing each other again, and he and my brother went over to her brother's for Christmas dinner, leaving me alone. Within a few months, they were living together again. Although he complained constantly about her to me, and sighed and said he wished he'd never married her, she had a hold on him much greater than I did.

When I did finally work up the nerve to call him, it was a Sunday, and he sounded kind but guarded, as he often did when Bettye was nearby. He said he'd received my telegram but hadn't yet had time to call Mr. Butterworth and explain the situation. He would do that this week. He himself couldn't send me any money right now, but he was sure I'd manage. I was always so resourceful.

His voice dropped to a confidential whisper. "The situation here at home is delicate at the moment," he said. "But call me if you are in real trouble, honey. I mean, *real* trouble."

He didn't mention the phone call I'd tried to place to him earlier, and neither did I.

After the $50 from Janet was exhausted, Leanne began loaning me money. It was nothing to her, she said. She had plenty from the settlement, and obviously my situation was just temporary. What banker wouldn't respond to the letters and wires of a young person stranded in London, especially if my father got in touch with him and explained? I was no longer so sure. Every day, sometimes twice, I went to the American Express office, and every day there was no letter from my father, no wire from the Bank of Battle Creek.

I tried to keep my spirits up, in a way that involved not spending money. I discovered that the YWCA had a library and that I could check out books. Here was where I discovered Virginia Woolf's *A Room of One's Own* and reread some of my favorite Jane Austen novels. I became friendly with the librarian, who liked me because I never seemed to check out anything "modern." She did not care for modern writers, she told me. The library in fact did not seem to have many of them. I wrote out long sections of *A Room of One's Own* in my journal while sitting in the Y's tearoom, drinking milky tea and eating buttered scones. "All I could do was to offer you an opinion upon one minor point—a woman must have money and a room of her own if she is to write fiction."

That this book was published in 1929—forty years ago—was almost impossible to believe. Why hadn't the world changed more than it had? Why had I grown up not knowing about Margaret, Duchess of Newcastle, and Aphra Behn? Why had I never thought about what would have happened to Shakespeare's sister in rough-and-tumble Tudor England? And why had I always thought Virginia Woolf was only a novelist, a prissy one at that, when she was not only a brilliant essayist but a feminist?

Why, I wondered, as I dropped marmalade on my notebook page, had it been left to a righteous but decidedly unpoetic soul like

Betty Friedan to make the case for women's liberation, when Woolf, lucid-minded, effortlessly erudite, had made it so well long before— and much more humorously and succinctly? Her touch was light but implacable; she didn't shy away from the pointed questions: "Why was one sex so prosperous and the other so poor?" Woolf asked. "What effect has poverty on fiction? What conditions are necessary for the creation of works of art?"

What did it mean to write as a woman? Should one? Could one? Her irony was a refreshing tingle—as if the brain were plunged into a saltwater bath—but the irony was only in service of larger questions: What was the effect of discrimination on a writer's mind, particularly a woman writer's mind? How could a mind transcend all impediments to become not just self-confident but truly free?

I could have read in the room upstairs, but it was very likely that Leanne would be there, and if she were, she'd want to talk to me, because, as she often exclaimed, I was "the best listener she'd ever had."

We were an unlikely pair. She spent an hour every morning putting on her makeup and refreshed it several times through the day. She manicured and polished her fingernails and toenails daily to match her clothes. She wore giant hair curlers to bed. She had three suitcases filled with dresses and slacks bought in Raleigh, augmented by scarves and shoes from Paris. I'd been interested in makeup briefly at the age of thirteen or fourteen and had worn lots of mascara and white lipstick (and a scarf through my pageboy); then I'd become a hippie and had given up wearing bras and shaving my legs. Now, after months of travel, my long hair was even longer, and my clothes were in tatters. I had two pairs of bell-bottom jeans and my Mexican blouses, now stained and faded, a sweater, and one dress, a shiny black crepe number I'd bought secondhand at the St. Vincent de Paul in Monterey. I sometimes wore the red shawl I'd bought in Madrid.

Still, in that odd way of people stuck in elevators or marooned on lifeboats at sea, Leanne and I became very close for a time. I was very grateful to her for loaning me money, and she was grateful to me for my apparently bottomless interest in all things to do with her life. As the days went on, Leanne seemed to spend more and more time with Manny. He took her to the Savoy for tea and boating on the Thames. He escorted her to expensive restaurants, which she liked, and operas, which bored her. I was glad to hear more about their outings instead of so much about Ralph and Raleigh, but it was hard not to be envious when she arrived back late in the evening with stories of delicious dinners.

Manny had grown up in Tehran but had lived in London for some eight years, since he began medical school. Like Gunnar, he was twenty-eight or twenty-nine. Manny had a medical degree but was following postgraduate courses at the Royal College of Surgeons and had an easy schedule that summer. He had been unfailingly sympathetic about her love for Gunnar without pressing for the details. "He's a perfect gentleman, very reserved but kind underneath. He's very well-off, and has excellent taste," Leanne said. "He's very intellectual. I've been telling him about you—he thinks you sound *fascinating*."

After a week I finally met him, in the lobby of the YWCA, as they were heading out to Sadler's Wells and I was on my way to hear another lecture by Borges.

Leanne had said Manny wasn't a conventionally attractive man, and this was true. He had a large, serious face, with big ears, slicked-back receding black hair, and thick glasses. There was something of Velázquez in his high forehead and hooked nose, his full, womanly lips, which he kept a little pursed. His hands were beautiful, real surgeon's hands, long-fingered and perfectly manicured. He wore a beautiful suit and a tie.

His voice was accented, but not much. He shook my hand and smiled, said he was sorry that I couldn't go with them. I wondered suddenly why Leanne had never suggested inviting me, when she knew all I could afford was a sandwich in the evening. Perhaps she was embarrassed at the way I looked. Standing in the lobby beside them, Manny in his suit, Leanne in one of her many black dresses, heels, and her hair up in a French twist, I thought the two of them seemed like real adults. Although Leanne was only three years older than me, because of her Southern upbringing and because of her determination to re-create herself as a sophisticate, she often seemed to belong to another and more formal generation.

"Oh, but I'm going to hear Jorge Luis Borges," I said animatedly. "I wouldn't miss it for the world."

"He's in all the newspapers," said Manny. "I'd be interested to see him, too."

Leanne sighed just slightly, and he took her elbow. Outside was an Austin, and he opened the door for her. They waved at me and drove away, two grown-ups from a film about the sixties.

The topic that night was "Books in My Life," but it seemed to reiterate and circle around some of the themes of his first talk. Again he spoke of Stevenson, Wells, Scott; he mentioned the Father Brown stories and Dickens. Again he talked about how influenced he'd been by Anglo-Saxon writers and how reading them had brought him to Old Norse and a study of the poetry, myths, and sagas of the Icelanders. I was slightly disappointed that Borges repeated himself, down to using some of the same phrases. The audience tonight was much larger, the atmosphere less intimate, and I was put off by the mood of reverence I felt around me before the lecture began. Two men behind me assured each other that Borges was the greatest writer alive today. They mentioned the film *Performance,* which had Mick Jagger quoting from "Tlön, Uqbar, Orbis Terris."

Mick Jagger quoting from my favorite Borges story, the one I'd read over and over on my travels through Spain and Italy! I'd believed that Borges had been my secret find in an obscure bookstore in Córdoba on a narrow street leading to the great mosque. I'd delighted myself by imagining that the discovery of *Labyrinths* was an example of the reach of the civilization of Tlön, which made itself known in our world as a brief mention in an encyclopedic entry on the mysterious country of Uqbar but whose creators, creating new encyclopedias, had gradually infiltrated and changed what we think of as reality. I didn't like to think that Mick Jagger had discovered Borges, too.

I was in a mood to be contrary. I'd now finished *A Room of One's Own,* and it seemed clear to me, in a way I'd never managed to put into words before, that there was something *male* about all Borges' talk of daggers and swords and knife fights and struggles between two men, who were the same man, mirrored. The adulation of the crowd fed into my irritation. Would a woman writer get the same attention?

Borges, Woolf's translator, had impelled me to seek out *A Room of One's Own,* but in doing so, he'd also unwittingly set in motion a sense of indignation that was now turning me against him. Woolf had removed the blinders from my reading eyes. Of course, I'd read Colette, Austen, Elliot, and the Brontës, but I'd never thought of reading them as a woman. Nor had I read male authors as a woman. But now, and increasingly through the seventies, I'd find it difficult to read as anything else.

Leanne had decided, and no sooner had she decided than she acted. She was going back to Reykjavík whether Gunnar liked it or not. "The whole time I've been away, his wife has probably been working on him to get back together," she said. "I know what he and I had was real."

I accompanied her to the airport. I had given her my blue vinyl suitcase, since she'd done more shopping in London, and now she had four pieces of luggage. She put £10 into my jacket pocket. "I know your money will come through soon," she said. "I can't believe that they're holding it up like this."

In spite of the fact that I wasn't sure what would happen to me once I couldn't depend on her loans, I couldn't help agreeing with Leanne and encouraging her to leave. For it seemed to me that it was the country of Iceland that drew her as much as Gunnar. On that unlikely rock in the middle of the sea, Leanne had glimpsed the possibility of reinventing herself.

"Call Manny up when I'm gone," Leanne urged me at the airport gate. "In case you're in London for a while. At least you'll get a good meal."

When I called Manny two days later to express Leanne's regrets that she hadn't had time to say a proper goodbye, Manny told me he had a spare ticket to an orchestral concert. He picked me up in his Austin and asked about Borges to put me at ease. He was dressed in a suit and tie and seemed very elegant. Afterward he suggested we have dinner and drove us to a French restaurant in Soho. Manny commanded the attention of the maître d' with a £5 note pressed into his hand as we entered, and ordered a rich and plentiful meal of escargots, quail with juniper berries, and a bottle of champagne.

"Now," he said in his almost perfect British accent, with an encouraging smile that erased any thought I'd had that he was ugly, "tell me about your travels. Leanne said you'd been in Italy. How marvelous."

Instead of telling about hitchhiking and difficult encounters with men and boys, I talked of museums in Florence, chapels in Assisi, and the Vatican treasures. Of walking the streets of Verona imagining *Romeo and Juliet,* of spending the day in the Roman Forum, sketching and recalling *Daisy Miller.* Leanne hadn't been as interested in any of that. She'd scarcely been interested in me at all, it seemed now, as I began pouring out my impressions of Italy to Manny. Under the influence of several glasses of champagne, I talked too of Laura, and how I was missing her.

"It was Easter," I said. "And the candy stores and cafés were full of huge, decorated chocolate eggs, some of them a foot high. We were obsessed with these eggs. We wanted to know if they were full or empty, and, if they had something inside, what was it? One afternoon, sitting in a café in an out-of-the-way street in Orvieto, where no one was paying any attention to us, we were right next to a glass shelf full of those eggs, most of them wrapped in colored cellophane and ribbon.

"'I dare you,' Laura said.

"And in a flash, I grabbed the hugest egg and ran out the door. She ran after me and we tore down the street clutching the egg, certain that the café owners and the police would be after us. We were laughing like crazy. We went back to our room and cut the egg open."

"What was inside?"

"Nothing! Just some little plastic toys. It was very disappointing!" I paused, in the midst of my dessert and coffee. "I wouldn't want you to think I'm a thief. It was—I was going to say I ran off with the egg for the fun of it. But, really, I don't know what possessed me. It was sort of . . . the way Laura and I could get with each other sometimes."

Manny laughed. "Did you and Laura go back the next day and apologize?"

"God, no! What if they'd arrested us? We didn't even have the nerve to mail them the money for the egg. Of course, we didn't really have the money."

But I could see he didn't understand what that meant. He just thought, he told me later, that I was a delightful storyteller.

It was after eleven when Manny dropped me off at the YWCA in his large car, and as I moved to get out, he stopped me and said, "Leanne told me a little about your situation. The least I can do while you're waiting in London is to give you a good dinner from time to time. It's a favor to me—I love the company."

And then he pressed, oh, so discreetly, a £5 note into my hand. "Just until the bank comes through," he said. "Please don't think I'm presumptuous."

"Oh," I said, embarrassed that he might have thought I was angling for a loan. "I'll pay it back."

"Shall I pick you up tomorrow evening?" he asked. "The Joffrey Ballet is at Sadler's Wells. I happen to have a spare ticket."

"Something to look forward to," I said, blithe and grateful.

❧ EIGHT ❧

Bleak House

Soon I was going out with Manny every evening, and there was no
further pretext that he had an extra ticket to anything. We attended
Boris Godunov at the English National Opera and *Così Fan Tutte*
at Covent Garden. We listened to symphonies at the Royal Albert
and string quartets at Wigmore Hall. Manny adored Schubert and
Bruckner, but of all composers Gustav Mahler was his favorite. I found
it hard to concentrate listening to these concerts; my mind would often
drift off, especially during Mahler, and I'd come to only at the end,
when suddenly, the clapping began. I was remembering my travels
with Laura and missing her intensely. I was worrying what I would do
if Mr. Butterworth were to remain truly adamant. I much preferred the
theater, where the story took my mind off my problems.

The first week or two I was often gleeful at my sudden good
fortune. Now I wasn't just listening to Leanne's stories of delightful
outings, I was experiencing them myself, in a *Gigi* or *Sabrina* sort
of way, a spinning film collage of fancy locales where a young and
inexperienced girl is introduced to an elegant manner of life beyond
her wildest dreams, with Maurice Chevalier singing and champagne

corks popping in the background. Manny, with his open wallet and his sophistication, was a sort of Humphrey Bogart–like figure, with dark hooded eyes, large ears, and a sense of mystery behind the good manners. In his swift way of moving into a restaurant or buying tickets from a scalper outside a theater, I saw power but not arrogance, and certainly not the defensiveness of a stranger in Britain. He acted as if he belonged in London, yet there was a sense of the outsider too, the outsider who is superior. Of course, Manny wasn't as good-looking as Bogart and lacked his charm and particularly his smile. I thought his eyes were lonely sometimes, and once or twice I saw them flash with anger, though not at me.

In addition to all the evenings out, we took day trips on the weekends. One Saturday we drove to Stratford for a performance of *Romeo and Juliet*. We ate lunch in a hotel where Manny introduced me to carved roast beef and Yorkshire pudding, with strawberry tart thick with cream for dessert. Another Sunday we headed south to hear a musical afternoon program at Chichester; we had China tea in flowered cups, with plates of crustless sandwiches and lemon curd tarts while sitting on lawn chairs, surrounded by men in pin-striped summer suits and women in enormous hats. I wrote about all this enthusiastically in my journal, the one I'd begun in Italy, which also had descriptions of being taken out to dinner a few times. Laura and I once had had a memorable five-course meal with two businessmen en route from Bergamo to Verona; I considered my meals with Manny not only food but cultural experiences, which I recorded so as to be able to have my fictional characters eat the same dishes one day.

One evening we drove to Regent's Park with a hamper Manny had picked up at Fortnum & Mason, and a cloth to sit on. We were going to attend an outdoor production of *A Midsummer Night's Dream* and were both in good spirits. We ate pâté and gherkins and roast chicken in mustard and gloucester cheese with Carr's water biscuits, all washed down by champagne in plastic champagne glasses as we sat on the manicured green lawn surrounded by English couples and families. I prattled on, as I often did in those first days, about writing and my past travels. Manny liked to hear the details of my time in Paris and Barcelona, though I emphasized the architecture and discounted the boyfriends. I talked to him a great deal about Laura, but only as my madcap traveling partner, who had gone on to Greece. Talking about Laura, even in a way that disguised our relationship, assuaged my longing for her.

As the evening slowly darkened and we moved into the stands to watch the play, Manny took my arm to help me up, and it didn't feel proprietary but only thoughtful, avuncular. I thought what a fantastic story this would make somehow; how, at the very end of my travels, I'd been taken to see all these plays and concerts that I couldn't have afforded on my own by a selfless benefactor who simply enjoyed my company. Of course, I knew even then I was fooling myself.

The play began, set against a background of trees, from which the gauzily dressed fairies and clever sprites emerged and vanished. I was enchanted by the story of Oberon and Titania and the lovers who kept missing each other and running through the grass in various states of joy and distress. The night was cool and the air spring-sweet, scented with the last lilacs and new roses. Manny squeezed my arm a couple of times as we laughed, and I didn't draw away. Thinking that there wouldn't be many of these occasions, I tried to enjoy them. It was only as time wore on that I wearied of the nights out, of the endless concerts and dinners afterward.

The restaurants were all small and usually French; we often had champagne and dishes that weren't on the menu but that Manny quietly insisted to the headwaiter that the chef knew how to prepare.

I took my cues from Manny and tried to act as if this life were natural to me. Of course, we were unlike everyone else in the restaurant—Manny, dark, foreign, elegant, and me, wearing the short black crepe dress, shiny at the seams, from the thrift store. Instead of a coat or sweater, I wore my red Spanish shawl, which made me feel protected. Manny always wore a suit, well pressed, and a tie. He had a particular manner of speech, cultivated and slightly pedantic. When he spoke to others besides me he had a way of sounding both assured and impatient. He didn't like to be kept waiting and was sensitive to slights. To waiters he was politely condescending; they saw the money in his eyes and clothes and were obsequious back. He always seemed to have a wad of bills in his wallet, big notes.

I accepted Manny's generosity, not just in the form of concerts and plays and dinners out: I also took money for my bed at the YWCA. There was nothing that either of us could do to disguise that, and although he was so discreet, perhaps Manny didn't want to disguise the gift. For he always put the money in a heavy linen envelope, square, ivory, embossed with his name and address, and he set the envelope on the dark dashboard after we had come back to the car from the concert hall or restaurant, and there it would lie gleaming softly and speechlessly all the way back to the fusty brick Victorian facade of the YWCA. At some point, before I got out of the Austin, I would have to reach for that envelope and decide whether to say thank you or nothing. And in that reaching, in that decision to show gratitude or nonchalance, there was the knowledge that I was a woman and he was a man and I was taking money from him.

It was always the same amount. It was always £5. The nightly cost of a bed, including breakfast, was £3, or £3.50, depending on whether I stayed in the dormitory or had a double room. Every morning I had to arrange for another night and usually had to lug my rucksack and increasingly heavy bag of books to another room or down into the luggage closet. We weren't allowed to check into the rooms until later in the afternoon, and I almost invariably had to check into a new room. The women at the desk knew me—after all, by this time, I'd been at the Y almost a month—but they weren't sympathetic. They had seen it all, had heard every excuse over the years. Now that it was summer, the rooms were in great demand, and often women had booked ahead, so I had to beg and wheedle for a place to sleep; sometimes, with my rucksack in the luggage room, I didn't know until late in the day whether I could stay.

"If only you had *told* us you'd be staying for another night *yesterday*," the one gray-haired, tight-lipped woman would say, and the other, thinner, with a pale peach-colored permanent wave and eyes that were that particular color of piercing English blue, chimed in, "If you're really planning to stay in London for a while, you should move to our residence hall."

I'd never been to their residence hall, which was in South Kensington, but I pictured it as something out of *Jane Eyre*, rooms of neatly made white beds, girls like me being forced to kneel to say our prayers, the whole of it presided over by ladies like these two, only far more terrible.

"I expect to be going home any day now," I told them, trembling with the wish, which they did not see as a wish but as a kind of lie that they couldn't bother themselves to expose. They never asked where I got the £5 to stay every night, and only £5, but they had seen the Austin pull up in front, had seen the extremely well-dressed foreign man come into the lobby to claim me.

The £5 paid for a bed at night and for lunch; with what was left over I sometimes went to Foyles and bought a book. Why should I need more, I who was departing any day now, and why should

Manny, who was basically a stranger, give me more? The fiction between us was that soon, very soon, a draft from the Bank of Battle Creek would appear and I'd be hopping on the first plane back to Los Angeles. The reality was the ivory linen envelope gleaming softly on the dark dashboard. Five pounds was generous. It was more than enough for one night. But £5 wasn't enough for two nights, as Manny well knew. I could have gone without dinner and saved up, but I didn't have the nerve to tell him I didn't want to see him; nor did I want to sit on my bed in the Y at night, dinnerless, listening to one or another roommate chatter about her travels and ask me about mine. This meant that I had to see Manny every day, had to go out with him every night, had to reach for the envelope at the end, had to decide whether to be cheerful and easy about accepting it or show the gratitude that was increasingly uncomfortable.

How many times can you visit a museum, how many times can you look at Westminster Abbey or the Tower of London? As May began to turn into June, I walked the city endlessly, but this time, in contrast to my visit in December, with less and less interest. Tourists in shorts and sandals, wearing badges and clutching guidebooks, crammed the museums and careened through the streets on red sightseeing buses. Germans with expensive cameras and French women in dark glasses, Indians in saris, Africans in dashikis, Australian hippies, and Canadians with maple-leaf flags sewn to their hats, jackets, and backpacks so they wouldn't be mistaken for Americans, thronged the streets and squares. And of course there were thousands of Americans, rushing around Piccadilly Circus and Trafalgar Square, snapping pictures of each other, changing money at the American Express, and exclaiming and sharing travel stories in accents I now found flat and twangy but that made me homesick all the same.

Among the vacationers I felt lost, and forgotten by everyone at home. I wondered sometimes which London the incoming floods of summer tourists were seeing, which London they had imagined and were superimposing over the city. Was it Swinging London or Tudor? Was it Buckingham Palace or Bloomsbury? Was it the London of Samuel Pepys or the London of the Blitz? Or were some of them, as I'd been last winter, looking for vestiges of Charles Dickens in the warrens of Lincoln's Inn Court and Chancery Lane?

There was rarely any mail for me at the American Express, for everyone thought I'd be home any day. Aside from Mr. Butterworth, the person I most wished to hear from was Laura. She wouldn't have known to write to me in London, and though I sent her a letter c/o the American Express in Athens, I couldn't be sure she'd get it. She hadn't wanted to be pinned down as to where she was going and what she planned to do in Greece. She thought she might sail to the islands, but which islands, I didn't know.

A letter had come from my father with $20 enclosed and the bad news that Mr. Butterworth was proving intractable. My father said that I might have to stay in England until my birthday in October and should think about getting a job. "Of course, you could always write to the bank yourself and plead your case," my father ended. I had the feeling he was washing his hands of me, and that was Bettye's doing. I always found it easier to blame Bettye.

I had begun, in fact, to think of getting a job but wasn't sure where to start. The stamp in my passport specifically forbade working in the U.K., and I had no English friends to help me. Only Manny, who was against the idea.

"You'd be unlikely to get a work permit," he said. "The English are horrid about that. They make me jump through hoops to stay. They don't want to let me practice medicine here, only to keep paying fees to the Royal College of Surgeons to do further study. Besides," he tried to cheer me, "you might as well enjoy London as long as you're here. Let me help you do that."

Manny said that he'd been talking over my situation with Elizabeth Thorne, his friend and landlady, and that she'd suggested perhaps I might move into the house across from them, which they owned and rented to an Australian couple, the Taylors. The Thornes lived off Finchley Road in West Hampstead, and Manny had boarded with them for many years, since he'd first come to London as a medical student. Mr. Thorne was a dentist and Elizabeth Thorne a thin, correct matron who gave the impression of having been livelier once but having tamped it down. They had two children and several large dogs. Once I'd been there for dinner and Elizabeth had taken me aside and said meaningfully, "We've known Manny since he first came to this country. He's a very special man. We want him to be happy."

During the meal Elizabeth plied me with polite questions about my family and upbringing. She pretended to be surprised that I had not graduated from college. "Manny tells us that you plan to become a writer, or that you are a writer now, I'm not sure. I've not heard of writers skipping college."

I made an awkward, pretentious reply about experience being the real teacher, and anyway, I was going to go back to Spain and enroll at the University of Granada. Then I became completely tongue-tied, used the wrong fork, sloshed some of my red wine on the tablecloth and drank a bit too much, after which I tried to show off by speaking Spanish to their au pair, Consuela.

After dinner Manny took me up to his rooms for the first time. They were small and masculine and studious. His record collection was enormous and the stereo system very swank. We drank some cognac and listened to Mahler.

"Symphonies are so perfect," Manny said at the end. "So balanced. Everything is stirred up, then resolved. Life's tragedies don't enter into it. Music compensates."

For what? I didn't ask. I had been looking at him during the Mahler symphony, with his eyes closed and his full lips a little open. He had large ears, and I wondered if that made him hear better. I found him ugly, in a fascinating kind of way. It was one of the few times I really was curious about him. He had told me a few stories of his childhood in Tehran, but mostly he seemed not to want to speak of the past, though once he told me I reminded him of someone at home. He joked that the Thornes were his family; he'd been living with them for six years, and although he could afford a flat of his own, he didn't want to leave. He said he didn't really feel welcome in England, which I found astonishing. His money should make him welcome everywhere. He said he didn't feel very grown-up sometimes, and I found that completely unbelievable. To me he was a grown man, a wealthy surgeon. I was the one who wasn't grown-up. I was just a girl.

I didn't feel I had much of a choice whether to move into the Taylors' house or not; after all, I couldn't pay for the YWCA myself. This way, I reasoned too, I wouldn't have to deal with the envelope every night. Manny had mentioned he would give the Taylors something for my rent but that I shouldn't worry about it. After I moved to West Hampstead, I came into the city less often and spent more time wandering around the posh neighborhoods there. Some days I hardly went out of the house but stayed in my room and read and moped. It was by now the middle of June and the weather was much warmer than I'd expected England to be. I found the sunshine and summery feeling very depressing, and my room, though the Taylors had fixed it up for me, had a storage-closet feel. There were many photographs of Fiji on the walls from a trip they'd taken, and a frightening mask or two, as well as random pieces of furniture and a somewhat saggy bed. The window looked out on a trim garden, very English, with a border and heavily clipped rose bushes.

The days were my own, but they were long days. The books I had with me, Borges, Colette, Virginia Woolf, seemed suddenly unsatisfying; my enthusiasm for their ideas mocked me now. Everything about my travels over the last six months seemed thin and unsubstantial. I tried to recall my delight in London and Paris last winter; my great happiness running around Barcelona with Monzo and Lluís; the long, slow days in Madrid with Laura; the museums of Florence; the Forum and pizza and gelato of Rome. Once or twice, just to re-create the warmth of Spain, I tried to make contact with Consuela, the Thornes' au pair, but she regarded me with suspicion. I was a friend—probably more than that—of Manny, and Manny, I'd noticed, treated her as a servant.

The Australian Taylors had lots of used Penguin paperbacks sitting around, including some well-thumbed Dickens. I picked up *Little Dorrit* first, then *The Old Curiosity Shop*. Eventually I went out and bought copies of *Great Expectations* and *Bleak House;* I began to reread those novels from the summer I was fourteen, all those novels of great expectations and great disappointments, of debtors' prisons and bankruptcy proceedings, of lengthy and useless appeals to justice, of worthy wards done out of their inheritances, of decent people reduced to shame and poverty, reduced to begging for their livelihoods. I lay on my bed in the room in Hampstead during the hot summer days, and it was strangely similar to how I'd curled up on my grandmother's sofa that summer, six years ago, in Battle Creek.

In those days I'd been able to lose myself in Victorian London, to forget about the life I lived and immerse myself in another. I read now for escape, but it didn't work as well. Often I found myself thinking not of Esther and Nell and Little Dorrit, the girls I'd once loved and identified with (imagining myself kind and self-sacrificing, which I certainly wasn't), but of the men who, out of greed and a love of power, squeezed and shadowed the hapless characters in the novels who had fallen, through mere human folly, into their debt. I shuddered to read of the lawyer Mr. Tulkinghorn in *Bleak House* and of Mr. Quilp in *The Old Curiosity Shop* and was relieved in both cases when they met their demise.

It seemed to me, as I reread those novels that June in West Hampstead, that Dickens was all about money and the havoc it wreaked in human relations. He understood the lack of it, and the power of it, and the threat of it, and the waste of it. He understood how some held their wealth over others, and some had to beg, and some pretended they didn't know anything about it. He would have understood why Manny put envelopes with pound notes underneath my door sometimes, and why I had to take them and pretend I hadn't. He would have understood why Mr. Butterworth felt the need to punish me, and why my father was so weak and my stepmother so strong.

Virginia Woolf understood it all, too—that poverty made women slaves, that you could have a room of your own but if you didn't have money you didn't have freedom, and without freedom, you couldn't write. What were the conditions necessary to create art? Why was it so hard for me to accept what Manny offered? What did it mean to have a room of one's own if that room was paid for by someone else, someone whom you didn't love?

As I read Dickens, I couldn't help thinking about my last summer in Battle Creek, the long, humid days, the walks to the library, the house full of the smells of laundry soap, cherry pie, and the misery of sufferers who came to the door in search of healing. I thought about how my grandmother had tried to talk with me about her own choices as a girl and how I'd tried to tell her who I was. I thought that if she knew where I was now, she'd be terribly disappointed in me; yet she never would have let me languish in London. A telegram that said "Desperate" would have brought a wire the next day, along with a fierce dressing-down. I felt such grief thinking of her— her upright morality, her stubbornness, her unfailing love—and of how I'd squandered her money (drinking!), that at times I lay on the bed choking with tears. My mother's death lay in a past best left unexamined and forgotten, but my grandmother's death, more recent, more graspable, left me suddenly bereft. I was stubborn, too, but to what avail was stubbornness without money?

I'd abandoned my journal from Spain and Italy and bought a new one where I recorded my thoughts on the books I was reading, my self-disgust, my irritation with Manny, my envy of Laura, probably having a wonderful time on some Greek island, even my renewed longing for Rob, the made-up Rob who was a stand-in for a real person I could love and be loved by.

Here I also wrote the rough drafts of my letters to Mr. Butterworth, which, because I was reading Dickens, took on an increasingly sensationalist tone. I'd tried many tones with Mr. Butterworth— apologetic, remorsefully apologetic, reasonable, abjectly reasonable, reasonable but outraged, and, finally, purely outraged—but now my letters, in addition to being accusing, grew more and more descriptive. Now I described the conditions in which I was living, not the real conditions, of course, in an upper-middle-class neighborhood of large houses and gardens and hundreds of thickly leafed chestnuts, oaks, and plane trees, but instead a kind of hovel based on Fagin's den, a place of disease and filth and rags piled up in corners with rats scurrying around.

"I sleep on a mildewed mattress on the floor," I wrote Mr. Butterworth one day, "with a blanket full of holes my only cover. I don't know what I'll do when the weather gets colder. For food, I eat whatever I can find in the garbage cans outside restaurants. The other girls who live here say I should do like them, and become a prostitute, but I hope it doesn't come to that. I know how prominent my grandmother was in the Battle Creek Christian Science church and I would hate for any of her friends to hear what I have been reduced to. You know I would work if I could, but as a foreigner it is impossible to get a work permit."

"Dear Mr. Butterworth," I wrote a few days later, "I was at my usual place, begging for spare change outside the American Express, when a man came by and asked me about myself. He was very surprised to hear my story and especially that it involved you, Mr. Butterworth, because he is from Michigan, too, from Grand Rapids, where he is chief of police. You may be hearing from him."

And I copied out a quote from *Bleak House* and sent it to him too: "In the question of how the trust under the Will is squandered away: the legatees under the Will are reduced to such a miserable condition that they would be sufficiently punished if they had committed an enormous crime in having money left them."

I did not receive a reply to a single letter. Mr. Butterworth no doubt surmised, correctly, that I had figured out some way to live in London, or else I would not be able to afford the postage to send him so many letters. I suppose he thought that I would just get over it eventually and stop bothering him. I'm not sure what he thought actually; he never told me.

Manny and I had begun to argue; at least I had begun to balk and sulk. "Do we have to go to another French restaurant?" I would increasingly say. "Can't we just have a bowl of soup or a sandwich somewhere?"

One evening in the kitchen of the Australians, Manny produced two tickets for a play and I said I didn't feel like going. I had never, since this all started, refused an invitation. The problem was, they didn't feel like invitations any longer; they felt like commands. I was sick of spending time with him; I was tired of trying to find things to say about the performance. I wanted friends my own age; I wanted to be back in Barcelona with Monzo and Lluís, on a Greek island with Laura, in Oakland with Ruthie, in Costa Mesa with Rob. Anywhere but here.

Now I added, "I don't like Shaw," for it was *John Bull's Other Island* Manny had tickets for.

At first he laughed, and asked me what Shaw I'd ever seen.

This angered me. It was one thing to look down on me for my lack of knowledge about music (in my earliest years my family had had only three records: *Tubby the Tuba*, the sound track to *Oklahoma!*, and *Bob Newhart: The Button-Down Mind Strikes Back*); but there was no reason to turn up his nose at my background in theater. How much Shaw had *he* seen, growing up in Tehran?

"I saw *Pygmalion* at ACT in San Francisco once. And I used to go with my drama class in high school to the Mark Taper Forum in Los Angeles. We saw *Arms and the Man*. I didn't like it."

"Theater in Los Angeles," sneered Manny. "Hollywood actors like your friend Rob, I suppose."

"Los Angeles has better plays than anything I've seen here," I said. "And Maggie Smith came touring as Masha in *The Three Sisters,* and I saw Marcel Marceau once."

"Fine!" said Manny, and his loss of control was faster and sharper than mine had been. He took the tickets of his pocket and ripped them up. "Fine, we'll sit home."

"Fine," I said, turning to go upstairs.

"But you have to eat!" he said.

"I'm not hungry!"

He became calmer. "Forget the play. Let's just have a quiet meal here. I'll cook something. And we'll listen to music."

"No!" I said. I felt as if I couldn't stand one single second more in his company. I kept walking away.

Then he grabbed my arm and pulled me toward him. He seized my shoulders and put his heavy, open mouth on mine. The kiss was huge and wet.

"Don't you ever do that again," I said.

"But it's been over a month that we've, that we've . . ."

"We've what?" I demanded. I wanted to lash out at him but was afraid. What would happen if the fiction burst open? Or worse, if he made it clear that there was a trade-off and that there were conditions? Almost running, I fled upstairs and, for the first time, locked my bedroom door.

Everything changed then and became awkward. A brief, formal handwritten apology was under my door in the morning, along with a £20 note. "Go into town and buy yourself something nice to wear," he wrote. I put the money back in the envelope, surprised at what a temptation it was, even after what had happened, to keep it, and slipped it back under his door.

I thought about a high-handed note back—"You can't buy me!"—but I didn't even want to put the thought into words. I wasn't a prostitute, no, but I'd become dependent on Manny, and the fear I hadn't acknowledged, that he was owed something for his generosity and that he'd someday want to claim it, was now real.

For a few days we were cordial and ordinary with each other, and one evening when he asked if I'd like to go to a concert with him, I agreed. We had a pleasant enough time and ate dinner afterward, but on the way back to West Hampstead from the West End, Manny took a circuitous route that brought us near a wooded lane where he pulled the Austin off the road.

"I want to tell you something," he said.

I was afraid, not just of what he might say but of his solid dark presence in the driver's seat. I believed, in the instant before he began to speak, that something terrible might happen, that he might even kill me. It was night in an isolated place, with only a streetlight casting a green glow through the heavy leaves of the thickly planted chestnut trees. My hand went in the direction of the door handle.

"Do you remember when—I said there was someone you reminded me of? Well, never mind. It was a girl, back in Tehran. Azar. I was sixteen, she was fifteen. Our parents didn't know about us. We wouldn't have been allowed to meet, you see. We were students at the same school, but I came from a very good family and she from a poorer one. It didn't matter to us, we understood each other so well. We talked for hours, we went on long walks and made plans. How I'd go to London to study and she would follow. How we'd marry and live freely, away from our families. She was such a beautiful girl, so alive, so adventurous, just like you.

"One day there was a holiday, and she and I took the opportunity to go into the hills for a picnic. Coming home, we passed a truck on the narrow, winding road. The truck was stopped. The driver was trying to turn around. He called out the window asking me to direct him. I told her to stay out of the way; then I told the driver how to turn, how to back up. 'Now,' I said. 'Back up against the hillside and you're free.' But somehow he went forward and too quickly, and Azar was in front of him with another hill behind her. It was all too quick. She was crushed. She died very horribly, in my arms. She was only fifteen."

Manny was crying. His hand crept over to mine. I held it reluctantly. I didn't want to be moved and, so, even though I was shocked (I saw it, the two young lovers, the dust, the truck, the hillside, the blood), I allowed doubt to enter in. Maybe Manny was making this up or some of it. Maybe he was telling me this in order to make me be kind to him again, to make me feel sorry for him.

I knew that Manny was waiting for my reaction, but all I could think to say was a rather subdued, "I'm sorry. That must have been awful."

That checked him slightly, but not more than a few seconds. The relief of speaking was so great, and his confessor so near, that he had to go on.

"I haven't met anyone since her who I could love. But you remind me of her. Won't you stay here in England with me? I've been so lonely. Won't you marry me? We could have a wonderful life together. You could write and we could go to concerts and the theater together all the time."

"No!" I said, in complete panic. Being raped and murdered would have fit my expectations better than a proposal of marriage. The surprise of it robbed me of any grace in my response. I'd read of proposals—in Jane Austen, for instance—but I had never expected to get one. "I'm too young. And I don't believe in marriage. And I wouldn't marry you. I mean, I don't want to stay in England. I hate England. I want to go home."

Manny didn't say anything. Then he started the car and drove me back to the Taylors' house without another word.

The next afternoon as I was lying on my bed, in my usual paralyzed torpor, trying to lose myself in Dickens, Mrs. Taylor knocked on my door. "Manny just called. He asked if you could come over to his room for a minute."

Of course I didn't want to go, but I got up obediently. All day I'd been replaying the scene from the night before in my head, blocking out the horror of Manny's story and the sadness of it and focusing instead on the presumptuousness of his hope. What right had he to put me in a position of such utter dependence and then use it against me! Going over to his house I was angry, because I was afraid. What if Manny was going to tell me that I had to move out of the Taylors' house? What if he said he would no longer leave pound notes in envelopes in the mailbox? What if the sordid scenes I'd been describing to Mr. Butterworth turned out to come true?

Manny was sitting behind his wooden desk that faced the door and, like an executive greeting a secretary, he gestured me to come in. Briskly he opened the top drawer and took out an envelope. He held it out. I hesitated.

"Your ticket from London to Los Angeles," he said. "You leave in three days. I'll drive you to the airport. I'm sorry; it was the soonest I could get."

"Oh, my god," I said. "Oh, Manny, thank you! Thank you! I'll pay you back. I really will."

"It's not necessary," he said, and then more softly, "It's never been necessary. And now," he turned back to his desk and bent over some papers, "if you'll excuse me, I'm rather busy."

The day before I was to leave for L.A. I stopped by the American Express in the morning, one last time, to leave a change of address. I'd spent the last couple of days rushing around the city, less from a sentimental urge to visit old places (I was thoroughly sick of everything to do with London by now) than from an excess of manic energy. I simply couldn't sit at home and read. I saw Manny not at all. He'd said that he would drive me to the airport, but until then he was unfortunately too busy to get together. He'd said this in a note with £10 enclosed. I'd spent the £10, in spite of a great desire to hand the money back to him.

At the American Express mail desk I gave them my address in California, c/o Rob's mother. "I'm leaving tomorrow," I couldn't help jubilantly telling the clerk.

"Are you, Miss? Well, here's one last letter for you."

It was from the Bank of Battle Creek. There was no letter, only a draft for $200.

I didn't go back immediately that day to Finchley Road, though I looked forward to the moment when I could hand over almost all the money to Manny for the plane ticket. There was no need now to cower in my bedroom, disappearing into the pages of *Bleak House*. London was restored to me that day, in all its happy glory. Now the tourists didn't bother me; I was one of them again. I took myself out to lunch and then decided to go over to the Victoria and Albert, where there was a continuing exhibition on William Morris.

Perhaps because of my almost uncontrollable relief and exhilaration, William Morris made a deep impression on me that day. I reveled in the depth and richness of his artistic and literary production; he was a poet, a novelist, a socialist, a furniture maker, a weaver, and a calligrapher. One of the Pre-Raphaelites, Morris designed wallpaper, tapestries, and fabric. He was a socialist, opposed to mass production, in favor of the handmade, who believed in the power of craft to transform ordinary objects from utilitarian to beautiful—for everyone, not just the rich. He had translated the Icelandic sagas! He had been to Iceland!

But as I wandered the slightly darkened rooms of the V&A exhibit that day, what struck me most were the glass cases displaying the books that the Kelmscott Press had produced, and the manuscripts that he'd drawn and illuminated. It was as if something about my long love of reading and handling books, my old interest in making books as a child, my newly fledged curiosity about Virginia Woolf and the Hogarth Press came together, and I thought, I could learn to set type, I could print, I could bind. I could produce books as well as write them.

I had a vision, standing in the museum, where carpets, walls, and chintz-covered chairs, all in different swirling botanical patterns of willow leaves and tulips, honeysuckle and jasmine, flowed together as if I were in a sort of drug-induced trance brought on now by color and decoration instead of LSD. I seemed to see how my life could be: woven together of many strands, richly colored, all the disparate, confusing patterns re-created into something whole, something meaningful and vivid, a large life, well lived.

Given Manny's new cold attitude toward me, I expected the drive to Gatwick Airport to be uneventful. When I'd handed him the money for the ticket, he'd taken it with the most perfunctory of nods, and thrown it into his desk drawer as if he couldn't be bothered with such small change. He didn't even seem surprised that I suddenly had money after weeks of poverty. Clearly, we were finished; he could no longer be bothered with me.

We had to be at Gatwick very early in the morning, and I was half asleep when we loaded the rucksack and two bags of books into the trunk. Until we were on the motorway Manny had said little either, but as the Austin gathered speed, the words began to pour out, a steady stream of contemptuous criticism.

"You are the most selfish and self-centered girl I ever met. I just want you to know that. I have never met anyone so ignorant who thought she was so clever. Do you know that Elizabeth and I used to laugh at you, you with your pretensions of being a writer? You! You're too stupid to go to university, and anyone who can't go to university can't be a writer. A writer needs to have intelligence and wit and compassion. But you're just a foolish little girl. You don't know about anyone else and you don't care.

"You thought I was attracted to you. You imagined I was in love with you. How stupid can you be! You are nothing to me. I was simply playing with you, as I played with hundreds of other girls before you. You couldn't have taken me seriously. I took pity on you, that's all."

For thirty minutes this went on, a minute catalog of my faults; scorn especially for my pretensions of being interested in Chekhov and Borges, writers I couldn't possibly understand, and for my dreams of becoming a writer, which I would never, not in a million years, have the talent for. I didn't try to defend myself as Manny raged against my self-centeredness, my stupidity, my dreams. I thought if I said anything it would enflame his anger and he might deliberately smash the car or stop it suddenly and throw me out. It occurred to me that perhaps this plane ticket was a forgery. That we were not on the way to the airport at all but to some out-of-the-way cottage where he would hold me captive or kill me. From the beginning, underneath his politeness, I had sensed this anger in him. Even after all he'd done for me, I still believed him capable of murder.

Instead of listening, I thought of William Morris and imagined myself back in the darkened galleries with rich patterns all around me. Like my grandmother, convinced of another reality, one in which God was good, and we were already healed before we had to ask for healing, I closed my eyes and saw tapestries of fruits and flowers. I had meant to tell Manny that in addition to becoming a writer, I now planned to make books as well. But now didn't seem to be the right time. Anyway, I hated him.

Not until we reached the airport did he wind down his diatribe. Inside the terminal I said, "Manny. You've been good to me. And it's been hard. And now I'm going."

"Oh, my little monkey," he said. His face crumpled; he looked like a little boy with his big ears and damp eyes; he looked like a bitter old man.

He bought me books, newspapers, chocolates for the journey. "When you next are in London, in the autumn, or anytime," he said, "I want you to call me. We'll go out, we'll have a fine time. Just like we did in the beginning."

I said, automatically, "Yes, of course I'll call you," and gave him the kiss he had wanted for so long, just before I disappeared into the tunnel to the plane that would take me back over the Atlantic and the country to everything familiar and longed for. I was a bird out of the cage again, another cage, now flying along with the clouds of heaven. For a little while at least I was suspended in the sky, safe and free, between cages.

I never saw Manny again, though I've been back to London many times. I still think of him when I hear Mahler or walk on Hampstead Heath. Once or twice I wanted to call him, years later, and thank him for teaching me so much about music and opera, for helping me when I had nowhere else to turn. I wanted to say I was sorry his girlfriend had died, and ask if he'd found someone to love who could love him back. I wanted to apologize for my self-centeredness and lack of grace. I wanted to shake him by the shoulders and demand, "Why did you make me wait for the money to go home? Why did you watch me twist in the wind in my own unhappiness? What did you expect from a twenty-year-old girl? Why didn't you see me as I was?"

Most of all I wanted to tell him, "You were wrong about me. I was a writer then, and I am a writer now. Didn't you understand that? Didn't you?"

❧ NINE ❧

The Looking Glass

ROB WAS NOW living in a houseful of actors not far from the South Coast Rep, which was located in a storefront on a charmless boulevard. In the small room Rob and I were sharing was a framed mirror, and in the frame Rob had stuck all my postcards. I hadn't realized I'd sent so many of them: There was a bright red London bus and a romantic Paris café, shot in the fog; there was La Sagrada Familia in Barcelona and the Alhambra in Granada. There were many from Italy, perhaps because I felt guilty for prolonging the trip, and none sent from London these last weeks, when I had nothing left to say except *help*. Every time I looked at these cards, which of course was often, since they were in a mirror, I felt troubled. At first it touched me that Rob had put them up and made me terribly sad to think that I'd experienced so much without him and hadn't even wanted him there with me. Then it began to anger me that the cards were there, reminders of a freedom I'd once enjoyed, a happiness that was now gone.

Rob had picked me up in Los Angeles and had kissed me ecstatically with tears in his sea green eyes. He'd found another girlfriend while I was away, I'd find out soon, but had dumped her when he received my telegram with the arrival time. On the long freeway drive from LAX to Costa Mesa, on a smoggy July day, he didn't ask a single question about what I'd been doing for the last seven months. Of course I hadn't written anything much about Manny in my letters, but had said I was living with some Australians who'd taken me in. He threw himself on me in the double bed shortly after we arrived. Afterward he tried on the matador's jacket, but it was too small.

Waiting for me at the house had been two aerograms from Laura. The first, written in mid-May from Athens, several weeks after we'd parted in Rome, was a lively account of her adventures with the captain of the ferry from Italy to Greece. For almost two weeks she'd stayed in his cabin and had gone back and forth across the Adriatic. The second aerogram was troubling in a different sort of way. She said that in Athens she'd met a Frenchman selling jewelry in a market; he had a van and she was setting off to travel with him in Yugoslavia. The letter was dated early June from Sarajevo. Now it was almost August. I called Laura's mother and found out that Laura was back in Athens, with some medical problems. She'd been in the hospital and would be flying back to New York shortly to stay with her sister for a couple of weeks.

"I'll tell her that you said hello," said her mother.

I didn't ask what sort of medical problem; her mother's tone seemed to imply that I didn't need to know. Eventually I'd find out that Laura, who'd brought no birth control with her to Europe, had had a tubular pregnancy. The Frenchman hadn't let her out of his sight to see a doctor; finally, very sick, she'd run away from him and called her mother, who wired her money to get back to Athens. I found it as unbelievable a story as my own prolonged stay in London, though far more dangerous.

I told Rob about it and he said, "Laura always had a reckless side." He said it as if he knew something about her that I didn't, and I was reminded that he'd actually made love to her while I'd never quite managed it.

The days when I had quoted poetry to Laura seemed long ago. Sometimes I took out Machado and reread his poems, but already the Spanish seemed harder to follow. I looked again for my English translation, the one I'd done with the poet in Granada.

> Last night when I was sleeping
> I dreamed—Oh blessed vision!—
> that a fountain flowed
> deep within my heart.
> Tell me, water,
> By what secret channel
> have you come to me
> A spring of new life
> I've never drunk before?

I sometimes thought that it was Laura herself who'd been my secret fountain, the spring of new life from which I'd wanted to drink but hadn't dared. How distant those days in Spain seemed, how distant that sunny afternoon on the Plaza Mayor, when I'd told her, "I can't bear to have you leave without me."

I should have never gotten on the train in Rome.

Rob didn't want to know much about our travels together, and when I brought up something about Spain or Italy, he was likely to look vague and change the subject back to himself. He especially didn't like to hear about all the plays I'd seen in London and would try to top me by telling about productions in Los Angeles. "Women have served all these centuries as looking glasses possessing the magic and delicious power of reflecting the figure of man at twice his natural size," Virginia Woolf had written. Rob was delighted to have his looking glass back at home. All the same, he needed to remind me often to do my reflecting correctly.

I planned to get a job of some sort, but not quite yet. I wanted to go up to Oakland, where Ruthie and her boyfriend Doug were living now, but couldn't work up the courage to tell Rob I wanted to leave so soon after arriving. I dithered around most days, rearranging my books, from *Zen in English Literature and Oriental Classics* to *Labyrinths,* and paging through my journals and sketchbook.

I had so much material for stories; I had what I had gone to Europe to find. And still I sat there, on our double bed in the small room, unable to write a single line. Rob was out much of the day, rehearsing, and out in the evenings too. Late at night, all the actors would come home, smoke dope, drink, and tell endless stories of the theater to impress each other, the way actors do. I could tell Rob was disappointed in me because I was so silent most of the time and because I never seemed to do anything, much less write. He'd told people I was a writer; now everyone asked me about what I was working on and if I'd been published.

In the mirror of that small room I saw myself, and I looked older somehow, not so fresh or wide-eyed. I had my hair trimmed to my shoulders and went to the beach to get a tan. Compared to the vivacious and attractive women working at the theater I felt fat and wan; my unhappiness showed on my face. In front of the mirror I tried to see another girl, a lively, pretty twenty-year-old, one who'd been followed in the streets by men, one who'd been kissed on the streets of Paris, one who'd walked arm in arm with Laura in Madrid. But I failed. The worried face looking back at me from the mirror reminded me of the face of my adolescent self, mired in self-doubt and unbearable memories, the self I'd gone to Europe to escape.

Sometimes, in the evenings when Rob was rehearsing, I took one or another of the postcards out of the frame and read what I had written, those sprightly messages from the traveler to the stay-at-home, that always ended, "Miss you. Love you." One evening I noticed a card from Rome, a photograph of the Forum, that I suddenly didn't recall sending. I plucked it out and saw that it was addressed to me, in Costa Mesa, and was dated early May:

> I just saw you off at the train station. How strange it seems without you. How lonely! I've been walking around, eating ice cream, but it doesn't even taste the same. Tomorrow I'm off to Greece, and new adventures. But I wish you were with me. I hope your last couple of days in London are fun and that the flight is fine too. I wonder how it will be to be back in the States. Is it strange? I miss you very much. I love you. Laura.

I curled up on the double bed with her postcard in my hand and cried.

PART II

UNIVERSIDAD DE GRANADA
FACULTAD DE FILOSOFIA Y LETRAS
CURSO DE ESTUDIOS HISPANICOS

Tarjeta de Identidad, núm. ...., de

D. BARBARA WILSON

matriculado como alumno en el

EST.HISP. (15- X -19 72 a VI 19 73)

V.º B.º
El Decano,

El Director del
Curso,

Firma
del interesado

❧ TEN ❧

Incognito Street

"WHY NORWAY?" asked Leanne dramatically, waving a Carlton.

She wasn't asking me why I'd just arrived in Oslo on this cold day in February 1972 but explaining her own past six months in Scandinavia. "Everyone wants to know why I've come here. And what someone like me can possibly be doing working as a maid."

With her black hair in a long pageboy, red lips, darkly made-up eyes, and, of course, the long, polished fingernails, Leanne looked as sharkishly feminine as I remembered from London nine months ago. She was pale from a sunless winter, dressed in belted slacks, and a navy blue sweater, with a red scarf around her neck. When she met me at the airport, she'd also sported a beret and a stylish black wool coat; she'd stood out from the crowds of Norwegians in their snowflake-patterned pullovers and ski pants.

"I tell them the truth," she continued, "that I never want to set foot in America again. That I don't even think of myself as American any longer. I know I'll be in Norway the rest of my life. There's no problem with the language, and everyone finds me exotic because of my dark hair and Southern accent. The men are so tall too."

"No problem with the language?" I repeated stupidly, half overcome by jet lag. "But it's—Norwegian here, right?"

"Oh, everyone speaks English. It's like Reykjavík, only much *much* better than Iceland."

Gunnar? He was long out of the picture. She'd returned to Reykjavík and found him still separated from his wife but not at all interested in resuming a relationship with Leanne. She'd managed to find a job for a month or so, then had taken a leap and traveled to Norway with a Norwegian friend who had offered to put her up for a while. She'd arrived at the end of August and had fallen in love with the country. Leanne had told me all this in letters, and now she told me the whole story again, cigarette punctuating the main points, smoke obscuring some of the pain of rejection and the obvious fact that she'd spent most of the insurance money and was now forced to work a menial job.

We were sitting in a large room carved from the attic of a very large house high in the hills above the city center. An open closet was full of little black dresses and chiffon peignoirs, but otherwise the room was rather stark, with a plug-in kettle, narrow bed, and springy old sofa on which we sat with our pot of tea and plate of biscuits on the table before us. Nearby was my Hermes typewriter in its hard sea green case and the large new suitcase in which I'd packed as much as I could of my old life.

"This is only temporary," Leanne said. "In fact, it's probably a *good* thing, because the Holmen family is so very rich and well known—they're the Holmens of Holmenkollen, one of the most famous ski jumps in the world. I might be their maid, but when they have parties, I do meet their friends, and what that means is that I meet interesting men with money. Kari works me hard, but she has connections. She's a very good person to know."

I thought back to Leanne's wonderful letters about Norway, with their stamps of fjords and mountains, and how they'd begun to arrive in late summer, little blue signals of hope, into my often lonely and sometimes anguished life first in Costa Mesa, then in Long Beach after I'd left Rob. "Picture a dark blue fjord sparkling in the sunshine, with small white sailboats fluttering like moths all over its surface," she wrote, and I did picture it and was envious of Leanne. *She* hadn't just sat around in Iceland being miserable when Gunnar dumped her; she was on to new adventures, ravenous for life, claiming the title expatriate proudly. When I spilled out my dissatisfaction with being back in America, my unhappiness with Rob, my irritation that the trust money *still* hadn't come on my twenty-first birthday in October, so that I wasn't able to begin my year of study in Granada as I'd hoped, Leanne had written: "When you do get the check, why not come to Norway for a few months? I'd love to see you, and you can get a job if you want and save up more for Spain."

Through the window of Leanne's attic room I saw a black sky with a full moon at barely four o'clock in the afternoon. Last week I'd walked along the beach of my hometown at sunset, feeling the sand cool under my bare feet, smelling the sharp, familiar saltiness of the ocean. I'd looked down the length of the shore to the Pacific Coast Club building where I'd had swimming lessons. I looked at the palm trees on the bluff above and remembered how often I'd come to this beach as a child with my mother, who had been dead now for nine years. My tiny studio on Coronado Avenue was only a few blocks from the mortuary where I'd last seen her when I was twelve, lying in her coffin, and where my father and brother and I had sobbed and held each other and my father had said, "I'll take care of you. I'll be your mother now."

Like Leanne, I felt when I boarded the airplane out of Los Angeles that I, too, was never going back. I was here in Europe to stay.

Oslo's center seemed very small to me, packed into snowdrifts like a Christmas present in tissue paper. In size it was completely unlike London or Paris, even though it was a capital city. There wasn't much traffic; trams crisscrossed the city, often with multiple pairs of long wooden skis attached. The morning after I arrived, while Leanne was washing dishes and doing laundry under Kari's critical eye, I took the tram down to the center and walked around until I grew tired. I had on my tall suede boots from a Florentine market last year and a long white canvas coat, quilted inside, that I'd bought a few days before when I visited my friend David outside of Boston. I had never seen this much snow before, not even in Boston, for there the streets were plowed and the sidewalks scraped clean. These streets were hard-packed with snow and so were the sidewalks, which gave the city a seamless look of white. Oslo looked almost built of snow, deep-frozen, with a very long, wide boulevard running through it, some stately old hotels, a theater, and even a palace right in the center. All was white, even the sky, and strangely silent; by afternoon, snow was falling through the darkening blue air, and the world grew even more muffled and private.

I bought a Norwegian phrase book and some English translations of the sagas, *Njal's Saga* and *Laxdæla Saga,* and took them with me to a *konditori* where I had coffee with cream and Danish pastry. The language of the sagas was swift and clear; reading the opening passages of *Laxdæla Saga* brought to mind Borges and William Morris, who had both, in their separate ways, made me receptive to Leanne's urging to come north. The North that had once been imaginary was now real. It wasn't as cold as I'd expected; the dry air invigorated and the whiteness dazzled. Damp London had been far chillier and gloomier last winter.

Over and over I told myself that first day, I'm in Europe, I'm back in Europe. Yet it was a far different Europe than I'd known last year. The people were tall and reserved, efficient and intelligent looking; a race of engineers and architects, they seemed. They wore knit hats, thick sweaters, and parkas, and some of them seemed dressed for the slopes, in woolen pants that came only to the knees, with thick wool stockings and boots. The language swung up and down like a seesaw, even when they spoke English; everyone did speak English and seemed amused when I referred to my phrase book and tried to sound out, "How much please?" "*Vær så god,*" they said when they handed me my change. "Be so good." I bought a red wool hat with a pattern of reindeer, and new wool gloves, and breathed deep of the crystal-cold air on my way back to Leanne's. California already seemed a dream, my old life decisively over, a new life beginning. What would happen to me here?

I wasn't in Oslo much more than a week before I was offered a job as an au pair in the town of Hamar, about two hours north by train, on the shores of Lake Mjøsa. My new employer, Elisabeth Helland-Hansen, had been a Holmen before marriage. One day she was in town and made a visit to her brother and sister-in-law, Kari, who told her that I was looking for work. While Kari had long blond hair and was the very picture of Norwegianness, with bright blue eyes and red cheeks from skiing, Elisabeth was tall and thin, with a brown complexion, curly light brown hair, and hazel eyes that often looked amused.

"You could come home with me," Elisabeth said suddenly as the four of us sat around the kitchen table, Leanne and Kari smoking and all of us with strong coffee and something new to me, *lefse,* a thin griddle cake spread with butter, sugar, and cinnamon, folded and cut into triangles. "I have three boys and a husband. The littlest boy, Knut, isn't in school yet. I could use some help babysitting, shopping. It would be more like you were part of the family."

"But—then you wouldn't be in Oslo!" Leanne dismissed the idea with a puff of smoke.

"I could come back on weekends sometimes—if I lived there," I said. I wasn't sure what was so attractive about the idea of Hamar, except that there was something about Elisabeth's smile when she invited me to join her family that seemed so kind, and I was in great need of kindness. My first week in Oslo had made me face reality: that although Leanne was generous, Kari was less so. Leanne was her employee and I could be Leanne's guest, but only for a short while. Kari had suggested that I move into the youth hostel after a couple of nights here. Sleeping in a dorm room and being locked out of the hostel every day from noon to four had begun to pall. I sat in *konditoris* and read the sagas and began to worry. How would I make my way here? I'd felt rich when I left Long Beach with a wad of traveler's checks, but Norway was far more expensive than England or the Continent had been. Whenever I paid six times for coffee what it would have cost in Spain, I seemed to see Grandma Lane's stern frown. I'd promised myself that I wouldn't fling my money around as I had on my first trip but would hang on to it as long as possible.

I looked straight at Elisabeth and smiled back. "I can be ready to go back with you today."

Later Leanne told me she'd been shocked how quickly I decided to leave, shocked I'd consider living anywhere in Norway outside Oslo. She was disappointed too that her confidante was disappearing on her. She'd thought, when she wrote suggesting I come to Norway and get a job, that I'd live in the same city, that she'd have someone to go to films and bars with, someone to compare notes with about affairs and relationships. But it had become apparent to me, after just a week, that Leanne and I were on different paths. When she said she loved the country, what she loved was Oslo, with its shops and restaurants and men who seemed to have money to burn. What I was coming to love about Norway was something completely different.

I knew, the first morning I woke in Hamar, in my room in the big yellow wooden house that looked just like something out of a Carl Larsson painting, that I was in exactly the right place. The walls were wainscoted with painted blue gray wood, and the floor was painted the same color. The room had a wooden single bed, with a striped blue seersucker cover on the down comforter. Most important, there was a pine table in front of the window, a table for writing. The sun streamed in that morning on the table, where I'd placed my journal and typewriter, sunshine made brighter by the abundant snow outside, but still a northern sun, low in the pale blue sky, filtered through bare branches.

How do you get to know a country? Who can teach it to you? In high school I'd applied to be an exchange student with the American Field Service. I'd imagined living in France with a new mother and father and siblings, going to the market with a wicker basket strapped to my bike. I hadn't been chosen, but somehow, at the age of twenty-one, with a wealth of adult experience behind me, I'd found myself secure within a family in a foreign country, learning everything about Norway from the ground up.

Knut, my snub-nosed, sturdy, blond two-year-old charge, didn't understand I didn't speak his language. He had only learned recently to speak himself. He could say bread slice: *skive*. With brown cheese:

med brun ost. He could say pee: *tisse.* And amazingly he could say, "I want to go skiing." *Jeg vil gå på ski.*

Bundled up in his snowsuit, with red plastic skis, he already could propel himself over and down the small snowdrifts around the house. I strapped on a pair of old-fashioned wooden skis and accompanied Knut around the yard, along with the big black dog, Buster. Knut couldn't understand why I, a grownup, was always in a tangled pile. How could I explain that I'd been raised in Southern California and had never seen snow like this?

My spoken Norwegian was constructed on ordinary speech. "Knut, come here and I'll put on your shoes. Knut, time for a nap." The first full sentence I ever learned in Norwegian was *Vær så snill å sende meg smøren.* "Be so kind to pass me the butter." I learned all the words for food first, then for clothing and for weather. Neither the syntax nor the vocabulary was so difficult, since they were much like English and there were many cognates, but the intonation was initially almost impossible for a monotone American. How did you hear and reproduce that peculiar singing quality? How did you know to go up on certain words, down on others? Compared to Spanish, which had fit my mouth so easily, Norwegian often seemed composed of tiny beads, words two and three letters long, strung together in a necklace that waved up and down.

"Why Norway?" Elisabeth wanted to know as we sat down in the kitchen after the flurry of getting two of the boys, Bjørn and Geir, and her husband, Thor, off to school and work. We usually had a cup of Earl Grey tea before doing the dishes and some basic tasks like laundry and sweeping the planked wooden floors. Unlike Kari, Elisabeth was no taskmaster; she was more glad of the company. Her voice held a laugh, and she had an accent in English that was partly Norwegian and partly Scottish. She'd been an au pair herself, in Edinburgh, fifteen years before.

I knew that she liked me as much as I liked her but that she found me oddly resistant to talking about myself. This had been a habit of mine since I was ten and trouble had come to my house. I kept my secrets and over the years had collected more and more of them. I wanted to present myself as an average girl to Elisabeth but knew that I wasn't and hadn't been for many years. In fact, I wasn't a girl anymore; I was a woman who'd lived with a boyfriend, who'd been in love with another woman, who'd traveled and lived on her own. But in Elisabeth's company I wanted to present my life as simpler. I wanted to begin again, and she let me.

I spun a story of always having wanted to travel and learn languages, of having planned to be a writer, of having been given an unexpected gift by my grandmother. I often emphasized my ties with Grandma Lane to Elisabeth, as if to prove that there was someone in my family who had never let me down. I mentioned my mother's death from cancer, leaving out her Christian Science beliefs and mental breakdown. I said my father had remarried and I didn't get on well with my stepmother, that I had a younger brother but he had left to get away from Bettye as well. I didn't say no one knew exactly where he was. Family was so important in this new country that I couldn't bear to explain how estranged we all were from each other or how I'd felt so homeless for so long that I never even thought of my departure from America as leaving home.

"Why Norway?" Elisabeth probed again. "In winter?"

"I needed to get away," I said when I knew her better, and I told her a little about Rob, with whom I'd finally split when he took up with the choreographer of *Tommy,* about six weeks after my return. Strangely, for all my ambivalence about him, he'd still managed to wound me. Everyone knew about the affair but me, and that was one of the most painful parts—to feel so foolish. Rob wasn't remorseful or guilty, only angry that someone had spilled the beans. Even after I left him and moved into the studio apartment on Coronado Avenue in Long Beach, he would still come over and stare at me with those black-lashed green eyes and say, "You know we have a connection that nothing—that no one can destroy, don't you?"

Heartbreak Elisabeth could understand. She told me that I was young, that I'd recover. But there were other heartaches I couldn't so easily share.

Laura had finally returned to California at the end of August, after spending some time in New York. I'd flown up to Oakland to stay with Ruthie in early September, and Laura had driven over from Sacramento. We met again on a hot Saturday, in a kitchen full of Ruthie's friends, and our hug seemed over too quickly. It was four months since we'd seen each other, and after hearing what she'd been through on the phone, I expected her to look terrible. But she was healthy, even radiant; she'd kept her curly hair short, but it seemed to suit her better now, and her smile kept turning into the irrepressible laugh of someone deeply happy.

We went out on the sagging front porch to be alone. Ruthie's house was in a run-down part of town, where a new overhead BART section was going in and the sound of jackhammers echoed noisily from two blocks away. Kids played in the street, kicking balls and shouting; their mothers sat on stoops, just like us, trying to get some fresh air on the smoggy day, some waving fans. Oddly I was reminded of the old-fashioned shops around the Plaza Mayor, with their displays of fans, mantillas, and shawls. What a long time ago our leisurely days in Madrid now seemed.

To my surprise Laura didn't want to dwell on her hard times with the Frenchman who'd practically kept her prisoner for three weeks, nor on the emergency surgery she'd had in Athens. She was hardly more interested in my tale of Manny and only said, "That sounds tough. But at least you got to see all those plays and things."

She had other news. Better news. News she hadn't wanted to tell me on the phone but to share in person: She was in love. It had just happened, just a couple of weeks ago, in New York. Her sister had a Greek friend, an actor; actually her sister had been seeing him. But Laura and Georgiou had fallen in love on the spot. He was returning to Crete for a while, to live with his family, and Laura was going to join him. She'd be leaving in two weeks.

"When are you coming back?" I was dumbfounded, my eyes fixed on the blue eyes that didn't quite seem to see me.

"Maybe a year," she said. "Georgiou is also thinking of moving to London next year, to try to get in one of the acting schools." She had the dreamy look of a woman in love, content and self-absorbed. I felt pathetic next to her radiance, my own unexpressed hopes suddenly dashed. But hopes of what? Surely I hadn't really expected us to make plans together for the future.

"Are you still going back to Spain?" she asked.

"I want to. It depends when I get the money from the bank."

"And you're writing. Of course."

"Our place is small," I excused myself.

"One of these days you'll really leave him," she said wisely. "And find someone you can truly love."

Soon Laura remembered she had to get her mom's car back to Sacramento and we said goodbye, hugging on the street in front of the curious children and the women with their waving fans.

For just a second I smelled the familiar scent of my Mermaid; then she was gone.

Ruthie threw up her hands when she heard that Laura was headed back to Europe; with me she took a sterner tack. This fall, she told me, I really had to take hold of myself. I needed to return to school and finish, preferably with an English degree, and stop all this talk of going back to Spain. She'd transferred from UC Berkeley to the California College of Arts and Crafts last year and was going to graduate in the spring with a degree in applied arts. During my time in Oakland she was always busy knitting sweaters or embroidering bird motifs on black velvet or playing Bach on her viola or hoeing around her tomatoes or baking whole-grain bread or making chocolate-chip cookies for her dozens of pot-smoking musician friends. The sight of me in her living room staring disconsolately out the window with the poems of William Blake in my lap was abhorrent to her, and she asked me to end my visit early. After I returned to Southern California to find that Rob had taken up with the choreographer, Ruthie wrote me a sharp letter about my lack of stick-to-itiveness and my tendency to live in a fantasy world. It was the kind of letter meant to send a wake-up call but harsh and critical enough to disrupt a friendship.

From time to time I'd go to Oslo on the old-fashioned train, with its compartments of heavy wooden trim and hard seats. I'd stay in the attic room of the huge house in Oslo's tony West End, drink coffee, and listen to stories of Leanne's latest conquests: An industrialist had flown her to Bodø up in the north on a business trip; a poet and Marxist loved to upbraid her for the war in Vietnam even as he was screwing her brains out; a married man wanted her to run off with him to Torremolinos for a vacation in April. Compared to her, I felt like a nun in my little room at the Helland-Hansens'.

"But what do you do there?" Leanne demanded.

Like the rest of the family, I had a dose of cod-liver oil in the morning with my two slices of whole-wheat bread on which I squeezed some bright orange fish eggs from a tube like toothpaste. I used an *ostehøvel* to shave off slices from the top of a big rectangle of jarlsberg or brown goat cheese. For lunch we ate exactly the same thing. For dinner there were meat cakes—or fish cakes or spongy white fish balls with white sauce—with parsnips or rutabagas and boiled potatoes, followed by a dessert of cornflakes and cultured milk. I joined in the late-evening snack of a slice of bread with cheese or sometimes fried mushrooms or even pancakes with currant jam. I drank multiple cups of coffee with cream throughout the day and, on special occasions, cakes built up with layers of whipped cream. At first Norwegian meals seemed strange to me; I'd come so lately from a world where oranges hung on the trees in winter and grocery stores were full of fruits and green vegetables, but gradually, like so much about the country, the food seemed just the way it should be, providing comfort and sustenance without a lot of flavor or flash.

Like the others, I put on my woolen long johns and ski hat to go outside and slipped off my shoes when I came in. I took the dog on walks, and I went to the local store for Elisabeth, sometimes using a sort of kick sled on long runners, called a *spark*. Sometimes I put Knut in the little box on the sled and brought him with me. I spent a lot of time getting Knut in and out of his snowsuit. Unlike Leanne, who was busy from morning to night keeping Kari's home spotless, I had only light tasks at the Helland-Hansens', mainly washing up and sweeping. Elisabeth and I did many things together, talking all the while. We changed the covers on the *dynes,* or down comforters, though I never mastered the way that Elisabeth had of shaking the *dyne* into the inside-out sheath in a single quick movement. On sunny days we hung the *dynes* out the windows and put the rugs out on the snow. We cooked the evening meal and the Sunday meal, which was slightly grander, with perhaps a chicken or a whole fish.

I had several hours in the afternoon free and often used that time to write. I took up smoking small cigars like George Sand and sat at my pine table clattering away on my typewriter. I experimented with short pieces first and then a novella called "The Iceland," a story of love and loss told in a spare and mythic style that had much to do with the Icelandic sagas and something also of Borges's story "The South." In his tale, a man who's almost died of septicemia in Buenos Aires leaves for the wide emptiness of the South and a ranch he's bought there. En route, in a little hole-in-the-wall, he's challenged to a fight. The story ends with him walking out into the night, into his destiny, almost certainly to his death. In my version, a dark-haired beautiful woman from the South, Quita, comes to the far North to forget her previous life. Embroiled in a love triangle in the dead of winter, she knifes her rival to death.

"The Iceland" began with a quote from a minor saga, *The Deluding of Gylfi,* by Snorri Sturluson:

> Then Gangleri said: "The sun moves fast and almost as if she were afraid; she could not travel faster if she were in fear of her life." Then High One answered: "It is not surprising that she goes at a great pace; her pursuer is close behind her and there is nothing she can do but flee."

Its plot was melodramatic and convoluted, with a great deal of cold weather. It was peopled with Kjells and Astrids, all of whom had high cheekbones and spoke in somewhat stilted English like that of the saga translations. I was never to write anything remotely like it again, yet it absorbed me completely for a month or two.

For the first time I had something approaching discipline in my creative life. The most important thing about "The Iceland" was that I worked on it almost every day. During the fall in Long Beach, when I'd lived on Coronado Avenue, I'd often tried to write at my kitchen table in the evenings after I returned from my job as a cashier in a discount store, but I was often too tired and too out of sorts and never knew when I might hear Rob's knock at the door. It was the first time I'd ever lived alone on purpose, and it had often unnerved me more than freed me. It was not the room of one's own I'd dreamed of in London after reading Virginia Woolf.

But my room at the Helland-Hansens' big yellow house was that room of my own. It taught me that I didn't have to be completely solitary to write; in fact, I liked the sounds of the house around me: the boys back from school running up to their rooms opposite me to change into soccer uniforms and then out again; Elisabeth's humming as she came upstairs to the laundry room; Thor arriving home from work, snatching up Knut in his arms: "How's it going, little friend?" All those sounds were happy sounds, and although I sat in my room, smoking cigars, looking out at the snow, and typing versions of a story about revenge on the choreographer (now transformed into the evil Astrid), I felt like a member of the family, a youthful, artistic auntie or even another child, well taken care of.

"Do you ever go out in the evenings?" Leanne wanted to know. "Aren't you bored out of your skull? I could never stand it." But then, Leanne did not eat with the family. She served them in the dining room and then retired to the kitchen for her own meal. Kari was very clear that Leanne was the maid.

In Hamar we ate dinner around four, in the Norwegian fashion. Bjørn and Geir did their homework. There was a single channel on television: at five was the children's program, at six the news. Later there was something cultural—the Bolshoi Ballet doing *Giselle,* or something trashy, like the American serial *Dynasty.* Sometimes all of us sat around reading. Often in the evening I took Buster out for a walk. Away from town, in the farmlands nearby, I took him off his leash and together we ran along the hard-packed snow roads. Sometimes I'd walk into a field and lie down and look up at the constellations. I felt perfectly safe, and it occurred to me that there were few places in the world where I could feel as safe as this. I never thought of Rob during these times, or Laura or Ruthie. I thought only of the night, the stars, and the cold, and the warm, wet nose of Buster, who would eventually get tired of running madly in circles and would come and lie down beside me.

During the time I was at the Helland-Hansens', Norwegian television was showing a drama in several parts based on one of the novels of Cora Sandel, *Alberta and Freedom.* The drama was in Norwegian and I didn't know enough to understand it. But Elisabeth explained as much of the plot as she could: A young woman, "a writer like you," left the north of Norway to go to Paris around 1910. There were scenes of bohemian artists in garrets, of cancan girls, and smoky cafés on the Boulevard Montparnasse. A blond girl slipped anxiously through the streets, en route to a modeling job. But there were also scenes of her hunched over a desk, scribbling. "She is trying to be a writer," explained Elisabeth. "No success."

The Alberta novels were based on Cora Sandel's own life, Elisabeth told me. Sandel had been born in 1880; her family had moved far north when she was around twelve. Her real name was Sara Fabricius; she'd taken a pen name when she finally published. Early on she had a talent for art. After studying in Oslo, Sandel eventually found her way to Paris in 1906 and managed to live, much like Alberta, a poor but not quite disreputable life among the Scandinavian art community. Sandel learned her French from advertising signs and newspapers, later from French novels she read while standing in bookshops. She married a Swede, a sculptor, and returned with him to Sweden after the First World War. There she left him and began to support herself through her writing.

Later, when I read her short stories and novels, Cora Sandel would become immensely important to me. For now I memorized her name and the titles of her books and added her to the small pantheon of women trying to be writers.

After I'd been in Hamar a month or so I got to know the Munck family, which consisted at the time of a divorced mother and her six children, all of whom had grown up on an estate outside São Paolo. The family had been transported abruptly to Hamar after their father was discovered in bed with the maid. The Muncks had a famous relative, Edvard Munch. They were from the side of the family that was not artistic and had changed its name so they wouldn't be called "munch" abroad. This branch of the family went into manufacturing and made cranes. One factory was in Brazil, where Mr. Munck had stayed on with the maid, and the other was in Hamar. Elisabeth's husband, Thor, was the factory director. The Muncks seemed very un-Norwegian. They spoke to each other in Portuguese, and most of them had violent tempers. They liked to eat and drink, and the house was generally in a tumult when I went over there. I became most friendly with a girl of sixteen, Ida, who had bright blond hair and was a great reader, in three languages.

They were another part of my life that was increasingly hard to explain to Leanne. She was impressed that they were related to

Edvard Munch, but she couldn't understand what I was doing playing with children. "You taught them to play softball? You let them call you *Bra-Bra?*" Knut, not being able to pronounce Barbara, called me that first, and it had caught on. I found it charming, for *bra* is the Norwegian word for "good."

It was difficult to tell Leanne that in Hamar I'd found a way to return to a childhood that had ended when I was ten. I'd found a way to erase the intervening unhappy years and find the solid ground I'd missed so desperately once my mother got sick. Being in a family again restored to me in part the happy-go-lucky nature I'd been born with and soothed the anxiety about my choices in life. Elisabeth took it for granted that I was a beginning writer who would gradually improve and publish. She heard me typing. She read "The Iceland" and pronounced it "very much like the sagas." She didn't expect me to be living with them forever, but while I was there she took me in and treated me like a dear younger sister and encouraged me and loved me. My thirsty heart soaked up her affection, which came so readily, without strings attached.

More and more Leanne and I drifted apart, and when we met in Oslo it seemed as though we were living in different countries. One day in May, with the snow finally almost melted, we met up in an outdoor café in Frogner Park. Leanne looked very glamorous, in heels and a longish skirt slit up to her knees, a Hermès scarf that was likely a present from a beau. Some of the softness of her face was gone, but that only made her more beautiful. I sometimes wondered why I never felt attracted to her; I suppose I found her an alien species of womanhood, like certain dashing socialites I'd known in high school. It reassured me that I felt the same about Leanne as I'd felt about those girls—fascinated but repelled. It reassured me that I'd only ever been in love with one woman, Laura, something that perhaps wouldn't happen again.

It was about five in the afternoon, and the sun was bright still on the fresh green trees of the park. The return of the light had been extraordinary to us both. Leanne ordered a martini, in English, from the waiter. I had hot chocolate. As usual she began telling me about some of her recent dates. It never made her uncomfortable when men she liked bought her meals or took her on business trips. She'd never understood, though I'd explained it as well as I could, what the big problem had been with me and Manny. Of course, Leanne wouldn't have let it get to the point I had. She was able to take care of herself, to get what she wanted, and then move on. She never bothered even to rationalize it; it was the way the world worked. Or so I thought when I was irritated with her.

In fact, Leanne and I had more in common than I would admit then. We'd both come to Europe to shed some of our pasts and to make a fresh start. I didn't really know what she was running from or who she thought she wanted to become. I didn't know why she would choose another country to reinvent herself in, when she could have so easily married rich and erased whatever humiliations she'd undergone in Raleigh. But I suspect that, in spite of all the talking, Leanne didn't tell me her whole story, just as I never told her mine.

That day in Frogner Park we chatted about our summer plans. Kari had introduced her to a friend who ran a tourist agency. Leanne was going to be a tour guide for them, escorting Americans in buses around the beauty spots of the country.

"But you don't like to speak Norwegian!" I said. "How are you going to manage with all the logistics and hotels and everything? Besides, you haven't even seen these places you're going to be showing the tourists."

"I'll wing it, the way I always do," she smiled.

I was going to work in the tourism industry as well. I wanted to see more of the country and felt I needed to earn a salary as I was doing it. Elisabeth had seen an ad in the Oslo paper advertising for the manager of a souvenir shop at a hotel up in the mountains. "You'll be perfect," said Elisabeth. Together we had composed a letter in Norwegian to the hotel owners and I had received one back, hiring me. My plan was to spend the summer working, then head to Spain in September, to finally begin the course for foreigners at the University of Granada.

Leanne and I parted that sunny late afternoon with a cheek-brushed kiss and a promise to write over the summer. Then she went off to meet one of her dates at the Theater Café and I took a long walk back through the city to the train station where I'd catch the train for Hamar. My walk took me in the direction of the palace, along Incognito Street, past the Incognito Clinic, a place I was always going to put into a story someday. I imagined my character walking into the clinic with one self and walking out with another. The story's outline wasn't really so different from the plot of "The Iceland." A woman wants to leave her past behind her. She develops a new voice, new personality, even a different past. I based the character on Leanne, but it was really myself I was describing.

Why Norway? Chance, luck, or destiny, who knows? I can only say that, in the late winter turning into spring, with the sun shining on the packed white snow, the whole country looked to me like a clean sheet of paper, one that was only waiting for me to write my new story, my fresh beginning, onto its page.

❧ ELEVEN ❧

A Glacier Summer

I SPENT THE SUMMER in the high mountains of central Norway, a landscape known as Jotunheim, or "Home of the Giants." Elveseter Hotel was in a green valley on the road that wound from the coastal fjords through high plateaus, ice fields, and the tallest mountains in Northern Europe. In earlier times the hotel had been a large summer farm; it was still owned by the original family and had retained much of its traditional character with many outbuildings around a central hall. Although in 1972 there were two long motel-like structures for the guests, there were also numerous small huts characteristic of a Norwegian farm: storerooms, saunas, and bakeries, built of logs with grass roofs where goats were once tethered. A fast-moving river ran below the farm, so loudly that in the beginning it seemed to drown out all other sound. Above the farm lay other *seters,* or summer farms, alpine meadows, and glacier-covered peaks.

Aside from four Norwegian students who worked as maids and drivers during the day and performed folk dances for the tourists at night, almost all of us who worked at the hotel were foreigners (we often speculated that the Elveseters had chosen non-Norwegians intentionally, to push us around more easily). Of the foreigners, I was the only one who could get along in the language, which is why I'd been given the job of managing the souvenir shop, a tiny glass room off the restaurant that was packed with hand-carved wooden trolls, delicate silver jewelry and pewter bowls, as well as postcards, film, and sundries. Of the Norwegians, only one seemed interested in getting to know the foreigners. That was Leidulf, a student who studied engineering at the shipbuilding school in Trondheim. He had thick bronze hair and red lips and was graceful when he danced. I noticed him right away and he noticed me.

We all had to wear costumes at work. Mine was a striped blue and white skirt, a white blouse with puffed sleeves, and a blue bodice that laced in front. My Australian roommate, Felicity, who ran the hotel bar, wore a version in red. We looked like something out of *Song of Norway,* and tourists often remarked how authentic we looked—until we opened our mouths. Our lack of fluent—or even basic—Norwegian took Norwegian travelers by surprise, but, in fact, native tourists were few and far between. They preferred to stay someplace less authentic and were usually up in the mountains for serious hiking, not for buying hand-carved wooden trolls and for folk dancing after dinner. What Elveseter catered to were busloads of European and American tourists on package tours who usually stayed only one night on the way from Sogndal to Otta.

The hotel was quite remote, and from the beginning, life there had a dreamlike, disorienting quality. Although the foreign staff had arrived with the idea of seeing Norway, the grandeur and isolation of the landscape were intimidating. We were all from urban centers like Sydney, Newcastle, Cincinnati, and Los Angeles, and few of us were really prepared for the light nights, towering mountains and what seemed, at first, an overwhelming lack of anything to *do.* The eighteen of us formed a close-knit society—six men and twelve women, mostly students. Felicity was the oldest of us at twenty-three; she and I roomed together in the second story of a *stabbur,* or storehouse. Traditionally, it was the unmarried women of the household who lived there during the summers and drew the ladder up every night against prospective bridegrooms. Grass and wildflowers grew in profusion on the roof, and the ladder gave us not a little trouble that summer. Almost every time we had a party someone lost their footing and tumbled to the bottom.

The hotel was in the Bøver Valley, twenty-five kilometers west from the nearest village of Lom, which, other than an old white-painted church, had little besides a café and a few shops. The closest large towns were at least a day's journey by bus or hitching, and it was difficult to arrange time off to visit them, though several of us made it to the spectacular Geiranger Fjord. The Elveseter family—wild-eyed husband, stern wife, and lonely, obnoxious son—worked us exceedingly hard. We had very little time off, and to make sure we didn't run away they kept our wages for us, to be paid at the end of the summer. Meanwhile they docked us constantly for being late to work or sneaking into the walk-in fridge to steal some food. For although the guests exclaimed at the bountiful tables of sliced roast beef, shrimp, and huge strawberries, we who worked at the hotel ate only bread and cheese, cream porridge, and reindeer stew with potatoes. We spent many mealtimes obsessing about pizza and Chinese food.

Our small society went through various fashions and passions during the three months of the summer season. The first weeks of June were cold and rainy, and we spent a considerable amount of time indoors, drinking and getting to know each other. We often stayed up all night because it never really got dark, and plotted ways to get alcohol cheaper than Mr. Elveseter wanted to sell it to us. Lom didn't have a state-owned liquor store, so two of us were dispatched, list in hand, two hundred kilometers to Lillehammer, to order bottles in bulk. Our boxes of alcohol arrived by bus one day, much to the consternation of Mr. Elveseter. But when these bottles were gone—almost all on the big blowout party we held around a bonfire on Midsummer Night's Eve—a more sober period set in, and we turned to cheaper and more innocent pleasures, such as learning folk dancing from the Norwegians and stitching traditional bell pulls from packages we bought in Lom. Even I, notorious non-sewer, produced one of these objects. Felicity decided our minds were rotting. She wrote to Foyles in London and ordered some books, which is how Sylvia Plath's *The Bell Jar* made its depressing way through a dozen young women that summer. Eventually Felicity fell down the *stabbur* ladder while carrying a pile of newly received art books that had been sent by mistake. That was the end of Foyles.

I'd brought with me the sagas, which I loaned out, as well as a Dover edition of Thoreau's excerpted journals, which I'd bought after visiting Walden Pond with my friend David. I didn't loan it out because I had underlined many things that I felt might expose me as someone other than the adventurous and lighthearted young woman I wished to appear.

"My Journal should be the record of my love. I would write in it only of the things I love, my affection for any aspect of the world, what I love to think of," Thoreau wrote. I had begun a new journal in Oslo as soon as I arrived, and I had tried to put in more description of the external world as opposed to writing only of my inner hopes and dreams and fears. Yet, more often than not, I wrote of the things that irritated and puzzled me, instead of simply recording what I saw, much less what I loved. I was no longer in the grip of Anaïs Nin; I was learning to describe people as separate beings, not only in their relationship to me. I wrote about Leanne and about the Muncks; I wrote about the books I was reading and even described Oslo fairly thoroughly. But I spent little time, until I encountered Thoreau, in trying to give a sense of the natural world and in showing affection for it.

Although there was no place and no time at Elveseter to continue writing stories, and I never took my typewriter out of its hard sea green case, I did try to keep a small journal while I was in the mountains that summer. It was much more difficult than I'd imagined to train my eye to look outward and observe nature, rather than to look inward and describe emotions. The religion I'd been brought up in eschewed the physical and exalted the spiritual. Early in my childhood, I had to leave the schoolroom whenever the rest of the class took out their science books. I spent the hour in the library while they learned about osmosis and photosynthesis, while they fed the gerbils and raised avocados in glasses of water. The founder of Christian Science, Mary Baker Eddy, was a nineteenth-century woman with an abhorrence of the medical profession (a distrust well founded in the days of dosing patients with mercury and sawing their limbs off without anesthesia). The Christian Science Church was in part built on the belief that the world in which we lived and moved was not the *real* world. I had almost no knowledge of the life sciences, no eyes to see the world except poetically, no understanding of the forces of nature around me. Even after my mother died and my father switched us over to Lutheranism and I enrolled in chemistry, the workings of the natural universe remained something of a mystery. I'd never been taught to cultivate a sense of wonder about the world; I looked at it like a two-dimensional painting, and although I smelled, tasted, heard, and touched the landscape around me, my descriptive writing tended to be visual and metaphoric. The world existed to be put in a poem, as background for the dialogue and action of a story.

When I wrote about the valley at the beginning of the summer, the river was loud as an airplane, was cold as if a thousand ice-cube trays had been dumped into it, was full of stones like gems in a fluid necklace. The mountains around me were white at the top, with glaciers old as time creeping down their slopes like stealthy polar bears. Or they were green as paint, spattered with tiny speckles of flowers. Did I know the names of any of the flowers? Not yet. My botanical studies were in the future, as was my interest in physical geography. Nevertheless, I pushed myself that summer to begin to see what was around me, to become a writer, hard as it was, a little more like Thoreau.

Toward the end of June the sun came out, along with giant mosquitoes, and the days were hot and long. Our group began to get its bearings and to become more adventurous. None of us had ever climbed before and a few had never been in snow, but the dream began to grow on some of us that we should be trying to conquer the peaks around us. The two gay cooks from Bournemouth firmly declined to know the heights and so did two of the women, but the rest of us gamely began to hike above the farms to the upper pastures, traditionally where the sheep were taken for the richer grass. As the snow retreated, lupines and columbines, bluebells, and dozens of flowers I didn't know the names of bloomed extravagantly in the meadows. Above the pastures there were plateaus and peaks, and the tongues of glaciers licking expectantly at our feet.

One sunny day four of us decided to join a guided group on the ascent to Galdhøpiggen, one of the mountains across the valley and the tallest peak in Norway, over 8,000 feet. We were all quite unprepared. Paul from Sydney wore sneakers and a sweatshirt. David from Hull had on jeans and a windbreaker over his T-shirt, and Sue from North London had on shorts and a sweater. In spite of having spent a snowy spring in Norway, I still assumed that when the sun shone it was hot, especially in summer. I had thought to wear two pairs of socks and had the only pair of mittens in the group, but my suede boots had little tread and soon became soaked. None of us had the foresight to wear a hat.

A bus from the bottom of the valley took us up a twisting road to a hostel at the base of the mountain, and as the bus wound upward our excited joking diminished slightly. There was a *lot* of snow, we noticed, hard-packed and glittering, and although the sky was blue it was definitely *much* colder than down in the Bøver Valley. Paul was too macho to give up, and although Sue admitted later she had hoped the guides would refuse to let us go, none of us spoke our worry as we attached crampons to our shoes and roped up. A crystal-cold, warning breeze seemed to come off the ice, and as we skirted one bluely gleaming crevasse after the next, and as we saw the guides tap at the pockmarked surface under us with ice picks, our jokes stopped entirely. David's beard was soon frozen stiff and Paul shivered in his Foster's Lager sweatshirt. Sue's plump little knees turned blue, and I lent her one of my soggy mittens. A wet cold fog descended on us from the top of the mountain, so that even when (after hours it seemed) we reached the summit, we didn't have a view. We bought some hot chocolate from the little kiosk and cards postmarked "Galdhøpiggen," and Paul, his red nose running, said this mountaineering stuff was highly overrated, give him a pint down at the pub any time. By the time we got down from the mountain the four of us were giddy with something approaching hypothermia, but on the bus going back, Sue said to me a little shyly, "I see we have the same day off. Shall we buy some proper gear and try again?"

Then, for the next six weeks, on our days off and sometimes in the afternoons, Sue and I began to explore the high plateau of Jotunheim above the green valley. We bought sturdy leather hiking boots, long underwear, woolen hats, and gloves. We bought sweaters with reindeer designs and extra-thick socks and Freia milk chocolate bars. Our legs got strong and our faces sunburned.

The high plateau was glacier country, full of enormous granite boulders and the rubble of glacial till left by the retreating ice. Above the tree line there was no vegetation except yellow green lichen and a stiff, scrubby heather. Here and there were streams and small lakes, milky with glacier flour that scattered the light. It was a bare but beautiful landscape, not so much desolate as simplified: In the absence of numerous things to look at, you could look better at the few things that were there.

Paths marked by cairns crossed and recrossed the plateau, and you could walk for hours sometimes without seeing anyone. Up there everything looked clearer somehow, more real and hard and definite in the thin, high air. The sky seemed close, light porcelain blue, though sometimes storm clouds came up unexpectedly, and we had to huddle against wind and rain in our ponchos.

Often it felt as if we were on the very top of the world, and our minds cleared out and freshened, as did our lungs, as did our hearts. We used to walk miles without saying a word, and then sit and share an orange by one of the ancient-looking cairns and ponder which way to go when every direction looked the same. Sometimes we climbed higher and came to the moraine at the base of a glacier, and the glacier itself, which was like a frozen wave caught around boulders big as sofas and small houses. We walked a little ways on the glaciers, but never far, for we were full of stories of people vanishing in crevasses that suddenly opened up, and occasionally we heard the creak and break of ice and skittered back to the safety of the rocks. Sometimes if it was sunny and we were tired, we lay down on the boulders trapped in the ice, or on the tongue of ice itself. Glacier ice has no air; it is densely packed and bubble-free. From a distance glaciers look like smooth coverlets of white, but up close, especially at the edges, they are banded with dirt and honeycombed with pockets the sun has made. Yet the density of the ice makes it seem not to melt, just as the glacier itself seems not to move but to be hard and firm like an inviting stone.

Sue and I often napped on the glaciers, and we both had strong dreams. When we woke the sky was still blue and the silence was endless still, echoing hugely, and there was a cool wind blowing off the glacier, telling us it was time to keep walking. Sue usually dreamed of horses; she'd worked at a stable before coming to Elveseter and wanted to be a vet. I sometimes dreamed of Rob or Laura, or of Elisabeth and the house in Hamar, but surprisingly often I dreamed of Ruthie.

I had answered her sharp letter in the fall with one of my own, describing how I was living and what my plans were. I defended myself against her criticism by saying, "No one knows the best way for another person to become an artist. Maybe your way is to get a degree in art; my way is to read and travel." I pointed out that her parents were paying her college tuition and that her chances of becoming a self-supporting artist were about as remote as mine were of being a writer.

She responded with even more anger than the first time she'd written. She told me that my grandmother's money was the worst thing that ever happened to me, that it only encouraged my tendency to fantasize about the future instead of living in the present. Her parents' paying her college tuition wasn't the same; they were investing in her future. She said my life was slipping away as I dreamed of returning to Spain. She wrote, "You say you're living alone and reading Proust and Jung and working in a discount store. That you're taking a bookbinding course, because you 'want to somehow, someday make books.' *Somehow. Someday.* That about sums up your life. And it's not *good* enough! Don't you realize, that you're never going to become a writer like this? You can do so much *more* with your life."

The worst was that I feared Ruthie might be right. I had been drifting, waiting and waiting for the money, which finally showed up in January. How to explain to her that I was learning something from Proust about narrative and memory, from Jung about the inner life, that bookbinding was connected to William Morris and the richness of the exhibit in London on the Kelmscott Press? I used to take the bus to Los Angeles once a week for the bookbinding class. It was also a chance to see my father, for he and Bettye had moved there to be closer to their jobs. He and I sometimes had dinner by ourselves, and he'd spill out his unhappiness to me, as he'd been doing since I was sixteen.

"I wish I could just disappear," he told me. "I wish I had the strength to leave." "You *can* leave," I told him as I'd always told him.

But he just continued complaining. He'd be complaining about Bettye until the day he died many years later.

I didn't answer Ruthie's letter until I was in Norway and had finished the first draft of "The Iceland." Then I wrote, coolly, that I was living outside of Oslo, learning Norwegian, and writing daily. I made a claim for the life of the imagination and said that although I didn't always make the most obvious choices, I was convinced that I was on the right path. She answered pacifically, but the damage was done. I never saw Ruthie again, though eventually we got back in contact some years later. It was of small comfort to hear that, with her expensive art degree, she'd become a masseuse.

Sleeping on a glacier in Norway, I was still arguing with Ruthie in my dreams. Thoreau, that "inspector of snowstorms," was on my side in the argument, telling me there was a value in simply being in the world and noticing it closely. Ruthie, besides having been my closest friend for many years, was also a voice in my head, urging me to produce and to achieve. I could see now that the steady habit of writing daily could net me a pile of paper. But how could I write daily at Elveseter? How could I stay inside on my one day off or my free afternoons? The world was calling to me with its rivers and glaciers and fields of wildflowers.

Perhaps I dreamed of Ruthie because Sue reminded me of her. Not in the obvious ways: Ruthie was Jewish, with a wide mouth and lovely curved nose. Sue was short and stocky with freckles and a big laugh. But I felt comfortable with Sue, the way I always had with Ruthie. Sue made me laugh with her accent and her decided views. Sue, who was nineteen and lived at home, couldn't imagine my former life and asked me sometimes to tell her about drugs, open sexuality, and the Vietnam War protests, about growing up wearing a bathing suit and dancing to the Beach Boys and Motown. Up there in the mountains everything I'd done and lived through before I arrived at Elveseter seemed as strange to me as it did to her.

Sometimes we walked all day and didn't return to the valley below but stayed the night in hostels and huts where we put our sleeping bags on the floor among all the other unknown travelers and slept the wonderful, deep sleep of physical depletion.

I could have gone on walking high on the top of the world for days, for weeks. But there was always the souvenir shop to return

to and my blue and white striped skirt and bodice to put on and my
trolls to sell and the tourists to talk to ("You speak English so well!"
"Thank you!"). My thoughts were always *outside*. Sometimes, if I
had only a free hour or two, I'd go sit on a rock in the middle of the
swift river and I'd lose myself completely. Above me the mountains,
around me the roar of the river. I'd grown up swimming in the Pacific
Ocean, and that had always been my private wilderness. Now I was
learning another wilderness: snow, rocks, rivers, and forests.

Diane was another young English woman at the hotel that summer,
the sort with deceptively pink cheeks and mild blue eyes, who
nevertheless had no sense of physical danger. Diane had taken
naturally to climbing and had far surpassed the rest of us with her
exploits in the highest ranges. One weekend she talked me into
accompanying her and two Norwegian mountain guides she'd gotten
to know up a mountain near the Jostedal Glacier. She flattered me
by telling me I must be in really great shape after all my hiking with
Sue, and I forgot for a moment that what Sue and I mainly did was
stroll along cairned paths and take naps on the glaciers. I hadn't been
actually glacier climbing since the Galdhøpiggen misadventure, but I
forgot and said, "All right. I'll go."

Leidulf was also persuaded to go, and shortly before the trip we
became a couple. He assured me that he wouldn't let me fall into a
crevasse and that if, by some misfortune I was buried in an avalanche,
he had seen a special on Norwegian TV about how to dig people
out of the snow, no matter how deep. He had also taken advanced
mountain-climbers first aid and knew how to set broken limbs and
apply tourniquets and deal with hypothermia.

The Jostedal Glacier is an ice field eight hundred feet square that
sits between the Nordfjord and Sognfjord. We were planning to hike

up to a mountain called Fannaråki, along a skeletal black ridge, to a small hut on top where we would stay the night.

Because we got a late start, the two guides decided that we should skip the slow approach to the summit, which climbed up the ridge (and to my eyes looked steep enough), in favor of a faster frontal assault. This route would take us straight up the side of a mountain that looked made of white glass and black obsidian. I was embarrassed in front of Diane's eager assent—"Oh, what fun"—and agreed. I put on crampons and tied the rope around my waist. With an ice pick in hand (relinquished when Diane told a cheery story about someone who'd fallen and poked out his eye with the deadly tip), I somehow kept from falling to the certain death I imagined at every second. We crawled up past blue-walled crevasses and sheer slopes of hard-packed snow, at certain places hacking steps in the ice and hauling each other up.

I was so afraid that later I had almost no memory of the experience. I couldn't have been afraid of the height, because I never looked at anything except my hands and feet and the next step. Later I did recall wanting to retrieve the ice pick and to use it on Diane, especially when she called to me encouragingly, "Only a few feet more to the next flat bit!" but mostly I felt hopelessly dependent on my companions and touched by their belief in me. "You can do it! We're almost there!"

When we finally reached the summit, it was sunset. My legs gave out briefly and my calves and arms quivered like uncoiled springs. Leidulf helped me up, and after a few minutes I managed to stumble with him supporting me to the other side of the ridge, where the great white ice field of Jostedal spread out before us like an immense sea turning gold and rose and lavender. Further out, beyond the ice field, was the sea itself, the arm of the Nordfjord, glittering blue violet in the late sunshine. It was the perspective you get when you fly westward above the clouds on summer evenings, and the plane keeps up with the sun, so it never seems to quite set, or only slowly, by degrees, and everything—the clouds, the sky, the sun—remains the same, almost timeless. None of us said anything, you couldn't, and then we had hot chocolate, and I found that my fingers couldn't hold the cup.

Once during the night I woke up and went outside to pee. It was August and getting dark for a few hours now, but still not very dark. A half moon swung in the east, and there were stars, blue and white, and the glaciers were pillowy comforters of dreamy ivory that lay softly on the legs and arms of the giants all around. I knew that tomorrow would be filled again with fear—we had to get back down!—but that night it seemed as if you should be able to just float gently off the peak into the snow below and, falling, never feel a thing.

After my ascent of Fannaråki, I was content to rest on my laurels, and I went back to hiking at lower altitudes. Every day I could hardly wait to get out of my skirt and bodice and into my jeans and boots. I went out hiking sometimes with Leidulf, but we rarely had the same days off. Felicity and I went often to the hillsides to pick blueberries, and Sue and I continued to sleep on the glaciers. But there were more cool evenings now and more cloudy days. Summer was ending; the wildflowers were long gone, and the leaves on the birches were turning golden yellow. Darkness came earlier, more and more quickly, at ten, at nine, at eight.

At meals now we discussed fall plans: Felicity was planning to return to Australia after a short trip around Europe; Paul was going to London and back to bartending; the two gay cooks were heading to hotel school in Switzerland; Kay had fallen in love with Norway and was returning to Kentucky to pack up everything and move here; Sue would look for a job with a vet in St. Albans. Most of the others would return to their colleges or universities, and I, too, was beginning to look forward to a year of studying, to being back in the enchanted city of Granada with its Gypsies and Moorish past.

Leidulf always looked sad when I talked about Spain, and he began to urge me to give up my dream of studying in Granada and to just stay in Norway. Soon we'd be driving through the country to visit his family in Arendal, an impossibly clean and charming town perched on Norway's south coast. There his family would take me in, we'd pick berries and eat ice cream, swim in the late summer sea, and I'd try, without entirely succeeding, to convince Leidulf and myself I was doing the right thing by leaving Norway for Spain. "I don't understand you," he often told me. "We could be happy here."

Before the summer ended, everything we foreigners had complained about at Elveseter became beloved. The gluey-sweet cream porridge, the *stabbur* ladder, the sound of the river, the strange Elveseter family, the silence and isolation. We worried what it would be like to be in a city again, how noisy and dirty it would seem. We all promised to write and keep in touch, perhaps to come back the following summer or to work somewhere else as a group. But except for Felicity, who visited me in Spain some weeks later, and Leidulf, whom I saw in Trondheim the following summer, I never saw any of those friends again.

One afternoon, a week before the hotel was to close for the season, I took a bike and made a circuit through the mountains behind Elveseter. I could feel as I rode uphill how strong my legs were and how much stamina I had. In the high pastures the leaves of the trees had not only turned yellow and red but were falling thickly, and the snow was creeping low again. I felt as if I'd come to belong there in Jotunheim, to belong in the mountains as I'd once belonged in the ocean when I was growing up. I remember resolving that I'd never let this feeling go, this lovely, intense *outside* feeling.

That day at the very end of August it rained. I took refuge with my bike in a barn, with an old man whose dialect was so strong I hardly understood him. It didn't matter; he gave me some cheese and I gave him some chocolate, and when the sun came out we both smiled to see there was a rainbow. When I got to the highest peak, I took a deep breath and started to fly downhill. It was a five-kilometer stretch of joy, where green and gold rushed around me like a tunnel I could sense but not touch; the mountains were all around me, and the sound of the river was loud as always, but so familiar I no longer heard it as anything but the rush of my own heart.

❧ TWELVE ❧

Winter in Granada

CRISTO DE LA YEDRA, the street where I lived for the first four months of my stay in Granada, began its steep wind into the brown hills at a tiny plaza with two benches and a Madonna in a plaster seashell. I often began the trek up to my apartment with a stop at the bakery, where I bought a stick of warm bread in the evening after my classes at the university. At night the street was randomly lit, and the potholed asphalt gave out after two blocks, becoming rocks and dirt. In 1972, there were still streets like this in the city, dusty or muddy depending on the season, not so different from how they would have been in the nineteenth century. Cristo de la Yedra led into the hills where the Gypsies still lived in caves, and I often saw the *gitanos* on the street in the evening, along with students in maroon jackets, workers in berets and patched trousers with ropes for belts, and black-clad women with shopping bags. After a block or two I passed a garage, where much of the work was done in the street to the accompaniment of radio pop music, and two woodworking shops, where the smell of sawdust and black tobacco replaced the sweet fragrance of bread, and burros carried away scraps of wood and machinery in straw hampers.

"*Hola, rubia,*" the men in the garage and carpentry shops *psss*ted me, no matter how many times they'd noticed me before, no matter that I always averted my eyes. My conversation teacher, Manolo, had talked about the Andalusian tradition of the *piropo,* a compliment in couplet form, for example: "Your eyes are as blue as the Virgin Mary's cape." But I seldom heard *piropos,* only the eternal, reflexive nest-of-vipers hiss, which meant: *Woman, I see you, in all your inferior, oversexed femaleness.*

After a *frutería* and a workers' bar came a small cinema that advertised its dated and censored American films on luridly colored posters; in front of it, from early in the morning to late at night, an ancient woman sat on a stool with a basket full of candy and nuts. On opposite corners of the second block were two small shops. I'd made friends with the man who sold eggs, milk, and candy from a tiny storefront. In his late twenties, Juan already had the look of an aging family man, with turtleneck sweaters stretched over a rounded belly and glasses he removed when I entered. Juan had worked six years in a Swiss factory in order to marry and set up shop; he was part of the Spanish exodus from Andalusia to more prosperous countries, a work force that was now returning, exiled back home by economic slowdowns in Northern Europe. The only way he could make any money was to open early and stay late. "It's not the work of a serious man to sell candy to children," he moped. I bought lots of eggs from him. The Spanish *tortilla,* a thick frittata packed with potatoes and cut in slices like a tart, was one of my few culinary achievements.

I often stopped in the evenings at the small grocery across the street from Juan's, where tough yellow chickens swung above our heads along with fat strings of garlic and papery red peppers. The shelves went up to the ceiling and were stacked with canned goods. It seemed impossible, given the space, for more than two people to fit in front of a counter of cheese and sausages, with baskets of onions and potatoes on the floor, but there were usually about eight or nine women and children when I crammed my way inside in the evening, and I had to add my voice to the din, shouting for what I wanted through a crowd of aggressive short ladies in buttoned-up sweaters over their dresses and aprons. This was good practice for me, pointing at cans and repeating their names. I always tried something different: marinated anchovies, stuffed olives, artichokes and eggplant, until I was on to *pulpo a gallego* (octopus in the Galician manner), *bacalao al pil pil* (reconstituted dried cod in tomato), and *berechos en escabeche* (cockles in sauce). My curiosity and extravagance made up for my lack of eloquence and speed getting the words out. The owner liked to see me coming. Some of those cans on the top shelf had probably been there for decades—*antes de la guerra*—"before the war," as people said when they wanted to place an event in the long-ago past.

I lived about halfway up Cristo de la Yedra, next to a bodega that recalled a Western saloon, with a pair of swinging doors that belched tobacco smoke and male voices. The bodega began to grow lively only in the evening; during the day old men with glasses of *tinto* would sit outdoors in the sun. Even the old men had it in them sometimes to *pssst* me.

My two-bedroom flat, on the second floor of a small apartment building, was cheaply furnished with a vinyl couch, a plain table, a few chairs, and several beds, but it had a sunny balcony and a view of the snowy Sierra Nevada. Without the sun the rooms were cold and dreary. The walls were greenish, the linoleum floor cold. The only heat came from a stout butane gas heater called an *estufa,* which could be rolled around the apartment; the butane smell made me dizzy, so I left it off as long as I could stand the cold. Off the kitchen and one bedroom was a dank interior courtyard; olive oil and garlic frying came through the kitchen door—along with the rapid, often comforting sound of Spanish spoken among families—which opened out onto a tiny porch with a sink and clothesline. This was where I, too, had to wash my clothes and hang them out, though sometimes I took them up to the roof, which had a view of the mountains and the city.

When I moved in, the landlord had explained the times when the water was turned off, and when to put out the garbage on the street, and the fact that I was responsible for washing the building's stairs in rotating order of every six weeks. The water supply was shut down just when you'd expect the tenants to be using it most, from about five PM to past midnight. That meant that in order to have enough water to prepare dinner, wash the dishes and brush your teeth, you had to fill up a bucket or two of water before the shut-off time. I forgot about this my first evening and around eight PM tried to make myself some tea. I turned the tap back and forth vigorously before I remembered, then went out to a café.

Around two AM that same night, I heard the doorbell ring loudly. "*Señorita! Agua!*"

Through the pounding there was a sound like a waterfall in the kitchen. I suddenly remembered I'd never turned the tap back off; I got up and went to the door, where I found a plump housewife and her six-year-old daughter. The water had been pouring out my kitchen door to the balcony and on to their balcony. I spent an hour mopping up the kitchen. Later I got to know this family, whose six members lived in a space the same size as my own.

Although in Granada I looked at a snow-covered mountain range every day, I missed Norway violently, and especially Jotunheim and its deep valleys and rivers and glaciers, where I'd learned to feel so physically free and at home outdoors. Over and over in my journal those first weeks back in Spain, I noted how shabby and poor Granada seemed and how the men bothered me. Neither poverty nor dirt had upset me when I was here a year and a half ago, but now, after many months in pristine Norway, the city was noisy, dusty, and invasive. Men young and old spoke to me on the street and sometimes followed me for blocks, so that I rarely felt at ease. Motorbikes roared and burros brayed and people talked at the top of their lungs. Everywhere I turned were dogs with flies in their eyes; Gypsy women with one hand out, the other around a baby, "*Señorita, por el niño, por favor*"; blind people sitting on stools with lottery tickets in their laps; and beggars on the sidewalk itself, beggars missing legs and arms, who had been young once, *antes de la guerra*.

I was often lonely my first six weeks back in Spain and thought I'd made a mistake in leaving Norway. I poured out my dissatisfaction to Elisabeth Helland-Hansen in letters; she wisely counseled me to give Granada more time before I gave up. I kept my disappointment from Leanne and Leidulf, who would only have said, "I told you so," and "Take the first train back north." My Australian roommate from Elveseter, Felicity, stopped in Granada en route from Greece back to England and home to Sydney. For several days we did nothing but sit in cafés drinking and reminiscing about what a wonderful time we'd had in Jotunheim. As soon as Felicity returned to Sydney, she happened to meet a Norwegian man and married him instantly.

I tried to capture the magic of the city I'd held in my imagination for so many months by revisiting the palace of the Alhambra, and there, amidst the courts and patios with their reflecting pools and sound of running water, I often did feel the old enchantment and a sense of peace. It was sometimes a hot climb up the road to the

Gate of the Pomegranates, but once I was inside, the stroll through woodland up to the palaces and fortresses that made up the complex of the Nasrid sultans was shady and usually quiet, except for the birds singing. From one of the many crenellated towers or horseshoe-arched windows in the palace, the city of Granada down below was calm, white in the sunshine, roofed with red tiles, peaceful in its gardens and small squares.

Long ago, in the mid-thirteenth century, the first Nasrid ruler, Mohamed Ben Alhamar, had caused water from the Darro to be brought to this high hill and had turned it from a dry desert of cactus and prickly pear into a palace constructed of red clay, from which the Alhambra took its name. The bare clay walls were then plastered and tiled into a wonderland of repetitive ornamentation and geometric patterning. Ribbons of religious and poetic inscriptions in Arabic, rectilinear or rounded, were cut into the plaster, which was then gilded and polychromed. From many places within the complex, the honeycombed ceilings, the latticed windows, the slender columns supporting arcades of carved plasterwork created a sense of tranquility in repetition. The sun, even in early October, could be blinding on the white marble of the patios and the long, still pools, but within the dark arcades, the baths, the palace rooms, the temperature was cool and the breezes from the Sierra Nevada brought refreshment.

I thought of the poet who'd recited for me the Antonio Machado poem last year, and I thought more than I wanted to about Laura and our time in Spain. I'd heard from her, but not often, during her months in Crete. She described an idyllic life of living with Georgiou and his parents, where all they seemed to do was swim, drink ouzo, and eat yogurt. Now they were planning to go to England so that Georgiou could audition for drama school. "How fun," she wrote, "now that we're both living in Europe, if you could come to London and visit."

And she asked how it was to be back in Spain again and sometimes said she'd like to come back and do our trip over, "right this time."

I always wrote back, but cautiously. I wanted to see her of course, but not with Georgiou, and not in London. I supposed what she meant by redoing our trip was that she wouldn't have bronchitis, but maybe she meant she'd like to travel around Spain with someone other than me.

Sitting in the gardens of the Alhambra, I tried to be where I was. I tried to keep in mind that at Elveseter, with no real space or time to write, I'd dreamed of a place of my own in Spain, where life would be inexpensive, where I wouldn't have to work, where I could write in the morning and study in the afternoon. In this room of my own, I vowed, I'd rediscover the writing discipline I'd found in Hamar in the spring and lost over the summer. Now I did have a room of my own, I often reminded myself, as I whiled away the hours in the Patio of the Lions. It was up to me to make the most of it.

Classes began mid-October. Although I loved Spanish and was glad to be speaking it again, I was rusty and found the southern accent in Granada hard to follow at first. The Andalusians left the endings off many words; they slurred and flattened vowels. Instead of saying *Toda la noche,* for instance ("the whole night"), they'd say *To' la no'.* The first day of class, sitting in a lecture hall for three hours while each of our six professors, most of them very old and long-winded, introduced himself and his topic—geography, history, literature, art, grammar, and conversation—I could hardly make out a word. All around me, my fellow students were busily taking notes. Later I'd find out that many had felt the same sense of confusion at those lengthy speeches, but that wasn't a help the first day, when my one thought was to conceal my ignorance by not speaking to anyone.

I fell to studying with a vengeance and also began a piece of writing that I hoped would become a novel. I called it "The Travelogue" and narrated most of the story in the voice of a woman in her thirties named Alex, an American who lived in London, walked with a cane, and wanted to sail around the world. She had an intense relationship with a younger woman, Ruby, but also some kind of connection with Bruce, who was writing a book on the sixteenth-century explorer Richard Hakluyt, and with Sigurd, a Norwegian sailor. In Alex I tried to create the complex woman I hoped to become, and I spent many pages giving her and the other characters elaborate and lengthy backgrounds.

This novel didn't flow as smoothly as "The Iceland," where the saga-like motivations had been simple: revenge, guilt, atonement. "The Travelogue" aimed for something more complicated, but all I seemed to accrue were more and more scratched-out and scribbled-over pages about Alex's childhood in a remote Scottish boarding school, Bruce's Oxford education, and Sigurd's years on the high seas. Since I knew nothing about boarding schools in Scotland or anywhere else, Oxford, or ships, it was sometimes hard going. I knew that Alex's dream of sailing around the world had something to do with her limp. "She could not hike the Himalayas or the Rockies," I wrote, "so Alex imagined a small boat that would take her through the vast oceans to all the great ports of the world." I wasn't sure how Alex got her limp or whether a person with a limp could pilot a small boat around the world. Perhaps it wasn't a large limp. The important thing to me was that the limp was symbolic, though of what, I still wasn't quite sure.

I also began a journal, much more detailed than anything I'd previously kept, and wrote a number of my dreams, which were particularly vivid that fall. Sleeping nine to ten hours a day and writing down my dreams took a surprising amount of time; so did standing on my balcony and looking out at the city, thinking about Alex and her loves and longings. Gradually Cristo de la Yedra grew more interesting and even beautiful to me; I didn't mind the roar of the motorbikes, or the braying of burros, or the shrieks of the woman who sold fish from a cart, or the calls of the *butano* man who drove his open truck filled with heavy orange gas canisters up and down the ruts and rocks of the street. Only on Sundays did the cacophony cease; then came the tolling of the church bells calling everyone to mass.

I went out with Spanish men from time to time, but except for my conversation teacher, Manolo, most of them seemed childish and tiresome. They were the sons of the local bourgeoisie and the great landowners of Andalusia, the *latifundistas*. They had little access to international news and saw only the most banal of censored films; they carried an exaggerated sense of Spain's importance and were often ignorant of the outside world. Manolo was far more intellectual—he knew a great deal about Andalusian culture and literature—but he was provincial too; he once told me that the United States had no real universities—except Harvard perhaps—because our colleges offered business education and home economics. We had numerous Japanese in our class; they were astonished, but too polite to contradict him, when he asserted that Tokyo could not possibly have more than one university, and if it offered business degrees, it wasn't a university either.

Manolo was short and sinewy, with a round baby face deeply dimpled and a cap of tightly curled hair. When we walked on the street he'd link my arm through his and use it as a lever to keep my body close to his. He used to pinch my arm when something I said amused him. He also had a habit of pulling down his lower lid to express something like "Get it?" His favorite adjective for me was *competente*. He had a roommate, also named Manolo. I called them Manolo el Profesor and Manolo el Segundo in my journal.

They often compared me to the fictional character Nancy in the satiric novel *La Tesis de Nancy,* about a woman student in Seville, who was writing her thesis on Southern Spain and having an affair with a Gypsy and who misunderstood many key concepts of Andulusian life—such as *duende*—to comic effect. Eventually I read this mildly amusing novel in the form of letters by Nancy to a friend in America, but I never found it as illustrative of my character as they did, and some parts frankly offended me. Nancy overheard her Gypsy boyfriend, Curro, saying that he would never marry her because she'd lost her flower, and Nancy described it to her a friend as very sweet that the Spanish placed such a wonderful emphasis on flowers. Was Nancy—or more importantly her creator, Ramón Sender—an idiot to think Americans didn't know what that meant?

At first I hoped the Manolos would be my Monzo and Lluís, my pals in the city and my key to understanding the character of southern Spain, but they competed over me and each privately told me that the other had bad intentions, and I had to make a choice. Eventually that choice was neither, and I stopped seeing them altogether.

The Faculty of Letters was housed in a baroque old building in the center of the city. Gilt-framed religious paintings hung on all the walls, and we always seemed to be falling over two aged cleaning ladies washing the marble staircase or the parquet floors. There were no activities, because any gathering of students was forbidden, but there was a bar in the basement and some of the foreign students also hung out there. I gravitated to the European students, not the half dozen Americans who were here for their junior year abroad and were too wholesome for me. I often hung out with Bitten, a tall and beautiful *Sueca* in a leather jacket, but she moved back to Sweden after a month. Quite a few of the students seemed to drop out and return home during that first autumn, especially the girls. Some, like Bitten, said it was just too tiring to be the focus of attention every day. "No one ever *quite* touches me," she said. "It's just that I begin to feel their eyes crawling all over my body. I feel like I am naked." Even those of us girls not so curvaceous as Bitten knew exactly what she meant.

Other students just stopped coming regularly to class. The classrooms were unheated and, as winter came on, bitterly cold. The professors were often deadly dull, their topics circumscribed by the fact that (at least it was rumored) there were informants in most classes, to make sure the Franco regime was never questioned or criticized, no matter what sort of curiosity the foreign students showed. Our history class focused mainly on the Visigoths, and the Reconquista, or retaking of Spain from the Moors, followed by Spain's golden age and its colonization of South America. The twentieth century, in particular the liberal period that led up to the civil war, when democracy had tried to take root and literature flourished, was never mentioned.

My first friend in Granada was an anomaly among the students in the course for foreigners, because he was South American, fluent in Spanish, and much older—thirty-two. The other American girls didn't like him, for good reason; they said he touched them and suggested things and told dirty jokes. He'd tried those things on me at first, but with such a resigned good humor that it hadn't bothered me and soon he stopped. Periodically, throughout the months I knew him, he'd suggest we sleep together, but all it took was *"Hombre!"* and he'd leave off.

Miguel was a Quechua Indian from a village in the Bolivian Andes. Once I heard him speak Quechua to another Indian: *tchick, tchick,* very fast, accompanied by laughter. "Quechua is a very humorous language," Miguel told me. "You can joke about anything."

After leaving his village, Miguel had gone to La Paz and somehow acquired an education and had become a teacher. At twenty-four he'd immigrated to California, where he had become a busboy, learned English, and put himself through college. He'd just finished obtaining a teaching credential when he decided to take a vacation and spend a year studying in Spain. He'd gotten a scholarship of some sort, which is why he was nominally enrolled in our course instead of through the university. He never went to class but preferred to play the guitar and study flamenco. He was open to everything around him, which is why I liked him.

Miguel had a broad reddish face with high cheekbones and slanting cool green eyes that glinted when he told a story. His wide mouth was pale, surrounded by a red mustache and beard. His longish hair was red too, but darker. When he first came to California, he told me, he used to have his hair slicked back, and he wore glossy boots and flowered silk shirts. Now, like any American hippie, he wore flannel shirts and jeans. He had a motorcycle, and when I first knew him we sometimes went into the olive groves in the mountains around the city. It was November but was still warm enough so you could smell the dry, sweet smell of sage. We used to sit on the stony ground among red and orange poppies and talk about our lives. I told him of my travels and my longing to write, how hard I was finding it. "I stay up late, and then I get up late, and then I have to study. And suddenly it's time to go to class."

Sitting on the sunny hillside, Miguel was reminded of his childhood. He told me how he used to herd goats and llamas. He told me how his father had described over and over to him what a train was, until Miguel had grown so impatient that he had to see the train for himself. He and his father had set off and walked five days down through the mountains until they came to a city large enough for a train station.

We had a picnic of red wine and cheese and tomatoes. Miguel ate tomatoes by the pound. He said they sweetened the voice; he'd learned that in La Paz when he and his friends would sing serenades to the local girls. "*Ay,* how we would sing. Not only for the girls we loved. But for the girls we hated. Only we'd sing them a different kind of song—a black serenade, to darken their names!"

One day, after a miserable morning trying to write about my characters—Alex (was she going to take sailing lessons, or was she just going to talk and talk about her trip around the world?) and Bruce (I wanted him to sound pedantic, but not as boring as he came across)—Miguel and I ran into each other in the bar near the university where I was having a *café solo* to inspire myself for an afternoon of dull classes. I was in a glum mood and began to complain about Granada and mention I was thinking of packing up and going back to Norway.

"Don't leave yet!" Miguel said. "There's so much to learn from this country."

"But I don't know how to fit in here. I don't know who I am in Spain. I wanted to come here to write, but if I write I'm not living. If I don't write, I don't know what to do with my time. I don't belong."

"Why should you worry about who you are?" Miguel said. He switched over to English so I could understand him better. "Why worry about belonging or not belonging? Why should you limit yourself to being the person you thought you were? Anyway, we're not just one person, with one defined personality. We're consciousnesses with an infinite capacity for assimilation. We should have the ability to understand and express more cultures, more worlds, than the ones we were born into."

"Can't you lose yourself that way?"

"I haven't lost myself." He grinned. "Inside me is the boy in the Andes, herding llamas, and the dishwasher in the restaurant in Los Angeles. When I go back home I'll be a teacher, with a car and house. Now I'm a wild man with my beard and jeans, but very soon I'm thinking of trying to look like a *gitano*. I'll buy a pair of boots and a silk shirt and learn to sing *cante jondo*. Why don't you get some high-heeled boots and take dancing classes? All too soon you'll be somewhere else. You'll be looking back at your time in Granada and crying, *Why did I just sit in my lonely apartment trying to write a novel?* Why not explore a different way of being a woman in Spain? Why not really live here?"

I thought he was right, and stood up a little straighter listening. The next day I shopped for high-heeled boots and put my hair in a braid and stuck large hoops in my ears. I started shrugging when men *pssst*ed me and I tossed my head arrogantly as if to say, *You can shine my boots, shorty!* Sometime after that I put away my fitful attempts at "The Travelogue" and started trying to live where I was—in Andalusia—instead of in my imagination. The sailing trip around the world would have to wait.

Through Miguel I came to know some British students from Birmingham. Peter and I met at a party in early December. He was tall with a ginger mustache and wore little Lennon glasses, curiously opaque, to help his poor eyesight. He'd graduated last spring with a degree in political science and had been here for some months. His friends Tony, Julian, and Joe were all enrolled in the course for foreigners, though they never came to class. Peter lived in the old Moorish quarter, the Albacín, taught English to make a living, and spent his free time drinking and reading up on the civil war. He would have liked to be in one of the international brigades; he was a Socialist. The reason he was learning Spanish was so he could travel to Chile where the government of Salvador Allende provided a model of Marxism in action. Peter and I left the party with some others to go to a demonstration at the Plaza del Triunfo—the teaching assistants at the university were about to go on strike because they weren't getting their wages—but the Guardia Civil broke it up quickly. We wandered around the city for a long while talking about George Orwell and Communism and the Falange, stopping from time to time in a bar to warm up. Peter was a serious young man, who got more serious the more he drank. He had a pessimistic view of history; he suspected that even Salvador Allende, his hero, would not be around long (he was right, of course); the U.S. was a fascist state in the making, and only a revolution would provide a clean slate. "I'm afraid it will have to be violent," he said, in his rather posh accent.

At around four AM Peter had the idea of walking into the countryside to see the sun come up over the tobacco fields. A clammy mist enveloped us as we tromped along a dirt road through the green *vega*, the fertile plain that spread outside Granada's city limits. The most we could see was our feet in front of us and a surprising number of shoes in the ditches next to the road. There were so many that it got to be a joke.

"Here's another one," Peter said. "Another left one."

That made me recall a Spanish saying about men kicking off their left shoes when they died. The shoes were old; they could have been lying there for years.

"Granada was a Nationalist stronghold in a Republican sea, that's what they say," said Peter. "The Falange killed everyone they thought could be a threat, whether those people had borne arms and fought or not. They say at least three thousand people are buried in a mass grave somewhere outside of town."

My feet, in the high-heeled boots, were killing me, and more than once I wondered what I was doing here on a road to nowhere outside Granada with a man who believed in the violent overthrow of society. But there was a gentleness to Peter that I liked, and I felt touched when he confided that he'd come here to get over a broken relationship. "At first I thought I might go insane," he said. "Then I got interested in my own insanity. Then I stopped being afraid of it."

Around five we stopped in a little roadside café where he knew the owner, Maria. Just barely up herself, Maria came through a curtain of bright plastic beads. She wore a housedress and curlers. She gave us brandy and coffee, and Peter asked for *pan de chocolate*. Maria broke off squares of black bitter chocolate from a large bar and sliced open a slightly stale baguette and placed the chocolate inside. "*Que te aproveche,*" she told me. Peter smiled at me, and I suddenly felt a little bit in love. It was the best breakfast I could remember having in a long time.

Unlike the more puritanical Americans, who always seemed to be studying, the Brits were here to party as well as write a few papers for their tutors at home. Classes at the university ended for the holiday break, and although I continued to read—Spanish novels for the most part, but also English paperbacks that circulated around the foreign students—I usually spent my mornings with Peter, in my apartment or in his rooms in the Albacín, which had a stunning view of the

Alhambra. At night, lit up, the palace seemed to float in the dark sky like a vision from *Arabian Nights*. I continued to write in my journal, which began at this point to read like a social diary, full of parties and people stopping by my apartment and dinners at someone's house or other. My friends and I were remarkably casual about our drinking, which would sometimes begin at noon and continue long into the night. Occasionally, of course, I'd have a burst of guilt—at the aimless life I was living, at my lack of discipline. I often slept until ten or eleven, not surprising, since I was usually up until two or three.

Around lunchtime Peter and I would often meet up with Tony, Julian, and Joe and we'd walk out into the countryside to Maria's café. Maria made us *bocadillos* with ham or chorizo, and we drank carafes of *tinto*. We got to know a Gypsy family who lived nearby; Don Luís had a peach orchard in addition to tobacco. His fourteen-year-old daughter, Antonita, would often come by when we were sitting at one of Maria's outside tables, sheltered by rows of golden, drying tobacco, and she would hang on my arm and hug me and kiss my cheeks and drag me out for a walk, her arm wrapped around my waist, in the tobacco fields. The boys joking called her my girlfriend, and though I shrugged that off, the walks with Antonita were sweet to me. Her greatest dream was to have a long flounced dress with big polka dots; her second dream was to come and visit me in California, a word she always pronounced with wonder.

Sometimes we spent the whole afternoon at Maria's café, returning to town only to stop for cups of chocolate, steaming brown and thickened to a pudding-like consistency. Peter and I would share an order of *churros,* freshly made, and dunk the deep-fried sugary tubes into our cups. The combination of airy crunch and melting chocolate was sublime. The weather was getting colder and colder, in spite of the sunshine. Icy winds bore down on the city. I understood now why the Granadinos spent so much time in bars and restaurants; public spaces were far warmer than the badly heated homes.

In the evenings we sometimes went to a restaurant near the university that we called Chickenland. Its chicken dinners were awful, drenched in strong olive oil with chunks of garlic, but the decor made up for it. Along one wall stretched a prehistoric mural, in sad grays and puce greens, of dinosaurs and pterodactyls lumbering through tropical vegetation and flying through the boiling air. At their feet, barely recognizable, wandered three or four little chickens. Other walls were decorated with black-and-white framed photographs, most unappetizing, of a poultry factory, culminating in a series showing the assembly-line guillotining, processing, and packing of the birds. The coat racks were carved and painted chicken heads sticking out perpendicularly from the walls, one to each table. The food was very cheap, but we mostly enjoyed the restaurant's surreal quality.

During our excursions out to Maria's and our dinners at Chickenland, Tony held forth on politics and literature. He was short and slight, with bangs cut straight across his pinched sharp face, lower-middle-class, Catholic, smart as a whip, and sarcastic frequently to the point of offense. Like Peter, Tony was doing a degree in political science; he was particularly focused on the end of the dictatorship in Portugal and what that meant for the colonies in Africa. Salazar had died a few years ago, in 1968, but the transition to anything approaching democracy was rocky. The colonies in Africa were struggling to be free of Portugal. What would happen in Spain?

Tony hoped that Franco would die during the year he was in Granada, so he'd have a chance to experience the transition—or lack of one—himself. He could not believe Juan Carlos, "that young wanker," the heir to the throne but also a favorite of Franco's, would succeed. "There will be a coup. There will be blood running in the streets. We'll have to hide in the caves of Sacromonte and be airlifted out by the Royal Air Force. We'll have to make our way overland with burros to Gibraltar, where the Royal Navy will save us."

"I don't know why you're depending on the British Armed Forces," said Peter, nettled. "We obviously have to stay and help the Spanish people. This could be a second civil war."

Tony was a needler and provoker. He sometimes called Peter, who was very respectably middle-class, and whose name was Wandworth, Lord Wankworth, or Lennon (for the glasses). Joe from Bolton was Bolthole, while Julian was simply "old sot." Julian did drink more than the rest of us, but perhaps not much more. Joe went on benders and Peter often seemed to be in an alcoholic daze. Julian had the most beautiful coloring I'd ever seen on a man: thick rose brown glossy hair, down to his chin, and dusky rose freckles. He was bilingual in Italian, from his mother. His eyes were green and bloodshot. He could quote poetry in English and Spanish by the hour, and sometimes would, when we walked through the city at night, anything from Wordsworth to Lorca. He was the peacemaker in the group, and when Tony got on a roll about blood in the streets, Julian was likely to say placidly, "I say, I think that Juan Carlos is a better fellow than you think he is. Spain will be all right."

Now that I was part of the Birmingham circle, I had people to cook for. I purchased a cookbook and went to the market, where I bought saffron, rice, a chicken, chorizo, and all the ingredients for flan: milk, eggs, and sugar. My first dinner party was a disaster. I had no paella pan, so I cooked the rice in a saucepan, throwing in a teaspoon of saffron, a teaspoon being one of the only measures I knew, while I dealt with the whole bird, which, alarmingly, still had pin feathers in its cold, yellowish skin. I hadn't thought to ask the butcher to chop up the chicken and had to do that myself with a Swiss Army knife. I threw the non-uniform pieces in a cup of olive oil (a cup was the other measure I recalled from home ec) in the frying pan, and added the chorizo, which soon began to turn from red to black. When my guests arrived, they were fortunately all rather drunk, but still the sight of the stringy chicken chunks, looking like something just off the operating table in wartime, sitting on a hard-grained bed of rice stained a shocking circus yellow, made everyone pause.

If the main meal was inedible, the dessert was indescribable. The recipe was in grams and liters. I dumped eggs and several cups of sugar along with a bottle of milk into a bowl. I even cooked up some sugar in a pot, though it was more black than amber. I poured the syrup and then my custard mix into the custard cups I'd bought and then, because there was so much left over, into glasses and bowls. Finally I read an instruction that completely threw me: "Place the cups in a *baño de Maria* and bake in the oven." I didn't understand this at all. A *baño* was a bath or a bathroom. And who was Maria? There was no picture in the cookbooks, no clue as to what this thing was. Spanish Revereware possibly? Years later, when I read cookbooks with serious pleasure and came across the term *bainmarie*, or water bath, I belatedly understood that the dishes of custard should have been placed in an larger pan with an inch of water. My guests had been excited about the idea of homemade flan, and that had helped them get through the paella, but when the custard cups were unmolded, like rubber bath toys, onto plates pooling with syrup dark as motor oil, a silence more aghast than polite ensued.

"Just like Mother used to make," said Tony, bouncing his spoon off the surface of the flan.

"Beats spotted dick any day," said Peter, investigating the burnt sugar syrup.

"Bloody hell, woman, what is this mess?" said Joe.

And then we threw the lot out and continued drinking.

The Birmingham boys had discovered that my apartment building was next door to a bodega and that you could get bottles filled for mere pennies, and that took the edge off the dinner. Three giant vats with spigots, almost biblical, were behind the counter. One was white wine, one was red, and the third was *vino de Málaga,* the dark golden, raisiny-sweet dessert wine.

We had other meals together over the next few weeks, less ambitious and more successful. They brought olives, cheese, bread, and turrón, or nougat, while I fried up meats in the Spanish way; that is, I simply put them in a pan with a lot of olive oil and turned the heat on. Spanish food, it seemed to me, was a lot like the Spanish language. Just as words were pronounced the way they looked, food always retained its shape and substance no matter how it was prepared. No fancy sauces for the Spanish. Olive oil, especially in the south, was the ambrosia that flowed over everything, and I doused the food with a liberal hand.

In early January Peter received a surprising letter from his ex-girlfriend, Di, who said she missed him and wanted to try again. He'd mentioned me to her in a letter—that seemed to be part of the reason she wanted him back. He said if I asked him to stay in Granada, he'd stay, but I told him he should probably go. I felt comfortable with Peter, but my frisson of infatuation hadn't matured into anything more. For Christmas a friend in the States had sent me Doris Lessing's *The Golden Notebook.* I read it avidly, but it depressed me. I couldn't see a happy future for me with any man; I was too critical, too independent, too easily irritated and resentful. The character Anna wrote: "Resentment against what? An unfairness . . . It is the disease of women in our time. I can see it in women's faces, their voices." Resentment against what? A fundamental unfairness that seemed unlikely to change very much. All Lessing promised me as a woman was a cranky middle age alone, probably with a divorce behind me. I *already* had a divorce behind me, when it came down to it, with Rob, and I had feelings that I kept buried about other possibilities for me. Back in the fall, when I was writing "The Travelogue," I'd made a note about Alex that she was bisexual. It was hidden in a sheaf of unfinished papers. The experience with Laura was something I rarely thought about when I was sober.

Julian and I accompanied Peter to the station so he could catch the night train to Madrid, and afterward, although we were already somewhat drunk, we came back to my apartment and downed two more bottles of red wine. We talked about how things just wouldn't be the same without Peter, and together, tears in our eyes, we quoted all the poetry we could remember, ending with Lorca's lines: "The two rivers of Granada/ One of tears and the other of blood/ Oh love/ That vanished in the air."

Julian slept in one of the bedrooms, where I often put people up. The family downstairs, who'd been friendly to me the first month, inviting me occasionally to watch television, now averted their eyes from me and my guests in the downstairs hall. To them I could only be one thing: a *puta,* or whore.

Soon after Peter returned to England, I decided to move away from Cristo de la Yedra and to share a room with Gisela, a German woman. My apartment was cheap, but Gisela's would be cheaper, and I was trying to budget what was left of the rest of my money.

I left my apartment only four months after I'd moved in, though it seemed much longer that I'd lived there.

Yet, of everything I recall about my time in Granada, it's the walk up Cristo de la Yedra that comes to mind most vividly. I remember the days of October, when it was still warm and I had no inkling of the chill winter to come. I remember leaving my apartment for the university on a hot stale afternoon and finding the air perfumed with what smelled like boiling artichokes—it was the hops from the neighborhood brewery. Lunch over, the siesta was in mid-snooze at three fifteen when I walked to the bottom of the dusty street, went into a dead-quiet bar and, standing, drank in two gulps a short, sharp *café solo,* sugared, to knock the sleep from my eyes. I remember taking out my journal to write about my loneliness and describing Alex limping into her future, trying to find a name for all that she was and all that she hoped to become.

❧ THIRTEEN ❧

al-Andalus

Gisela lived on the far side of town, across the Genil River, in an area called Ciudad Jardín, Garden City. Many of the Latin American students at the university stayed in Ciudad Jardín, perhaps because it had a colonial look about it, with its small blocks of two-story pastel stucco houses, balconies, and red-tiled roofs. Palms and orange trees filled the gardens, and even in Granada's chilly months they cast a spell of southern abundance. Gisela rented from two Honduran housemates: Cristobal, one of the few blacks in the city, who was studying medicine, and Mario, who'd been doing his last year of law studies for three years. They were both anti-*Yanqui,* but they didn't put up a fuss when I took the extra bed in Gisela's large room.

My primary reason for moving in with her was to save money, but I also liked Gisela. Some of my friends found her too neurotic, but to me she just seemed German, a type familiar from my stay in Düsseldorf a few years before. My companions in the women's residence there were all worried and serious people too.

Gisela was very pretty, with blue eyes and lips that curled up into a natural smile no matter how depressed she felt, and long dark hair, which had a curious bald spot on top that she covered with a hat when going out. She pulled her hair out from the crown of her head when she was reading or writing; once she told me this was because her fiancé had died in a small airplane crash, an event that had almost destroyed her sanity and left her half bald for many months. She was from Alsace originally but had gone to university in Stuttgart and now lived there with her parents. Her French was perfect. She planned to become a professional translator, possibly a simultaneous translator of German, French, and Spanish, and this impressed me mightily, though I could see she rarely seemed to study and spent a great deal of time writing letters. She could speak excellent English, but she refused to speak it with me. She insisted we always communicate in Spanish, though sometimes, out of homesickness, she'd fall into German. Her grooming was lax, since she rarely went out; she shuffled around in flannel pajamas, a worn blue terrycloth bathrobe, and two pairs of socks. She never wanted the heat on. She was always making strange messes in the kitchen, like beef liver poached in vinegar. "Vinegar cuts all calories," she said.

Gisela was one of my small circle of women friends, along with Lolí, from Bilbao. I especially liked Lolí, the first—and only—Spanish woman I ever knew well during my time in Andalusia. Occasionally Lolí and I met on our own in her small room in the center of town, and I always went away feeling as if I'd learned something about Spain from a Spaniard, other than about bullfighting, the code of honor, and Opus Dei, that is.

Basque Lolí came from a banking family. She'd worked as an au pair in Brighton one summer and spoke English well; she was passionate about languages and linguistics, especially Spain's regional languages. She knew Galician, and some Catalan, and of course Basque, or *euskera*. It was perfectly fine, in the time of

Franco, to study other languages of the peninsula besides Castilian; the problem was to speak them and to consider them equal to what some called *cristiano*—the Christian language. In Bilbao, Lolí had been active in an illegal political group dedicated, she said, to restoring the Basque language and culture. She'd been arrested several times, and ultimately had had her passport taken away. That destroyed the plan she'd had of going to England—she'd been accepted at Cambridge—to study. Her parents had sent her down to Granada to keep her out of trouble.

Lolí was always neatly and somberly dressed in a navy blue blazer and oxford shirt. Her forehead was high and intellectual; she wore glasses and had short dark hair pulled back at the temples by two barrettes. She had none of the *alegría,* or liveliness, of the Andalusians; she looked like a photograph of Rosa Luxembourg. It's no wonder that she and Gisela were friends, because Lolí had something Germanic about her, that same thoughtful frown when she spoke, that same earnest intensity. From Lolí, who said firmly that she would never marry—in Spain anyway—I learned about Spain's Civil Code, which degreed that the husband must protect the wife, and the wife must obey the husband. *Permiso marital* meant that a woman needed her husband's permission to take a job or open a bank account. She had no say over finances. If she left home, for just a few days, without her husband's permission, her children could be taken away from her. Adultery was a crime. Other things were illegal in Spain too: divorce, abortion, the sale of contraception, homosexuality.

"If things don't change for us after El Caudillo dies," she told me across a small table, on which she'd laid a flowered tablecloth and placed a teapot and a pitcher of cream and a plate artfully piled with tiny cakes and sandwiches spread with imported marmite (Lolí loved the British custom of afternoon tea, which she never called by the

Spanish name, *merienda,* but always *teatime*), "I don't know what
my generation will do. We often feel so close to life being different—
but it's always out of reach. Just a year or two, we tell ourselves, he'll
die, and there will still be time for us . . . but the years go on. I will
never marry while he lives. My freedom would be at an end."

I liked spending time with Lolí; her seriousness was enlivened by
curiosity. She asked me many questions about the women's liberation
movement in the United States. I was sorry I couldn't tell her more
and wondered why I knew so little. I seemed to have been gone from
my country so long that I'd lost the habit of remembering what was
good about it. So many people I met in Europe hated the United States
for the war in Vietnam that it was hard to understand someone like
Lolí's admiration for America's progressive aspects. In feeling shame
for the war, I'd also forgotten the energy and determination of all the
recent movements, from civil rights to pacifism, that challenged the
status quo. But sometime in January that began to change.

Miguel, Tony, and Julian rented a spacious modern apartment in a
tall block at what was then the edge of town, on the big circular road,
the Ronda. After Joe went back to England, the three of them asked
me to move in, but it was more expensive than Gisela's, and although
I spent much of my time with these friends, I wasn't sure I wanted to
live with them. Instead, another American had moved in. Patsy was
one of the wholesome girls I'd avoided at the beginning of last fall's
term; she had long, straight reddish blond hair and a snub nose with
a few freckles. She shared her room for a month or so with a friend
from Humboldt State, who'd come to Spain and traveled with Patsy
over Christmas break. Bernie was an athletic ecology major who wore
hiking boots with her long skirts. Since the apartment was so large,
it had become an unofficial gathering place for many foreigners, and

I was over there all the time. We often had enormous group meals in the evening, where the conversation frequently turned to politics.

Tony spent his days reading newspapers and magazines and listening to the BBC World Service, so at dinner he was often the one to fill us all in, a role he enjoyed. He drew us maps on the paper tablecloth so he could instruct us, for instance, about Portugal's colonies abroad and Spain's past trade routes in South America. These maps often became more elaborate over the course of a dinner and turned into countries that did not exist, with fanciful names, such as Angorapackerstan or South Whossit. Bernie found Tony as arrogant as he found her naive—he said studying environmental science was the silliest California hippie thing he'd ever heard; she told him geography was more than sticking British names on maps.

For a very long time I'd been paying little attention to the news. Only when something enormous happened, such as the murder of the Israeli athletes at Munich last summer, did it seem to make much of an impact. When I'd left America a year ago, Richard Nixon was *Time*'s man of the year, and the Vietnam War, which already seemed to have been going on most of my life, was just as entrenched as ever. The war, in fact, had the quality to me of Francoism; someday, you thought, it might come to an end—but, then again, it might not. Franco's regime could very well continue under the restored monarchy. The U.S. might never leave Southeast Asia; the government might just continue warring with guerillas in Vietnam, Laos, and Cambodia forever.

Yet one day, when I went over to the apartment, Tony said, "There's a cease-fire between the U.S. and North Vietnam. This time it looks serious." He had heard it on the BBC. The Paris peace talks had produced results. The U.S. would begin withdrawing troops; the POWs would be coming home.

The prospect of peace was astonishing, but there was other news as well. Tony bought *Time* and *Newsweek* when he could get them on the newsstands, and there were always recent copies at their apartment, which I now began to read when I was over there. Spanish censors often cut out photographs of women not sufficiently clothed and there was rarely any news about Spain, but there was, of course, plenty about the U.S., which so often seemed a foreign country to me now. In early February came the report that, on the same day LBJ had died, the Supreme Court had decided in favor of women's abortion rights in *Roe v. Wade*. I knew little about the struggles that had led up to the decision, but I was very glad about it. I was glad too—and astonished—that *Time* now had an occasional section titled "The Sexes," which had articles beginning: "With increasing frequency, women are storming and taking once impregnable strongholds of masculine prerogative." One article told of a woman in Van Nuys, California, who'd tried to rent a rototiller and was told that only men were allowed to check out power equipment. Now she was suing. Another article mentioned that Germaine Greer, "the radical feminist," had written an essay for *Playboy* expanding the definition of rape to "daily brutalization of contact." And the ERA had passed the Senate.

Within a few years I'd be working on a leftist newspaper collective in Seattle and conversant with developments in the rest of the world as well as knowledgeable about all the ins and outs of every progressive movement in the country. But my interest in politics was only beginning that spring in Granada. I had been generally *against* the Establishment for many years, without completely understanding how my government worked. It took Tony to explain to me why the small matter of a burglary at the Democratic headquarters might be shaping up to become something important. "It's about executive privilege," he told me. "Nixon trying to control access to information by claiming it's his right as president to keep secrets; Congress debating whether that *is* his right. You know, the balance of powers, checks and balances, the Constitution, all that?" When I looked vague, he demanded, "Surely you know about the executive, the legislative, and the judicial branches of the U.S. government?'

"Er . . . of course," I said, scrambling to call up some remnants of the civics sections from a political science class. All those years of marching against the war and shouting and handing out flyers for Eugene McCarthy the summer after high school, and looking stern when people mentioned the military-industrial complex and feeling grieved when I thought about napalm and babies, and I really didn't have much of a clue as to the structure of my government. Washington was run by evil madmen, that's about all I could really confirm. As to how it was run—badly was all I was sure of. The story of this thing they were calling Watergate would soon blow over, I thought; Richard Nixon was too powerful to be challenged.

"The Sexes," with its suggestion that women's liberation was, to everyone's apparent surprise, actually getting somewhere, made me sit up. Suddenly politics began to seem more about me and my life, not just about men blowing each other up on the streets and in the jungles. I discussed *Roe v. Wade* with Patsy and Bernie and brought the news back to Lolí. I'd never been pregnant, but all of them had either had an illegal abortion or had worried they might have to seek help after missing a period.

Bernie wasn't with us long; she found the atmosphere in Granada "claustrophobic." She couldn't make her peace, as Patsy and I had done, with being followed and hissed at. She didn't care that we said the Spanish were basically harmless; they would never actually molest you. "Who cares if they rape you or not?" she said. "It's the fucking pain in the neck of being *followed* that I can't stand." One day she bought a beautiful knife with a carved handle in the market next to the Cathedral; she then pulled it on a man who was bugging her on the street. "I was afraid I was going to actually use it on him—I was so angry." The next day she made plans to go back to Humboldt County—"where a person can walk around without having to look over her shoulder constantly!" I missed her stories of walks in the redwood forests and friends who kept goats and used solar heating in their yurts; but at the same time I knew, and Patsy agreed, that there was something here for us that we wouldn't get just living in a safe hippie community in Northern California.

I knew why Bernie thought Tony obnoxious, but I still found him highly entertaining and brilliant. Like Miguel, Tony always opened himself to new passions and adventures. Tony and Julian traveled frequently—to Madrid, to Portugal, to North Africa, and wherever they went they seemed to meet people who often turned up at the apartment: Catalans, Madrileños, Australians, and Italians. Miguel was always bringing home new acquaintances as well. Sometimes the floor was littered with sleeping bags. To me, Miguel and Tony seemed to embody the spirit of old al-Andalus, a spirit that could be glimpsed through the rhetoric that described the Moorish "occupation" as backward and oriental. That spirit was tolerant and generous as opposed to rigid and pure; it was a time when Jews, Muslims, and Christians mingled and enriched one another's cultures. Miguel and Tony put a premium on mingling—but interestingly, as I got to know them more, I saw that they had few friends among the Granadine student population. We women were far more likely to be pursued by Spanish men; no girl from Granada would have ever gone out with Tony or especially Miguel. Miguel, of course, would have liked a Spanish *novia*—or two or three. Tony, I'm not so sure.

In spite of Tony's needling ways, he rarely made fun of me, though he easily could have. Once, he and I were walking down the street, talking of our futures. He planned to become an academic, "to satisfy me mum," but he also wanted to travel—to Africa principally. I was unsure whether to confide my dreams of writing, of having something to do with making books. I rarely spoke of becoming a writer these days—not the way I used to a year or two ago. It was more evident to me that in order to be a writer you needed the habit of writing and that the habit wasn't easily acquired.

My attempts last autumn in my apartment to write "The Travelogue" had often seemed like lowering myself hand over hand into a dark mine shaft, and then just as slowly and arduously hauling myself up, with only a piece of fool's gold to show for it. My character Alex, with her unexplained limp, her cane, and her interest in both men and women, was still down in the mine. Reading Doris Lessing had also alarmed me; in her new introduction to *The Golden Notebook* Lessing had written: "One novel in five hundred or a thousand has the quality a novel should have to make it a novel—the quality of philosophy." I felt so young, so inexperienced and callow; how could I meet that standard?

Without being too specific I said something to Tony about having written a short story or two, and maybe that being something I'd like to pursue in the future. I half-expected Tony, who delighted in sticking pins into others' pretensions, to mock me or dispute that, but he simply nodded.

"I can see you as a writer. You don't have the mind of a typical girl. I like that. You're not exactly well informed, but you think rationally. You have a logical mind, and believe me, that's rare in a girl."

It wouldn't have occurred to me in those days to ask what he meant by "a typical girl," or to be offended on behalf of my sex. I took it as a high compliment and for a long time, somewhere inside, was strengthened by his offhand faith in my logical mind.

Miguel had been drawn more and more into the world of flamenco; he had daily guitar lessons and now was about to start taking dance classes, to prepare for the upcoming *ferias* of the spring. With his usual charm, he persuaded most of us to join him in a class taught by a *gitana,* Luz of the long, lacquered red fingernails and blazing black eyes, with big pollywogs of black liner. Her black hair knotted at the nape. Her long back, visible in the polka-dotted black-and-white dress, was sinuous and shapely. She wore stiletto heels and told us (the girls) we could not dance without them and that we should wear dresses, too. I had high-heeled boots, but I couldn't bring myself to wear a dress, and that spoiled the effect—I knew that myself—of my proper role. A rumba danced in corduroy jeans and a long-sleeved shirt is not a proper rumba. Patsy also didn't want to wear a dress, but she bought a long fringed shawl of which Luz approved, and teetered on the highest heels she could manage—one inch tall to Luz's three-inchers. Tony and Patsy, more or less the same height, turned out to be excellent dancers; only Julian was clumsy—but that was because he'd often been drinking before we had our lessons. We learned the arm and hand movements of the *sevillana,* which always reminded me of Hindu dancing, and which perhaps, because the Gypsies were said to have originally come from India, wasn't so far off the mark.

More than any step or wave of the fingers, Luz imparted a notion of *la gracia,* one of those untranslatable words heard so often in the south of Spain. It wasn't like *duende,* a soulful mood that could be invoked only in certain circumstances from the depths of pain and beauty; *la gracia* could be cultivated, even by clunky, repressed

Anglo-Saxons. The dictionary defined it as wit or grace, but it seemed more like style, a quality that Luz possessed in abundance. It was the way you held your head upright, the way you responded to a glance of desire or answered an unspoken challenge, the way you whisked your flouncy skirt or rattled your castanets or stood, with a ramrod posture, your head lifted, waiting for the opening notes of the *sevillana*.

Our classes with Luz took place around eight in the evening. Afterward we sometimes went to one of the bars on the Campo del Príncipe, where smoke from Ducado cigarettes was thick as fog and the tapes ran continuously with flamenco, and where we practiced dancing the *sevillana* and rumba for an hour or two before heading up to the caves of Sacromonte. We rarely had dinner, only tapas, with small glasses of red wine. I never got drunk as I had in my early days in Spain; instead, I went for long hours mildly intoxicated, like many around me.

Sometimes we managed to get into the Peña de la Platería for a flamenco concert. In those days, pure flamenco was heard mainly in the *peñas,* or societies, around Andalusia. Granada's Platería was a long-standing institution in the city, half performance hall, half religious temple. It was a shrine to the purest of pure flamenco where you could hear Fosforito, Luís de Córdoba, Pepe de Argentina, José Menes and lesser-known names from one or another of the great Gypsy flamenco lineages. All the flamenco artists used a nickname or their first names with a modifier of place or family. Up in the caves above Granada, where once many Gypsy families had lived before the government forced them into apartment blocks, flamenco was performed for tourists, just as Laura and I had seen. There, on any night of the week, you could sit inside the whitewashed caves with a glass of rum and Coke in front of you and watch dramatic women fling their long black ponytails around and intense-eyed men in bolero jackets take poses with their arms upraised. The castanets clacked wildly and the tourists shouted "*Olé*" and went away relieved of some of their money but convinced they'd had an authentic experience of flamenco.

The Platería was different. It was a society of listeners, who sat in fold-up metal chairs every week paying close attention to one guitarist or another, to a dancer, to a singer. There were few resounding *olé*s at the Platería, only murmurs of approbation. Here we learned about *cante jondo*, or "deep song," which was as old in southern Spain as the Moorish occupation of Granada and had been influenced by the Arabs and Jews. The couplets were simple and expressive, drawn out in long syllables of grief and longing from the bottom of the feet up through the body and out the lungs. The tone was dark and piercing, gravel-throated, thin as a sharpened knife.

Although I spent a great deal of time with my English-speaking circle, I'd made sure to try to cultivate other friendships, with Lolí for instance, so I could continue speaking Spanish outside class. Now I began to learn a little Arabic as well. Miguel had introduced me to one of his friends, a Moroccan student, Abdelhaq, a dignified, reserved young man who offered to give me lessons in Arabic if I'd teach him English, and we were meeting twice a week. The first thing he taught me was the opening words of the Koran; the second thing was how to say "no" in Arabic: *la*. He told me it would be useful to know both if I ever traveled in Morocco. I sent away to Foyles for *Teach Yourself Arabic*, and Abdelhaq and I made it through lesson three by the end of February. I covered pages of my notebook in great sweeps of Arabic calligraphy and learned such handy phrases as "The merchant is the strength of the land" and "The donkey is the poor man's horse."

Gisela was very interested in Morocco, as well. Over the Christmas break, she'd gone to Rabat to visit a pen pal she'd originally met in a youth hostel once in Munich. Mohammed was a bureaucrat, and his family was connected in some way with the king of Morocco. She was eager to return there in March and suggested I go with her. She wanted to spend three weeks traveling around the country by bus, getting to know Fès, Marrakech, and the Atlas Mountains. I jumped at the idea; the longer I stayed in Granada the more intrigued I'd become by its Islamic past. Of all the cities and caliphates of al-Andalus, which once stretched over most of the Iberian Peninsula, Granada had remained under the rule of the Moors longest. It wasn't until 1492 that Isabella and Ferdinand drove out the last of the Nasrid dynasty, a date that was celebrated every January 2. We had learned a great deal about the Reconquest of Spain at the university, but of course what was always more intriguing, was how very long Andalusia had been Moorish— almost eight hundred years—and how that history was still to be seen everywhere in the city, from the grand architecture of the red palace on the hill to the very language, which held in vocal memory the sounds of the Berber tribes of North Africa.

I thought it would be a good thing for Gisela to travel; I could see she wasn't happy, that she was lonely. She didn't like my English friends—"I didn't come to Spain to speak English!"—nor the single other German woman at the university, who yearned to speak German with her. Gisela had been friends with her former roommate, Brenni, a Honduran girl who'd moved to Germany to study, but she wasn't much interested in Brenni's cousin Mario or in Cristobal. Cristobal, roundish and more African than Indian, was an excellent student, according to Gisela; he wanted only to finish his medical studies and get out of Spain, which he claimed was the most racist country in the world. Mario wanted to leave, too, so he said. He had been in Spain for eleven years, ever since he had impregnated an Indian girl on his father's estate and it was decided he should complete his studies abroad. Mario had gone back to Honduras several times: once to marry a girl of his father's choice and twice to visit the daughter they'd conceived on their Acapulco honeymoon. Mario's room was plastered with photos of the child, with tiny faded pink booties, ribbons, and crayon pictures. He was in his thirties, with a sparse mustache over his lip and a harried frown. According to Gisela, Mario had failed his final law exams twice. Although he studied, the night before the exam he invariably went out and got massively drunk and brought strangers back to the house.

The mood at the house was usually depressed. Gisela roused herself only rarely to change out of her blue terrycloth bathrobe and leave the house. On one of the few occasions when she accompanied me to a bar with my friends, she met a Spanish student who called himself Johnny, who came from a landed family near Andújar and was studying law. Like other *señoritos,* he exuded a sense of well-being and confidence, wearing his coat flung over his shoulders like a cape. Soon Johnny was established as Gisela's temporary *novio,* and there was talk of his returning to Stuttgart with her. She was worried, however, about breaking the news to her pen pal in Rabat, who was waiting for her visit at the beginning of March. All this conflict caused Gisela to begin pulling her hair out again.

Johnny had invited Gisela to visit his hometown one weekend. He'd spoken often of Andújar, where his family apparently owned thousands of acres of olive groves. Gisela thought this meant he was serious and wanted to introduce her to his family. But at the last minute she grew nervous; she asked me to come along and I agreed.

Aside from a trip to Almuñécar with Miguel on his motorcycle last fall and a recent excursion into the mountains by burro with my friends, I'd generally stayed close to home. Andújar was midway between Jaén and Córdoba, and I thought it might be possible to visit those cities too.

Johnny had a little Fiat and one Saturday morning he picked us up and drove us to Andújar. Gisela somehow had the notion we'd be staying with his family in the hacienda amidst the olive groves, but as soon as we got to town, he parked on a side street and directed us, in a cloak-and-dagger manner, to a *pensión* in the central square, where he told us we'd be very comfortable. He then departed to have lunch with his family, assuring us he'd be back in the evening, bringing a friend for me, so we could all have drinks and go to a disco.

"*Pero, pero, pero* . . ." Gisela sputtered. But, but, but . . . "I would like to meet your family."

"*Sí, sí, sí,* perhaps tomorrow," Johnny said evasively. "I will prepare them."

He jumped into his Fiat and left us in the very pretty main plaza. I wasn't particularly surprised, but Gisela chewed over Johnny's behavior all afternoon: at lunch, as we walked around, at dinner. "This is unforgivable," she said many times. "I have brought many people home with me to Stuttgart. My parents would never turn anyone away. Especially if I was interested in a boy. The boyfriend would stay with us."

About ten at night, as Gisela and I were sitting in our beds reading in the *pensión*, there came a shout from the street, and there was Johnny, looking like a gangster with his coat over his shoulders and his longish black hair slicked back, a cigarette dangling from his lips; his friend looked to me even more sinister. I expected Gisela to aim one of the flower pots on the balcony at his head after her diatribe all afternoon, but instead, she threw on her best clothes and urged me to do the same. Reluctantly I accompanied them for some hours of carousing in a surprisingly full disco where the song "American Pie" played incessantly and the "wheeskies" flowed.

Gisela and Johnny made up their differences, danced close, and he promised to pick us up at one the next afternoon for a tour of the olive groves, followed by a meal with his family, after which we'd all drive back to Granada. Gisela and I gave up the room in our *pensión* at noon and hung about the plaza, which was enlivened mainly by people coming and going to mass. We didn't have his phone number, and as two o'clock came and went, it became apparent that Johnny had had cold feet. "In Germany," Gisela said about a hundred times, "this would be very rude. This *is* very rude. Come on," she said finally. "Let's go."

She had a suitcase and I a knapsack; we decided that we'd hitchhike to Jaén and then catch the bus. We ended up walking through olives groves for a long time, while no cars passed. The province of Jaén had more olive trees planted than anywhere else in Spain—this we'd read and now we knew it for sure.

"When I see him in Granada, I look forward to telling him how offended I am," Gisela stoked her anger. "Now I am *definitely* going to Morocco in two weeks to see my pen pal. I hope you still want to come with me."

In view of how difficult I found traveling with her just on this short weekend in Spain, it still amazes me that I assured her I wanted nothing more.

We stood and walked. Cars of families passed us; no one picked us up. Eventually, however, our luck improved. A chipper Dutch couple in a yellow Fiat picked us up. They were on their way to a *jamonería* to pick up a special, locally cured ham. They invited us to come with them and learn about this particularly Spanish way of curing ham.

We stood at the counter first, eating olives, and homemade *morcilla,* black blood sausage, with tiny, cold glasses of thin, bright sherry. Then, from the hams hanging behind the dark wooden bar, the proprietor trimmed slices of *jamón,* so thin as to be almost transparent, for us to try, along with chunks of bread and more sherry. These hams weren't cooked or smoked, but had been covered with salt and hung in chill sheds, where the cold winds from the Sierras had cured them to a texture not exactly dry but not moist either, glassine in appearance and chewy, but melting in taste. Their colors ranged from fuchsia pink to wine red, marbled with fat. The best had a black hoof, a *pata negra,* and were from a special black-skinned pig. The Dutch couple bought one of these. They'd keep it in the dry cellar of their home in Dordrecht and slice off thin strips for months to come.

Suddenly Gisela was possessed by the desire to buy a large cured ham. Perhaps it was the sherry, for Gisela was mean with money. Although she had a stipend to study, and could have afforded to eat out regularly, she not only ate in but loved nothing more than to skip dinner several times a week, to save money *and* diet.

Gisela was protective of her ham once we got home. She kept it in a closet on her side of the room, under the pretext she was saving it for her mother, but little by little it began to disappear. A few times she brought the ham out to be admired, but later she grew vague about the whole experience. One day I found a black hoof in the garbage pail.

❧ FOURTEEN ❧

Simultaneous Translation

ALTHOUGH I WASN'T speaking Spanish as much as I would have liked, my reading ability had advanced, and I now began to discover the great wealth of Latin American literature from the sixties: Julio Cortázar, Mario Vargas Llosa, and especially Gabriel García Márquez. One day, on a friend's recommendation, I bought *Cien Años de Soledad* and was enthralled from the very first sentence: "*Mucho años después, frente al pelotón de fusilamiento, el colonel Aureliano Buendía había de recordar aquella tarde remota en que su padre lo llevó a conocer el hielo*" ("Many years later, as he faced the firing squad, Colonel Aureliano Buendía was to remember that distant afternoon when his father took him to discover ice"). The words had the same mythic inevitability of the opening of *Don Quixote*: "*En el lugar de la Mancha, de cuyo nombre no quiero acordarme, no ha mucho tiempo que vivía un hidalgo . . .*" ("Somewhere in La Mancha, in a place whose name I do not care to remember, a gentleman lived not long ago . . ."). They were like the musical overtures as the curtain rose on a scene of enchantment.

After a week or two of reading *Cien Años de Soledad*, I felt inspired to see if I could render García Márquez's story into English. I set myself the task of translating the first page from Spanish and found that it came more easily than I'd expected. This gave me an inordinate sense of mastery, as if I had double vision, able to read Spanish with one eye and English with another. In fact, I'd been curious about translation for a number of years. As early as high school French, I'd enjoyed the competitive act of word substitution. Then, translation was a kind of dictionary game for me, coming up with equivalencies and meanings. Mr. Heidelberg, our teacher, was ambitious for us; he had us try our hands at paragraphs by Rousseau and Montaigne. From time to time he suggested that there were words that had no exact equivalent, and meanings that could never be rendered in English: *l'esprit, l'honneur, l'amour.* In spite of the fact that reading French and trying to speak it gave me an unfocused but gorgeous sense of *being* French, I discounted emotion as a part of translation: *fenêtre* could never be anything but "window." Yet even in those basic exercises I experienced a hint of the possessiveness that can develop when you turn another writer's words into yours; that is, I often liked my translations better than another student's. When there were two English words to choose from, and neither was completely correct, or incorrect, you chose one, and that one word made your translation different—from the original, from someone else's.

I sat for long hours at the university library, which smelled, like everything else in the south of Spain, of bitter oranges, olive trees, and tobacco, lost in the world of Anacona, looking up words but reading eventually with more fluency. One of the things I discovered about reading in a foreign language was that it encouraged me to savor the language, word by word. I'd been mildly dyslexic as a child; it had once been almost impossible for me to see letters sequentially and understand their meaning. SEE DICK RUN was nothing to me all through first grade, and I sulked in the slow readers' group. I solved the problem for myself by learning to scan in clumps. My mind saw sections of the page and understood the words in groups. Years later, that was still how I was accustomed to absorb a text. I might write word by word, in sentences, but I still tended to read in paragraphs.

Now, the process of translation slowed my reading to a snail's pace, as I often had to look up the meanings of several words before I came to the end of a sentence. It also forced me to recognize that words in the dictionary did not quite cross the divide from one language to the next. Of course I already "knew" that; why else had so much ink been spilled on the concept of *duende*, for instance, much less on other minor words we were always quibbling about. Many words in Spanish described things that we didn't actually have in English-speaking countries—the whole vocabulary of bullfighting for instance—but it was more complex than that. When a Spaniard starting going on about *sol y sombra*, he didn't just mean "sunshine and shade" or which side you preferred to sit in at a bullring; it also had to do with the Spanish character, with philosophy, with the ways that phrase had been used in literature. When, as an English-speaker learning Spanish, you had a real conversation with someone, you could try to draw out the meanings of a word. You could ask, over and over, "Yes, but how *exactly* would you use that phrase?" And your conversational partner, if patient, would give you example after example, often with stories attached, and almost always with gestures.

In translating from one language to another, you could hope to convey only a fraction of the complexities of meaning. I looked at my page of translation from *Cien Años de Soledad* and wondered what I was missing. I had never been to the country of Columbia. I had never even been, though it was so close to California, to Mexico.

Nevertheless I was excited by my attempt and wrote to my friend David in the States that I'd discovered an amazing writer, and I enclosed the first page of my translation.

I asked, "If you wanted to translate a book like this, how would you go about getting it published?"

"Sorry," he wrote back kindly. "*One Hundred Years of Solitude* came out in English a few years ago. It's been a bestseller since."

Still, my attempt with García Márquez had given me a feel for being in two languages at the same time and had planted the idea of literary translation in my mind. About ten years later, in the same innocent spirit of adventure, I would decide to translate the stories of Cora Sandel from Norwegian into English, and that was a book that actually was published. I'd go on to translate two more books and oversee, as editor and publisher, the publication of two dozen more translations by women from all over the world.

"These sheets have been used!" said Gisela in her elegant, furious French. "Someone has been sleeping in this bed! The sheets are wrinkled!"

The proprietor of the small hotel in Fès bowed his head in acknowledgement. "*Oui, Mademoiselle,* but he was a very clean Mohammedan."

Gisela stormed out of the room and down the stairs to the street, and I followed tiredly. We'd been in Morocco two days, and Gisela had been almost continuously upset by one thing or another, often to do with cleanliness. Apparently when she'd been in Morocco over the holidays, the standards of her pen pal and his family in Rabat were much higher; she'd been driven everywhere in a chauffeured car and treated like a sultana by servants in the home. She wanted me to agree with her that Morocco so far was filthy. Dirty, yes, I said, but not filthy. And dirty we knew well from Granada. So what? To me, the dirt, the flies, and the ripe smells were part of what made this new country so marvelously different, so much richer and stranger than anywhere I'd been in Europe. From the moment we passed out of the Spanish colonial town of Ceuta on the North Africa coast where the ferry from Algeciras came in, everything changed absolutely. Most women wore Western dress, but some were swathed head to toe; their faces were veiled in the thin black material called the *nikab,* which stretched across the bridge of the nose and past the chin and was wet around the mouth. A number of men wore burnooses of thin wool or cotton called *djellabas,* with heelless leather slippers in yellow. On the bus, North African music, rhythmic and wailing, played incessantly; occasionally the bus came to a halt at a roadblock and we had to show passports. The King of Morocco had been threatened with a coup last summer and again this past January. Out the window, en route to Fès, the fields were emerald green with groves of oranges and date palms; the signs were elegant slashes of Arabic.

Our neighbors on the bus handed us almonds and dates; they asked us curiously about ourselves in French and sign language. They were eager to help us find a hotel in Fès, but Gisela dismissed them and instead, inexplicably, commanded me to follow a tout outside the bus station, who led us a long way into the medieval maze of alleys, some no wider than a single person could traverse, to this hotel. Obviously we weren't going to be staying here, and now we were lost.

Gisela fumed in rapid French, demanding of me, "Where are we going to find a clean hotel?" From the moment we'd set foot in Morocco, she'd stopped speaking Spanish with me and would address me only in French. I'd tried reasoning with her—"Gisela, I don't speak French anything like as well as I do Spanish, or as well as you do"—but she was adamant, even though this was nothing we'd discussed beforehand back in Granada. "This is your chance, then, to improve your poor French. After all, this is a French-speaking country we're in."

"Actually, they speak Arabic," I'd sniped. "And Berber." Abdelhaq, my friend in Granada, had told me that millions of people still spoke those tribal languages. I tried to hold out as long as I could in Spanish, but it was hopeless. Gisela would simply shrug, "*Je ne comprends pas!*" I don't understand you. And eventually I gave in. It *was* a chance to improve my French, even though it meant I was often silent the first few days. For the most part it often meant, at least in the beginning, that I was dependent on Gisela.

Eventually Gisela and I found our way out of the Medina and into the Ville Nouvelle, the French section of Fès, a parallel city created by the French during colonial times, with wide boulevards, shop signs in French, and outdoor cafés. We spent our first night in a clean hotel that might also have been a brothel, where someone banged on our door in the night and suggested he pay for the pleasure of our company, and there was some running and screaming in the hallways toward morning. The next day, a young man who'd been following us around town invited us to come and stay with his family in the heart of the Medina. I was skeptical, but there was no reasoning with Gisela; she wanted to get to know the Moroccan people and never for a moment thought of it as being a possible trap to lure us into slavery or prostitution. It's possible she imagined a home like that of her pen pal, Mohammed, in Rabat, but Gisela also had a contradictory quality. The more she feared something, the more she would go toward it. My own wishes were immaterial to her; she simply arranged things with others in rapid French and then explained to me what we were doing.

On this occasion she was absolutely right to be so trusting; I have no idea what Abdul's family thought of two Western women descending on their home, but for us it was thrilling. We slept on divans upstairs in a house with a central courtyard open to the sky and ate our meals with the incredibly hospitable family, all seated on cushions around a low table. For breakfast we had vegetable and bean soup; for dinner a huge silver platter was brought in, piled with light hot couscous, lentils, and a small piece of either chicken or lamb, like a treasure in the center. Only the father, patriarchal in his *djellaba* and embroidered cap, and Gisela and I were allowed to have pieces of the meat. The wife, in fact, didn't even eat with us, though the young daughters did.

Abdul was the oldest son; he spoke good French and wore slacks and sweaters. It was unclear to me what Abdul had on his mind, other than to get to know Gisela better and show us off to his friends. Perhaps he thought Gisela might be able to get him a job in Germany, for he seemed to be an unemployed man about town. He'd finished his schooling but apparently didn't want to take up his father's trade of shoemaking. His father ran a small shop in the Medina where the *babouches*, or heelless leather slippers, were sold. We never went out of the house without Abdul, because he assured us, and we believed him, that we'd never find our way back again. His home was on an alleyway with a hundred other white-plastered houses just the same and every street at first looked just the same, and seemed to lead nowhere.

The Medina was centuries old, one of the most intact medieval cities in the world, where crafts were still practiced in age-old ways. There were souks, or specialty markets, for everything you could imagine: streets where only rugs were sold, or leather goods, or jewelry, or inlaid wood boxes, or clothes. Abdul introduced us everywhere and supervised our purchases (perhaps he took a cut). We learned to bargain. I loaded up with silver bangles and necklaces, a belt and wallet in beautifully worked leather, a *djellaba* of my own. Gisela spent two hours deciding on a silver-plated platter; in the end she bought the largest one and then regretted it daily. We drank innumerable cups of tea made with fresh mint leaves and chunks from a sugar loaf while visiting in shops thick with red knotted rugs. We ate delicious street food—dried fruits, pomegranate juice, flat breads, and yogurt. Some parts of the Medina were nothing but food: big burlap bags of dates from the south of the country, or baskets of every herb and spice imaginable, from bunches of fresh mint to golden saffron.

French now supplanted Spanish, but it was a different French than I'd learned in school or practiced briefly in Paris, slangier and infused with Arabic words for food, drink, and objects. The Moroccans weren't snippy about pronunciation and would work with me to find the words for things I'd never learned in Mr. Heidelberg's class: I want the silver necklace with the tiny bells; one half kilo of dried apricots, please; that leather purse is not bad, but I couldn't pay what you ask, that would be laughable. Abdul had suggested that if I spoke French I would get far better deals than if I spoke English. The French were known for their thriftiness, the Americans for their naive profligacy. That was incentive enough. And so, French came back and, with it, skeptical smiles, shrugs, and conversational additions I'd long forgotten: puffs of air through pursed lips or surprised but not really surprised ejaculations, "*Oo la la.*"

Abdul took us here and there, but the occasion I remember best was one he and his male friends didn't attend. It was a party of only girls, one of whom was the fiancée of a friend of Abdul's. The girls were beautiful with long dark hair and bare feet and a scent of henna and French perfume. They put on Moroccan music and danced for each other, belly dancing just in their skirts and blouses but with sexy, sinuous movements, which didn't seem to be just flirtations but invitations. They pulled us up off the cushions and tried to get us to ripple our bellies, too; they served us mint tea and honey-and-nut pastries; and kissed us on the cheeks when we left. It was eye-opening to me that in this Arabic world, which seemed so male, female eroticism existed in a group of women, and that it seemed so openly acknowledged.

One day Gisela announced, "We're going." Abdul had pressed her a little too hard the night before; she wouldn't give the details, and besides, we had to see more of the country before heading to Rabat and the pen pal. We decided to take a bus into the Atlas Mountains and just get off when someplace looked interesting.

Night began to fall as our slow local bus passed through villages that looked too small to have a hotel and then several alpine resorts, which seemed almost Swiss with their chalets dusted with snow. We didn't get off in those places either, for neither of us had warm clothes and it seemed colder and colder outside as it darkened. I noticed, in the front of the bus, a man who looked Western, and told Gisela, "Let's get off when he gets off. We can ask him where to go." This we did, and the young American, who was in the Peace Corps, took us back to his small flat. But when we got there, a message had been pushed under his door.

"This isn't good," he said to me in English. "Another death threat. I suppose this isn't the best place for you two to stay."

He brought us over to the home of some friends, who were Frenchmen teaching at the local lycée. Gisela was in her element, talking politics for hours over wine and cheese, but I felt suddenly at a loss. My French, which had been improving by leaps and bounds in the Medina, was insufficient to discuss American imperialism, Marx, and the European Union. It was as if I had never studied the language at all; my brain went into a kind of dead zone. I sat there grimly, like a zombie, wordless.

The Frenchmen, though they were perfectly happy to talk about politics half the night, thought it best that we didn't stay with them either, so we passed the night on the floor in an empty room in the school. It was so cold Gisela and I had to huddle together, the closest we'd ever been. In the morning things looked much better. It was Tuesday and we were in Azrou, home to a well-known souk that happened only on that day. Berber tribesmen and women from all the surrounding mountains appeared at the outdoor market, many of them on horseback. Red carpets covered the green hillside, and the scent of fresh mint and sugar floated through the white tents. Gisela wanted to buy a carpet, but I persuaded her out of it; she already had her hands full with the outsize silver platter.

We took the bus back to the plains, to the old walled city of Meknes, and then we moved on to Rabat. Gisela had been preparing for seeing Mohammed again in Meknes by shaving her legs and underarms and getting her nails done. As soon as we arrived and were picked up by Mohammed, a tall, thin bureaucrat with a possessive air, Gisela informed me that I would not be staying with his family; I would stay, instead, with a cousin of Mohammed's and his parents in a house quite far from her. She told me this in French, as if it had all been decided in advance. "But for how long?" I asked.

"I don't know," she said dismissively.

"I'll wait for you for two days," I said. "Then I'm going on to Marrakech." This was brave of me, for in fact, I relied on Gisela because of her French and was uncertain how I'd fare traveling by myself.

Mohammed's cousin, confusingly also named Mohammed, took me over to his house, a French-style villa with Moroccan touches, such as divans in the rooms and only a hole in the floor instead of a toilet. His parents served us a Moroccan meal, but at a table with chairs, and spoke French with me and Arabic with their son. Then, I thought, rather inhospitably, they went off to another part of house, instructing Mohammed to show me to my room. He offered me *kif*, or pot, and refused to leave the room when I said I was ready to sleep. He was a university student and specialized in French literature. He thought he could get into my bed by quoting reams of Baudelaire, but this just annoyed me. Over and over I sent Mohammed out of the room, only to be awakened to find him sitting nearby, reading aloud from a poetry book, the room cloudy with the smoke of *kif*. In the morning, after a sleepless night, I asked him to take me to where Gisela was staying.

The house was in an upscale development, surrounded by a security gate. We buzzed the intercom, and after a short while, Gisela herself came on the line.

I spoke in English, angrily. "What do you think you're doing, leaving me with this guy? I'm going to a hotel. And tomorrow I'm getting out of Rabat!"

"No, no, no," she said. And in a whisper, in English, she added, "I seem to be trapped here. I think Mohammed locked the door from the outside."

"What? I'm calling the police."

"No, please. I think it's just a misunderstanding."

"I can't just leave you here."

"Go to a hotel," she whispered. "Mohammed will let Mohammed know where it is. I'll figure something out."

The Mohammed with me seemed not to have caught much of this. But then, he was still stoned from all the *kif* he'd smoked last night. He walked me back to town and helped me to find a hotel.

We spoke very little, and he seemed relived to see the last of me. "You seem *très agitée*," he said. "I did not think Americans were agitated persons."

If I had to be abandoned and alone in Morocco, Rabat was a better place than most. Because it was the capital, and because the king lived here and his life was threatened, there were security forces and police everywhere. The French quarter was very French, reassuringly so at the moment. I found bookshops, and where I found bookshops I found peace of mind. I bought a book, *L'histoire du Maroc,* and spent the evening reading in my hotel room. Although I'd told Gisela I planned to leave the next day, I knew I could never leave without her. I was already marshaling the phrases I'd need to approach the *Sûreté* the next day to explain that my friend had been kidnapped.

During what seemed the middle of the night, I was awakened by a noise at the window. After pressing my jumping heart back into my chest, I cautiously approached the window to see Gisela down below in the courtyard, clutching her silver-plated platter, with her suitcase by her side.

"Quick," she said in French. "There's a bus to Casablanca at five AM. We need to be on it."

Without asking questions, I quickly packed and checked out of the hotel. Only in the bus did she tell me her story. Mohammed said he'd locked her in for her own safety that first day. He told her that Morocco wasn't a safe place. She said she'd asked him why she couldn't stay with his large extended family, as she had the first time, instead of this house, which, it turned out, was only borrowed from a friend.

"And then he told me that his mother wouldn't allow it! She thought he was getting too serious about me. The family has already arranged a marriage for him, and if the fiancée's family were to hear of me returning again so soon after my last visit, they would realize Mohammed did not just have a pen pal! I asked was that why he invited me back to Morocco, saying he wanted to show me his country? It was so he could keep me locked up in a house for sex! That's not how we do things in Stuttgart with our guests!"

I was surprised to see that Gisela looked more irritated than petrified with horror, as I would have been. In fact, as the day wore on, and we changed buses in Casablanca and headed south to Marrakech, she began to seem remarkably pleased with herself. "I sneaked out the door, threw my plate and suitcase over the fence, and then climbed over it. Really, that's not such a good security system. Anyone could rob him if they liked."

All the same, she began pulling out her hair again, from the top of her crown.

It was in Marrakech that I finally relaxed. Gisela and I were there several days and generally went our separate ways. With all the tourists around, I didn't feel unsafe, but in fact, my time alone in Rabat had shown me I was all right on my own. Once, in Marrakech, a man followed me more closely than I liked. I turned around and quoted the first line of the Koran to him in Arabic, which made him fall back in dismay, either at my pronunciation or at the thought that I might be a Muslim convert. Morocco no longer seemed strange but only magical, and Marrakech the most magical of all the places we'd been in this enchanted country. The city, unlike Fès, was open and flat, hard to get lost in. Many of the walls were of reddish clay, and behind them were the mountains of the High Atlas, shimmering white with spring snow. The city was full of towers and minarets, palms and yuccas. I didn't say this to anyone, but Marrakech reminded me a little of Palm Springs, where my parents had sometimes taken us when I was a child.

Like most tourists I spent most of my time in the great market square of the city, Djemma el Fna, eating kabobs and pastries at the food stalls and taking in the sights. Around the huge square, blankets had been laid out carefully on the bare ground, and men sat cross-legged or on small stools with the tools of their trade around them. Each blanket was in effect an office, and the men in the middle of their blankets were offering services, whether that was getting a letter written, a prescription filled, or a fortune told. In other areas, snake charmers, jugglers, and musicians of all sorts entertained the crowds, and the haunting sounds of flutes and drums filled the air. The square was adjacent to the winding streets and souks of the Medina and there too I went on my own without fear, buying more jewelry after fierce happy bargains in French.

One day I stopped in front of a stall with carved and painted pipes. They were about a foot long, with tiny clay bowls attached to the end. "You want *kif, mademoiselle?* You want hashish?"

I wasn't much of a druggie, even during the days in the late sixties when everyone was smoking pot. Marijuana simply made me sleepy. But there was something irresistibly appealing about the notion of buying *kif* or hash in Marrakech. I wanted to believe myself sophisticated and adventurous, and I had a slight reckless streak that overrode my paranoia. Besides, Tony and Julian had been to Morocco; they'd bought hash and brought it back, bragging that no one ever bothered them in customs. They had asked me to bring some back for them. "You have an innocent face," Tony told me. "No one will think of checking on you."

Looking guardedly around, I bought the pipes, and then a small chunk of hash, and a little bag of *kif*. Back at the hotel that evening, Gisela was scandalized. "People go to jail all the time for drugs in Morocco."

I shrugged. After the Rabat incident I no longer trusted her judgment. I sat at the window in the balmy air, as the sun set with a crimson glaze over the reddish buildings and the palm trees and the muezzins called the faithful to pray, I smoked my pipe. I was thinking about Miguel last fall, who had raised the idea of dropping my American self and adopting, if temporarily, a Spanish one. Now I seemed to have let that Spanish self drift away, yet I didn't have a French self in place. French came and went. Sometimes the language was so easy, at other times I had no idea what Gisela was saying. A self based on language could feel at times so unbounded, at other times so constricted. I wondered why I had the longing to turn other languages into English; was it that I wanted to explore other ways of being, while still keeping the English-speaking self, the core self, primary?

Gisela was sitting on her bed, pulling out her hair and writing a letter to Mohammed, whom she had decided could still be her pen pal after all.

Drawing deeply on my pipe, I turned to her and asked, "How does it work, this whole notion of simultaneous translation?"

She stared disapprovingly at me, and I realized that I was speaking in English. But I persevered. "Just hear me out. I know you can understand me. I mean, you want to go back to Germany and find work as a simultaneous translator of Spanish and French. You've told me that many times. But, really, how can translation be *simultaneous?* You would have to have two mouths, both speaking at the same time. It has to be sequential, doesn't it? Really what you do is *rapid sequential translation.* Anyway, for the first time, I'm wondering, what is that like in your mind? Who *are* you when you're translating?"

"You are high."

"So what? It's still an interesting question. Are you a French version of Gisela when you're speaking French? Are you Spanish when you're speaking Spanish, a Spanish Gisela? What happens to your personality as you shift languages? Where does the German Gisela go?"

"It's not about personality. My personality does not change. I'm concerned with having the correct accent, and with making the meaning clear, especially where numbers are involved."

"Well, yes, you would be. But what's it like in your brain to have several languages there? I only ask because I don't think I could do it. If I speak one language all the time, I can't speak another. And I feel like I'm a completely different person when I'm speaking or reading Spanish. Or French. But if you're simultaneously translating from French to German and back again, what is going on—linguistically, I mean? In the place in your mind where words are born and die?"

"I don't understand you," she said in French. "If you study a language, you then know it, and you can speak it. Never quite as well as your own, but well enough. I plan to work in the business world, so I focus my vocabulary on business terms."

"*Bien. D'accord,*" I said ungraciously, and turned back to the window and the view of the High Atlas with the last pink alpine glow on their steep white flanks. The *kif* gave me a sense of my personality dissolving. I had wanted to come to Europe to learn languages, to try on new and different selves and to lose the old one. But what if, as the Zen masters said, there was really no fixed identity, only a shifting parade of selves? Now that would truly be freedom, not to be tied to a single identity and yet not to lose your identity, because there would be none to lose.

"I hope you are not becoming a drug addict," Gisela said, but I ignored her.

Essaouira on the Atlantic coast was our last stop. It was warm and windy, and the surf dashed up on a beach that was trodden occasionally by camels. By this time Gisela and I had almost no money left. We'd been eating simply, and drinking only bottled water. I didn't mind this at all; the yogurt was delicious, and so was the variety of dates and dried fruits. But Gisela was bored with yogurt. She wanted meat. An expert scrounger, she told me that in Germany what she'd do was go into a restaurant and take unfinished dishes off a table before the busboys got to them, but this I refused absolutely to do.

"Then we'll go to a fancy restaurant, order something very cheap, and wait until some rich men turn up. They'll invite us to eat with them, I assure you."

I was curious, so on our last evening I agreed to accompany her.

We sat for an hour over our shared salad, while white-uniformed waiters continued to ask us if we would like something "to follow," but eventually a group of French petroleum engineers entered the restaurant. Within five minutes, thanks to Gisela's beautiful French, we were seated at their table, enjoying sea urchins for appetizers and then a four-course dinner with several wines. Gisela had rack of lamb, and I had coquilles Saint Jacques. She sparkled now, as she hadn't during most of the trip, telling stories of our adventures. She even told the story, wittily, of how she escaped from Mohammed's friend's house, over the security fence. This was a Gisela I hardly knew, and it was hard to hold my own against her in French. In fact, as the evening went on, with dessert, fruit, cheese, coffee, and Cognac, my grasp of that language gradually faded out, so that I only experienced a wall of sound around me. Once, Gisela turned and whispered something secret to me in Spanish. I couldn't even understand that. I couldn't make the switch; my brain was numb. No, I would never make a simultaneous translator. Without English, I was like a baby waving my arms.

I needed it all written down. Even then I loved the idea of rebuilding an edifice of foreign words into my language, replacing each word of a writer's architecture with an English brick, so that the building or town would look the same, yet be subtly different and my own.

Then it was a long, overnight bus ride back to Tangiers to catch the ferry back to Algeciras. Worried at the last minute, I persuaded Gisela to carry my hash pipes through Spanish customs, because she seemed more bourgeois, with her suitcase, German passport, and perfect French accent, while I carried the actual small chunk of hash in a plastic bag in my underwear. We made sure to separate getting off the boat in Algeciras and going through customs. Even in my jeans and sandals, I slipped through easily. This was my famous *cara de ángel,* or "angel face," as Gisela said bitterly afterward. She, on the other hand, had to open her suitcase and was then led off to be strip-searched.

Even then, it did not occur to me to get rid of the hash, that she might point me out or that someone would have seen us together. In spite of seeing the signs everywhere about drugs being illegal, illustrated by people behind bars, it was hard to grasp that I could have been arrested and the key thrown away for years. When we met up outside the building, after I'd waited for her, more and more worried, for an hour, she was livid and I was cringingly apologetic. We took the bus to Málaga, not speaking, and arrived just in time for the last bus of the day to Granada. There was only one seat; I told Gisela to take it. It was the least I could do.

When I arrived back in Granada the following day, I didn't have the nerve to return to the Hondurans' house in Ciudad Jardín but went directly to the apartment of my English and American friends. They were having a big party and were excited to see me, wanting to hear about the trip and wondering if I'd brought drugs. "I have hash," I said proudly, and then remembered Gisela still had the pipes.

"Let's go over and get them," said Julian. It was about ten, which wasn't late by Spanish standards.

We walked over to the Hondurans' house and found it completely dark, the front door locked. I didn't have a key, because in general the door was always open. We rang the bell and there was no answer. Because Julian had been drinking, he thought it no problem to climb up to the balcony and see if he could get in the window of the room in front, which was Mario's. His hands were barely on the rails of the balcony, when there came a piercing scream of utter terror from the room. It was Gisela, screaming and shouting, "Help! Help! Thieves and murderers!"

Finally she pulled herself together enough to hear us calling her name and reassuring her. She came downstairs in her familiar blue terrycloth bathrobe, still badly shaken, to let us in, and told us that when she'd arrived late the previous night, she'd found no trace of Mario or Cristobal but instead a trail of blood leading from the entryway up the stairs. The house, at least the downstairs, had been ransacked. Eventually Mario had come home with a familiar tale. He was supposed to take his exams, but instead he'd started drinking and couldn't stop, and the last thing he remembered was inviting a group of Gypsies home with him. He didn't know why there was so much blood everywhere. He and Gisela cleaned it up, and then Mario vanished again. Gisela thought the ringing of the doorbell might be the bloodthirsty Gypsies again, and when she heard someone trying to get in the upstairs window, she panicked.

After Gisela heard all we wanted were the hash pipes, she handed them over with a furious look, now reminded of what she'd had to go through at customs and, in fact, for the last several weeks with me in Morocco, a country she had decided she would never visit again.

Julian and I skulked away into the night. I went back to the house only once when Gisela wasn't there to collect my things. Patsy had offered to share her room with me, and I moved in gratefully.

Gisela never spoke to me again, in Spanish, French, or any other language. I can't really say I blame her.

☙ FIFTEEN ☙

Cante Jondo

UNDERNEATH THE VIRGIN it was dark and sweaty; men cursed and joked. Miguel and I had crawled under the *paso* during a time when it was stationary. I was the only woman—it wasn't the kind of thing women did—but nobody threw me out. We stood up, holding the heavy wooden float with our shoulders and hands, and staggered off again, like galley slaves, all trying to match our steps, so the *paso* didn't jerk around too much. During these nightly processions of Semana Santa, Holy Week, painted statues of the Virgin or Christ, some of them very old, some garish with jewels and embroideries, others small and modest, were reverently placed onto flower-laden wooden platforms with drapery that concealed the men underneath and walked from one church to another. It was meant to look as if the holy ones were skimming through the narrow, crowded streets of the Albacín. Altar boys carrying censers walked in front of us; the evening air was warm with incense. In small plazas the procession heaved to a stop. A woman, sometimes in mantilla and comb, always with a flower in her hair, came out on a balcony and sang a *saeta*, a high soprano aria, and then threw another flower down to the crowd.

Miguel as usual had thrust himself, and me along with him, into the center of life. After we extracted ourselves from underneath the *paso*, we roamed along with the crowd and ended up in a bar with some Catalans. The whole city was alive with an exhilarating mixture of faith and high spirits. We went to bed at five AM. Julian, Patsy, and Tony had gone off to see Holy Week in Seville, for they'd heard that was the best of the festivals, but Miguel and I were content to spend Semana Santa in Granada, and especially to see the procession in Sacromonte when El Cristo de los Gitanos, the Christ of the Gypsies, would make his way up the road between the Albacín and the Alhambra.

I never wondered any longer where Miguel met people; he was so naturally interested in others, so hospitable, that he invited almost everyone he met for a drink or a meal, or to a party or a sleepover at the apartment. The day of the Sacromonte procession two wild-looking men, at least six feet tall, with lots of hair and heavy turtlenecks, turned up at Miguel's invitation, along with a passel of Catalans and other assorted friends. I understood, in the rush of introductions, that the two wild men were Germans, and decided to stay well away from them—after Gisela I was down on the whole country. Nevertheless, we all set off for the Albacín to have tapas and drinks before the Christ of the Gypsies began to get rolling later in the evening. One of the Germans, Karl, grew very animated after a few drinks; on hearing recorded flamenco in the bar, he beat his palm on the wooden bar, stamped his foot, and clapped. The other German, whose name I heard as Thomas, ordered mineral water and took a raw carrot—yes, a carrot—from his pack and chewed on it. He had a mop of brown gold hair and deep-set blue eyes; he was good-looking, in his mid-twenties, but his expression was stern, almost dour, a modern-day Martin Luther, and I had the uncomfortable feeling that he was judging and condemning all the festivity around him. *Did Christ our Lord suffer and die on the cross so that a rowdy bunch of fun-loving Spanish Catholics could prance around shouting "¡olé!"?*

I continued dancing the *sevillana* and eating olives and fried *calamares* (my usual dinner) and ignored both the Germans most of the evening. At ten or so we left the bar and made our way higher up the hillside. We found seats on a wall facing the caves, the red walls of the Alhambra at our backs. The hills were spangled with reckless bonfires, and the Gypsies sent up green and red flares that lit up the night. The *paso* carrying the painted Christ figure jerked slowly along the road below us surrounded by masses of people all surging along at the same pace. Instead of the mournful *saeta* the Gypsies played rumbas and clapped wildly, singing *"Son son sona, sera sera sera."* Two outnumbered members of the Guardia Civil on horses attempted to keep the crowd in line and one horse almost bit a dog. Everyone screamed: "We're being crushed!" The acolytes in front of Jesus smoked cigarettes and waved their pitch torches carelessly. A Gypsy woman held a burning branch above the crowd and sparks flew.

Faintly in the background, the Darro River rushed below in the ravine, and above us the moon was full. The night smelled of incense and cypress and that cold hint of snow that often seemed to whistle through the city at night. We all jumped down from the wall and followed the procession as it wound up the hills, and to get a better view we climbed along paths rather than streets, ancient paths I didn't even know existed. For a long while Miguel and I kept a tight grip on each other, but eventually we were swirled apart in another crowd. I only found the Germans because of their height.

Thomas fell into step with me. "I've heard you're American," he said after a while.

"Yes." Then, grudgingly, "Your English is very good."

He was silent.

"Where are you from?" I asked.

"I grew up in Mill Valley. Now I live on a collective farm in Marin County. But I've been in Spain for five months."

"California? You're from California?" I repeated stupidly, wondering how I'd missed the clues: everything about him shouted back-to-the-land hippie, from the worn Levi's and leather sandals to the backpack full of carrots.

"You probably thought I was German because of Karl? He's a guitar buddy of mine. Doesn't play worth shit, though, do you, Karl?"

"It is true," said Karl, coming up beside us. "I am very bad guitar player. Also bad at dancing. And terrible singer also. What can I do? I am a lawyer! I need to live in Munich and make a living. But if I could, I would be around flamenco day and night. I am now in Andalusia again one month on holiday. All day and night, music!"

Spare me, I thought. I didn't care for Germans, born-again flamenco aficionados, or, I was convinced, other Americans. Even Patsy got on my nerves sometimes, now that we were sharing a room. It wasn't her so much as that she reminded me occasionally of all I didn't want to be and was far too conscious, in spite of my months abroad, that I still was: a bit wide-eyed and effusive, too shallow, too optimistic, too *American*. I looked at Patsy in her long T-shirt in the morning and saw myself. Yet, clearly, I was homesick too. Which is probably why Tom seemed reassuring. By the time the three of us had walked all the way back down the hill and across the city to the apartment, Miguel and the Catalans and many more people were there. But somehow Tom and I had come to an understanding on that cold walk at three AM, and without discussion we went into my bedroom and closed the door.

Tom was a classical guitarist who lived about a half hour away in a small village up in the foothills of the Sierra Nevada. Canales was a stop on an old electric tram line, though you could also get there by car. The villagers were few; they raised goats and tended olive trees; there was only one shop and a single bar, and the women all gathered around a pump and stone washing troughs in the center of the village. The air smelled of pine and oak, and early wildflowers bloomed on the mountainsides. A whole system of granite channels brought water down from the Sierras to the city below, and stone cisterns and reservoirs held more.

Although he hardly spoke any Spanish, Tom had been living here contentedly over the winter. He baked his own bread in a clay oven he'd made himself from a design in the Whole Earth catalog. He washed his own clothes at the communal pump, and the women of the village told me he was quite a catch. When I began spending nights with him, they called me his *novia,* and it only would have shocked them to tell them I had no intention of being anyone's *novia,* now or in the future. But quickly he and I fell into a relationship, and from the night we met we were rarely apart for the next six weeks.

Tom was quite unlike Peter or, in fact, any of my other friends in Granada. He seemed, quietly and without much fanfare, to have a strong sense of who he was; he practiced his guitar for many hours every day and lived simply. He never ate in restaurants or drank too much, and in some ways, I suppose, my inner puritan was looking for a respite from my own months of relative excess. I'd stayed up too many nights listening to music and roaming the streets of the city with my friends from bar to bar. My health had suffered from secondhand smoke and drinking and poor nutrition (olives are not vegetables, and chorizo sandwiches and *chocolate con churros* do not a balanced meal make); ever since I'd arrived in Granada I'd had colds and coughs that lasted weeks, which I self-dosed with bottles of cough syrup. Tom gave me vitamin C pills and fed me potato-garlic soup and whole grain bread and played Bach to me on his guitar in the evenings. We ate a lot of carrots and almost never drank wine.

He'd come to Spain to order a guitar from a very famous guitar-maker in Madrid, who'd promised it would be finished by June. Until then Tom was playing on an inexpensive instrument that accompanied him everywhere. He taught me a Bach gavotte, which, with the enthusiasm of the novice, I played whenever he wasn't practicing. After Patsy, Tony, and Julian returned from Seville, I found that I used the apartment mainly for mail and a shower. The rest of the time I was up in Canales with Tom. We took long walks in the Sierras and started talking about traveling together. His parents were coming over in early June; they planned to rent a car and pick up the guitar in Madrid, then head over to France for several weeks. His parents had never been to Europe before and he worried how it would go. "They're used to the best," he said glumly. "My father has done very well for himself. It's going to be all four- and five-star hotels. Shit. But I promised my mother."

Before his parents appeared, he wanted to see more of Spain and even get over to Portugal. He and Karl had plans to go to the April *feria* in Seville and use that as an opportunity to visit some of the small villages of Andalusia and hear the "salt of the earth" singers of *cante jondo,* not just the better-known performers. Karl wanted to tape some spontaneous flamenco sessions and to interview a few *cantorares,* or singers, and guitarists, but his Spanish was poor. Tom suggested to Karl that they take me along; I could ask the questions and do the translating. By this time, classes were nearly at an end, and my attendance, like that of so many of the other students, was spotty at best. I, too, was planning to leave Granada in early June—to return to Norway to work for the summer and then decide what to do next. My longing for the north had abated over the last months, but I believed I might end up living there for some time. I still had some money from my grandmother, but not much. Soon I'd have to be working for a living again, and I was determined to enjoy myself for as long as I could. I was captured by the notion of traveling around Andalusia for flamenco's sake. The three of us, with sleeping bags and a tent and Tom's cooking gear and plenty of raw peanuts, set off for two weeks in Karl's old Mercedes.

The Seville I recalled from two years before was transformed by the fair. During the day men in short jackets and black, flat-brimmed hats paraded around on horses; women in red and white polka-dotted dresses, with their long, many-flounced skirts, perched behind their men, the flounces cascading over the horses' flanks. At night the fairgrounds, strung with lanterns, were transformed into small blocks of *casetas*, large booths with cordoned-off platforms for dancing and socializing, each constructed for the benefit of one family or another. Some were large and had real musicians performing, and others merely played tapes of *sevillanas*. Some had small bars with waiters pouring drinks and serving food, and in others there were simply some bottles of wine and homemade tapas. Almost all were closed to tourists; in spite of the fact that they rarely had walls, there was a clear demarcation: You couldn't simply walk into someone's *caseta* without an invitation.

Tom got bored after a few hours of this and went back to the tent we'd set up on the other side of the river, but Karl and I ran into Miguel and Julian and stayed up an entire night, wandering around the *casetas* and listening to the sprightly and infectious melody of the *sevillana,* the folk dance that had its home here in Seville. In the early hours things grew more lax and we made some friends, not only other shut-out tourists but some openhearted locals who'd imbibed a great deal.

After a couple of days of this the three of us drove to Jerez and Cádiz and then back toward Granada. We stopped in Alcalá and Utrera and Morón de la Frontera. We walked through the streets just listening. If we heard singing coming from a bar, we would go inside. There we'd quietly order ourselves a drink (*finos* for Karl and me, mineral water for Tom), eat a few olives, and pay attention. It was important to Karl that the locals not think of us as uninformed tourists, though I'm not sure how he thought that the three of us fair-skinned *payos,* as non-Gypsies are called, two of us over six feet tall, could be invisible. But Karl's enthusiasm was contagious, and after a while, he usually had permission to tape them on his recorder. Sometimes we were invited to someone's house, and he taped a grandmother or grandfather who was rumored to sing pure flamenco in the old way but who didn't get out much anymore. I did the negotiating for this, and my ear, though I was hardly a musician, became more and more attuned not only to the music but to the *jaleo,* the active listening and participation of the listener to the dramatic songs with their improvised ornamentation and abrupt stops and starts. The *jaleo* was the tapping of the foot, or the rhythmic clapping of one hand against the flat palm of the other, our response to the songs of death and lost love.

For *cante jondo* didn't come from the same place in the heart as rumbas, *alegrías, fandangos,* and *malagueñas. Cante jondo's* two main forms were *siguiriyas* and *soleares,* both of which placed the emphasis on the exposure of self, the catharsis of personal and universal pain. They weren't entertainment even though they bore a resemblance to highly stylized performance.

In Utrera we went to the home of one of the well-known singers of *cante jondo,* Bernarda de Utrera, a heavy-set woman in her late forties or early fifties who invited us in for a *copa,* or a drink, and allowed us to tape her singing for ten or fifteen minutes as she explained where she tried to go in order to pull up some of those sounds from her chest. She was the daughter of a man who sang flamenco, the granddaughter and great-granddaughter of singers, and it went back further than that, her connection with a past where music was the expression and the solace of having little and feeling much. She wore an ordinary housedress and apron, her face was brown-skinned and very lined, with black hair that was now graying a little and drawn back tightly. With the tape recorder on the table, Karl leaned forward as intently as if he wanted to disappear down her throat and live in her body. His attitude of focused listening reminded me of how Manny used to listen to Mahler, as if, by his attention, he kept the notes pouring through the instruments. Her voice filled the room with a robust woman's sadness, but she was singing only snatches for the tape recorder, examples of different styles and techniques. Why should she show her soul to us three travelers? To hear the true spirit of *cante jondo* you needed *ambiente,* and ambience wasn't just something you could call up by snapping your fingers. *Duende* didn't come on tap.

We stayed a day or two in Morón, a village even less prepossessing than Utrera but with a small colony of foreigners in residence. A thin American woman with hacked-off ashy hair leaned out of a window in a *pensión,* where we were looking for a German friend of Karl's, and invited us up. She was doing a PhD in musicology and had notebooks filled with descriptions of flamenco styles. I recall how intense, almost hysterical she seemed, and how she and Karl argued over the origins of flamenco. It was easy to see Karl as a prosecuting lawyer then, bludgeoning the defense with facts. He was certain that flamenco was pure Gypsy music, while she kept repeating that no, flamenco may have been brought to Spain by the Gypsies, but it had been strongly influenced by the Sephardic Jews. I remember Karl shouting, "The Jews contributed nothing to this music. The Moors, yes. The Jews, nothing!" and how I felt angry to hear him say that but didn't know enough or was too intimidated to argue back.

In that village we also met a young American man who took us up to his small flat and played flamenco in the rough Morón style he'd learned from his teacher Diego del Gastor. He revered his teacher and told us stories of his integrity and poverty. Diego del Gastor was for many years too poor to buy a really fine guitar; eventually a group of his friends collected enough to purchase one for him, a Santos. During the party that followed to celebrate the acquisition, Diego was unlucky enough to sit on it. Another time he set his guitar on a windowsill and it fell into the street. Diego might have *mala suerte,* bad luck, but he had *duende* in spades. "That's what we try to learn from him," said the American ruefully, "and that's the one thing he can't teach."

It was in Morón, for the first and only time, I felt that frisson of skin and soul that's the closest I ever got to *duende.* Tom and Karl and I were about to head back to Granada, when Karl said he heard music from somewhere near. We left off packing up the car and walked down a block to a dark, unprepossessing bar, which had no door, only a beaded curtain in the opening, and went in. It was after the siesta and a few men had gathered in the dim light. They were smoking and having a drink or two and playing around with guitars, ordinary men, Gypsies, with frayed shirt cuffs and cigarettes at the corners of their mouths. Then one of them began, seemingly out of nowhere, with a gravelly, broken-record guttural chant of *Ay yay yi* that stayed at the same tone for some bars, with the guitar following. The first *coplas,* or lines of the song I couldn't really catch, but when they continued again at a higher register, I heard isolated words . . . *"porque mi amor se fue"*. . . , "because my love is gone," pronounced with a terrible raw dignity by someone who has lost everything. Now the guitar began again, faster, ornamented. Tom leaned forward to admire the fingering, and Karl murmured a few words of encouragement along with the other men. Then at still a higher register came the man's voice again, like that of a torture victim. My hands clenched, as if I were trying to hold on to something. I flushed with sweat, and unbidden tears started down my cheeks. Perhaps if I could have put it into words, I would have said, "I can never see my mother again," or "I'm going to die, too." But all I felt was as if my pain was shouted out by someone else in a language I could understand.

I must have had a look of shock on my tear-stained face, as if something that protected me was suddenly ripped away, for one of the men looked right at me and nodded, more like a fellow mourner than a man who saw me as a woman.

I'd thought that I enjoyed flamenco. But this was more like being lowered into a grave, naked, with nowhere else to go. "The final blood-filled room of the soul," Lorca called *duende,* and after that I understood what people were looking for when they hunted those elusive chords and notes: that intimation of death while living that we call mortality.

After returning to Granada and Canales Tom and I spent a few days getting organized for the several weeks of travel in Spain and Portugal that would eventually bring us back to Málaga to meet his parents, at which time I'd decide whether I was going to travel with them all for another month or go back to Norway for the summer. We headed off to Madrid with Karl, who was leaving us there as he drove on to Munich. He had to stop at pay phones along the way and talk about his upcoming court case, which was scheduled to begin the day he arrived in Munich.

What a different Madrid this time than the city I'd been in with Laura two years before. It was warmer, far more summery in May. All the trees were filled out, and the Retiro was lusciously green and shady. We stayed in a *pensión* and I went to the Prado every day and sketched, something I hadn't done for months. In the evenings Tom and I ate vegetarian food in our room, with water. While he played the guitar, I read a novel by the Spanish Dickens, Benito Pérez Galdós, which conjured up nineteenth-century Madrid in all its squalor and glory. We visited the famous guitar maker, who showed us Tom's beautiful guitar under construction. Only three weeks and it would be finished. In the afternoons, during siesta time, we made love with the window of our room open, the blinds stirring in the breeze.

Tom was a lover like none I'd had before, patient and tender, and it made me angry sometimes to think of all I'd put up with before, especially from Rob. Tom was handsomer and taller than Rob, with his well-defined muscles and strong chin; he was a good catch, as the ladies in Canales had always reminded me. We got along so well too; we didn't irritate each other. He believed in taking his space and giving me mine. He believed in privacy, but he was also capable of closeness. He was interested in talking, before sex, after sex, any time I felt like it. I could feel myself falling in love, not hopelessly with a woman, not masochistically with an actor, but in love with an equal who was easy to be around. Because of his guitar, Tom always had a way of occupying himself no matter how constricted our space, and the soft classical music brought a harmonious *ambiente* to daily life, even on the road. No tenseness marred our decision-making, as it had when I'd been with Laura. He was never sullen as Laura had been, never was puzzlingly beset by unexpressed anger and hurt feelings. He was a man and I was a woman; the boundaries were absolutely clear. The edges were safe.

All the same, sometimes out of nowhere, especially whenever I was on my own in Madrid, I found myself thinking about Laura. I missed her laughter and the way we'd always egged each other on, the way she'd told me, "Oh, stop!" when I was making her laugh too hard. I missed the evenings we'd spent in the Santa Ana district, drinking our way from *taverna* to *tasca,* arms around each other walking home. Laura was only a little taller than me; she understood often what I was thinking before I expressed it. It had had never been easy to keep my inner life from Laura; it was all too easy with Tom.

I missed the Plaza Mayor so much that the one time Tom and I went there, I hurried him across its vast square without looking up once at the room with the grilled window and balcony where I'd sat in my red shawl writing, where Laura and I had made our pact not to get married to Rob, where we had whiled away an entire afternoon drinking and deciding to go on to Italy together. It was foolish to remember Laura. I knew that.

Tom and I tried to hitchhike out of Madrid, but no one picked us up, so we took the bus to Badajoz on the border and then another bus into Portugal to Setúbal and yet another to a fishing village. We lived on the beach for several nights, and every day Tom played his guitar and I read a Penguin copy of *Don Quixote* that I'd found in a flea market, even though it made me think of Laura, as did sleeping outdoors. I reminded myself that if I'd been traveling with Laura she would have made life miserable with her penny-pinching. Tom and I were thrifty, but it didn't feel like a crisis every time we stood outside a restaurant looking at the menu. He was so easygoing that nothing felt hard. We stayed in Lisbon another few nights, astonished by the warmth and color of Portugal compared to Spain. The language was softer, and the city more beautiful than anything we'd imagined. We listened to *fado* music, that infinitely sad music of Portugal, so different from the rough groans and high shrieks of flamenco, and Tom unbent and drank moderately and looked happier every day.

More and more often he spoke of the future and urged me to join him in Marin, on the communal farm. He would build a yurt; we would have chickens for eggs and a goat for milk. I would like the others who lived on the farm, all of whom were musicians. Having lived in Monterey three years before, I knew a variety of people who'd gone back to the land, mostly in the Carmel Valley. I was pretty sure that the rural life was not for me. But lying in bed on a hot afternoon during the siesta in a *pensión* in Lisbon, with the salt breeze of the Atlantic wafting through the half-open shutters, replete from lovemaking, with the sounds of Tom's soft guitar filling the dim room, it was easy to think that perhaps it didn't matter where I lived, as long as I was with this man, this man who seemed to think I was perfect for him.

Perfect—except he didn't really know me, didn't know what I was really like. I presented myself as brave, free-spirited, able to take care of myself, all things he admired. He didn't know much about my childhood or my adolescence, the insecurity that came from lack of family and lack of home. He knew nothing about Christian Science or what had driven my mother to try suicide. He knew about Rob, but nothing about Laura except that we'd traveled in Spain together. None of this was his fault; I'd long been accustomed to burying my past in anecdotes that seemed more palatable. When I told Tom I wasn't sure that I was quite ready to go back to America yet, I framed it in terms of not being ready to give up my adventurous life. I didn't say I was fearful that if he got to know me, he'd find out all the ways I'd hid myself, and that he wouldn't love me; he'd be repelled.

The problem of not really being a vegetarian paled beside the fact that, although music stirred me, I really didn't have much of an ear for it. I rarely knew whether Tom was playing a Bach or Handel arrangement, or whether it was a gavotte or a cantata. I'd learned my little Bach song but seemed not to get much further. Sooner or later he was going to notice I was practically tone-deaf and all thumbs when it came to playing the guitar. An even more complicated issue, not much discussed between us because it was embarrassing, was my writing.

I'd told him soon after we first met, after he'd asked me why I was in Granada and what I planned to do with my life, about my writing. Tom had nodded and asked me what I'd written, and if he could read it. "It's sort of in pieces," I said, thinking of the many beginnings to "The Travelogue" and wondering where the incriminating page was where I described Alex as bisexual. What would he make of Alex's going on and on about Ruby?

Instead I told him that I'd started a novel when I first came to Granada and then, after meeting Miguel and the British, had decided that it was more important to *live* than to *write*. "First I need to have the experiences; then I'll write about them," I said, but even to me that now seemed a tired explanation, one I'd perhaps offered too frequently.

It didn't convince Tom at any rate. "To be a writer you have to practice," he said. "Just like I practice my guitar." Even on the road, he played at minimum three hours a day. He certainly had noticed that, aside from writing a few times a week in my journal, I never picked up a pen. Although Tom was gentle, not contemptuous, as Rob had been, I felt the sting. I wanted to say, "Yes, if it was a matter of just moving the pen across the page in an artful fashion, like plucking guitar strings, then no big deal. But the hand is only the instrument of the imagination, and the imagination is a mysterious thing."

I didn't tell him that because I didn't have enough confidence in myself as a writer; I knew Tom was half right. A writer had to practice, just as a musician did. But for me, subject—that is, what the imagination dragged out in the open, what the imagination wanted to write about—was as much of a problem as ever. I knew if Tom read that Alex was bisexual, he would be curious about me. There wasn't much to confess on the sexual level; the problem was emotional. I didn't want to say I'd been in love with Laura. I didn't want to lie to Tom either. It was easier to pretend "The Travelogue" wasn't readable.

Back in Hamar last year I'd thought I'd conquered the art of writing at last. I had kept to a schedule for two months, I had made up a tale, and at the end of that time I had had a novella with a beginning, middle, and end. The subject was mythic, not realistic, so I didn't have to identify myself with it. But I hadn't found myself in such perfect circumstances again. Perhaps, perhaps, I could write on Tom's farm, but it was hard to envision. Instead, I saw myself having to feed chickens and harvest tomatoes and bake bread, surrounded by musicians and their "ladies," as Tom often called women friends. Secretly, my soul curled up at the thought. I'd once lived with an actor and his circle of friends in California. Was that how I wanted my grand tour to Europe to end, back in California with a guitar player, a man who wondered why I didn't finish my novel? A man from whom, if I were to write truthfully, I might have to hide what I wrote?

We traveled onward, to the ancient town of Ronda, perched precariously on a cliff, and then to Málaga, where we were to meet his parents at the airport. We found them what we thought was a nice hotel and made a reservation; then we checked into a cheap *pensión* for a last few days of sex and swimming. Tom went to a barber for a haircut and close shave. "I hope you've decided that you can join us on the trip—even just part of it. We can drop you off in Paris and you can go on from there. Please! I'm getting nervous at the thought of being around them on my own. And besides, I'll miss you."

I knew I would miss him, too. After six weeks constantly in his company, it would be a shock to be on my own again. And I questioned once again why I was so determined to head back to Norway when I could have a perfectly nice time with Tom and his parents in Spain and France.

"Málaga is too big," said Tom's father, when they arrived. "Our travel agent suggests Marbella instead," and suddenly Tom and I found ourselves in mid-size rental car, Tom in the front seat with his big, burly lawyer father, in a Lacoste shirt and shorts, and me in the back seat with his housewife mother, tan and dazed in white skirt and scoop-necked blouse, with gold jewelry. Tom had clearly told them—I'd heard him on the phone in Ronda—that I'd be with him, but they still seemed surprised to see me.

His mother asked no questions but sighed and smiled weakly whenever she looked at me. His father asked me what my father did. We arrived in Marbella and checked into the best hotel there, then sat on the terrace having a drink. Tom's father had a Scotch and then another and his mother a gin and tonic; Tom went for mineral water and I joined him. I began to understand why he wasn't much of a drinker. His mother asked what that man out in the bay was doing in a rowboat.

"He's rowing, Mom," said Tom. "He's probably fishing."

"Why doesn't he use a powerboat?"

"Because this is a poor country!"

"Well, I don't think a powerboat costs that much."

At dinner I translated the menu for them.

"Goat!" said his mother. "What kind of thing is that, to eat a goat?"

His father had a steak but was shocked at how thin it was. "This isn't a steak—this is like . . . I don't know what, with all the olive oil. Ask them to bring me another Scotch, by the way."

His mother decided just to have salad and soup. When the soup came, in a large wide bowl, she decided Tom had to try some.

"No, Mom, I'm fine."

"No, no, you've got to try it. It has the most *unusual* taste." She lifted up the bowl and tried to pass it over the table, managing to spill the whole thing on the tablecloth. The extremely reserved maître d' came over and supervised the cleanup. In Spanish I told him that the lady had wanted her son to taste the soup.

"But we could have brought him a small cup."

"I know . . . it's just . . . they're Americans."

He bowed his head in respectful disgust.

The excruciating days dragged on. I was taken aback that Tom couldn't seem to help turning into a gawky boy around them. I thought of him as a man, tall and rugged, quiet and able to handle any situation. But his mother called him Tommy and his father disregarded his opinions. "I don't think much of this Costa del Sol business," he announced. "I'm looking forward to Madrid and the Ritz." We ate in expensive restaurants where Tom's father was invariably disappointed in the thin steaks and where his mother asked the waiter, in English, "Has this lettuce been washed very carefully?" We went to an exhibition of flamenco dancing, which was everything Tom and I despised about the Costa del Sol and flashy tourist Spain and which wasn't satisfying to his parents, either. "I thought it would be more like ballet," said his mother. "They look so grim! And when they start singing—what is that? It's screaming, as far as I'm concerned."

Somehow the subject of whether I'd be traveling with them further to France never seemed to come up. Tom and I shared a room next to theirs, but I felt there on sufferance. At night, after quietly making love, Tom and I would whisper about the future, which seemed vaguer every day. All we could really decide on was that I'd write him from Norway and that at the end of the summer I'd make a decision about returning to California. I had to go to Norway and see my friends and work to make some money, I explained. And he apologized for his parents. "I knew it would be like this, but at the same time, I didn't think they'd be this bad. But I promised my mom I'd travel with them and I have to. They're my *parents"* he said sorrowfully.

On the way back to Granada from the coast, we stopped for a picnic in a grove of olive trees, with red poppies growing through the grass. We ate bread—good Spanish bread, not Tom's whole grain— and three cheeses, and *jamón serrano,* and drank a bottle of wine. His mother relaxed, and I could tell his father was warming to me as I told them about my year in Spain, editing out the unwholesome bits. I taught them to say *"Que te aproveche"* and *"Salud"* as we held up our glasses.

We spent a day in Granada sightseeing and then they dropped me off me at the door to the apartment building. I knew that when I went upstairs only Miguel would be left of our group and that he'd be gone soon, too. Tony and Julian would have returned home by now, and Patsy had flown back to Los Angeles early, for her mother was ill with cancer. Because of Tom I'd hardly seen my friends the last six weeks, and now I was achingly sorry. The whole year in Granada seemed to have speeded up after a slow beginning, and it was hard to imagine that I was really leaving Spain in two days. With Miguel beside me I'd go back to the Campo del Príncipe that night and have a few *copas* and eat all the unhealthy and delicious things I'd come to love. He and I would compare notes of the last month and marvel at the tourists pouring into the city now, and the growing heat in what had been such a very frosty town. Miguel I'd see again, the following summer, in Pasadena, where he had easily adapted to a new life as a Spanish teacher in a high school. He put on some flamenco records and we did a couple of *sevillanas* for old times' sake, but in a living room in Pasadena, with his girlfriend looking on, it was not the same. No food, no drink, no music consumed outside Spain ever tastes or sounds quite the same.

Tom and I were given a few minutes by his parents to say goodbye. We kissed passionately in spite of their eyes on us and promised that we'd write and that we'd meet again. At the last moment he asked his parents to open the trunk of the car and he pulled out his guitar and gave it to me. In another day or two he'd have the new classical guitar he'd waited eight months for. Tom had always told me that he had improved the sound of the cheap guitar by playing it well, that the notes hit the wood in the right way and helped create its sound.

It's a guitar I still have, and it still sounds warm and tender, even though I gave up playing it long ago.

❦ SIXTEEN ❦

Ripples from the Storm

The ad jumped out at me from the Trondheim classifieds:

SKIPSPIKE NEEDED IMMEDIATELY
ON THE COASTAL STEAMER

It was early July, and I'd been back in Norway about a month. After a happy reunion with Elisabeth and the rest of the family in Hamar, I'd hitchhiked up to Trondheim to see my former lover Leidulf, who told me he'd help me find a job. As it turned out, he was off backpacking in the mountains when I arrived, so I had to find one myself. I became a stock clerk at Domus, a big discount department store. All day I folded men's underwear and embarrassed the shy Norwegians who sidled up to ask me questions about briefs and T-shirts. My Norwegian was clumsy after ten months away; besides, these men spoke the Trondelag dialect, almost impossible to understand. "What size?" I kept demanding. "How big?"

A *skipspike* was a "ship girl," and that immediately recalled the seafaring stories I'd loved as a child, as well as my own unfinished novel about Alex, with her limp and longing to sail around the world. As for the coastal steamer, the *Hutigrute,* or "fast route," was legendary in Norway. Since the late 1800s the line had united a country with a coastline hundreds of miles long; the ships supplied the entire north, all the way from Bergen to Kirkenes, on what was then the border of the Soviet Union. I'd seen the ships of the line down at the fish-and-creosote-smelling wharves in Trondheim, where everything from cars to boxes of bananas and bales of magazines was unloaded. Two ships arrived every day, one sailing north, one sailing south.

Home from his backpacking trip, Leidulf was against my shipping out. "I don't understand you," he kept repeating. But then, he'd been hoping ever since I arrived that we could resume our affair from last summer. I was completely uninterested. Tom and I were writing, and I still thought there was a chance I might fly to San Francisco in September and join him on the farm. Or at least that's what I told Leidulf as a way of fending him off. In reality I was uncertain of my next step and sometimes wondered if I should go back to Spain, which I now missed inordinately. After longing to be back in Norway for much of the past year, I now found it disconcertingly silent, gray, and cold. Where were the lively bars, the brilliant costumes and decorations of the fiestas, the give-and-take with shopkeepers, and, especially, the heat and sun?

The rain poured down in Trondheim all that June as I sat in my small rented room in the flat of a divorced man and his teenage daughter near the Domus store; I practiced the guitar and reread *The Golden Notebook,* which I found just as disturbing and compelling as the first time. Why was everyone so terribly unhappy in this novel? Why did the men treat the women so badly? Why were the characters always joining and leaving the Party? Why wasn't Anna Wulf pleased that she could just live on the royalties from one book? Why did she seem to despise her own writing and think everything she wrote was false? How did all that square with the fact that Doris Lessing was a writer, and a famous one, who had written many, many books and lived from their sales?

I bought a new notebook, a red one, and tried to work on some stories set in Spain. I wrote sketches about Miguel and my British friends, and about the fiestas, the music, and the Gypsies, and about going out to the countryside to Maria's. I called the character who was myself Stephanie or Melissa. I stumbled, as I often did, with the plot. My stories began with either a departure or an arrival: "A few tears of farewell were still damp on Stephanie's face as she settled into her window seat on the charter flight from Los Angeles to London one morning in December." These comings and goings were the action of the story. Stephanie departed, she arrived, she departed again. And again. But, of course, a story should deliver a greater meaning. *Why* had Stephanie left home, for instance? To find herself, of course. "Stephanie had left home to discover who she really was." But once having written that, I was secretly mystified. How did you show a character discovering herself, and how could that manifest itself in a plot?

Stephanie came to Granada, she was looking for love, she met Miguel, and then she met Peter, and then she met Tom. I described Granada, I described the various men, I scrabbled for climatic moments, often involving a knife, a Gypsy, and a religious procession, then decided these were probably clichéd. In fact, everything I wrote about Granada had the faint tang of a lie, precisely because I'd tried to dramatize what were really very conventional interactions and puff them up with blood and poetry. Still here and there, as I look back, there's something interesting: a description of my street Cristo

de la Yedra and how the bread smelled in the evening at the bakery
when I came home from classes; a note about Tony drawing us maps;
another about Miguel telling me why he ate so many tomatoes; a
sudden warmth when I tell how my young friend Antonita, the Gypsy
girl, would kiss me on the cheeks and wrap her arms around me as
we walked in the golden tobacco fields. Details I put down quickly
and carelessly served me many years later to remember what that
forgotten place and time smelled and tasted like. The actual stories,
for all their arrivals and departures, went nowhere.

The city of Trondheim possessed a medieval history, a famous
cathedral, and some charming streets of red and yellow painted
wooden houses, but I had little money and only Leidulf for a friend.
I went to a few gatherings at his apartment on the campus of the
university. His three roommates, all shipbuilding engineers like
Leidulf, distilled their own alcohol from a homemade contraption in
the kitchen. They produced "flavorings" bought at the grocery store:
vodka, rum, and scotch. They added these to large glasses of colorless
grain alcohol and poured in tonic, Coke, or Fanta Lemon. After one
or two glasses, the young men, who'd been painfully wordless to begin
with, suddenly turned vociferous. They shouted, laughed, cranked up
the rock music, carried each other around on their shoulders, and on
one occasion heaved the sofa out the second-story window. Nothing
could have been more different from the conviviality of Granada,
with its streets of small bars, their counters spread with plates of
tapas, flamenco music in the background. The volume was loud in
Spain, but it was consistent. Spaniards didn't go from zero to ten
after a drink; they were always on high. That was their character.
These young Norwegians seemed to have split personalities, one
activated by drink. Leidulf was comparatively sober, and I felt too

repulsed by the scene to join in, but it was no fun *not* to drink at these parties. I usually left early and went back to my room on the other side of town. I felt, as I'd felt in Granada when I first arrived, that I'd made absolutely the wrong choice to leave one place for another. Moreover, I was stunned that Norway, a country that had seemed so open to me last year, so often sunny and invigorating, now turned a wet, dark back on me.

Leidulf and I had several hard discussions, though to a large extent they consisted of him staring silently at the floor or saying, "I don't understand you." I'd thought him good-looking last year with his fresh red lips and thick bronzy hair. He was very decent and cared for me and was honestly confused by my behavior; all that began to irritate me. It's no wonder that when I saw the ad for the ship girl, I immediately applied. I had a chest X-ray for TB and was given Norwegian seaman's papers on the same day. They needed someone right away, and even when I found out that the job was as a dishwasher, I was still eager to embark. The *Kong Olav* made port in Trondheim a few days after the ad appeared. I took my Hermes typewriter, my guitar, a stack of Doris Lessing novels from the library, a new blue notebook, and went aboard, bound for the Far North.

The *Kong Olav* was named after Norway's then king and had been built in 1964. The ship (it seems strange to call a king *she*) carried both cargo and passengers. Four cars could fit in the hold; they were lifted off and on by a crane secured onto the deck of the bow. This same crane offloaded food, dry goods, newspapers, and other necessities for the coastal towns and took on mail and boxes of frozen fish. The coastal steamer was, in those days, still a lifeline above the Arctic Circle, where no trains ran above Narvik and relatively few commercial planes flew in. Norway wasn't yet rich from the North Sea oil fields, and there weren't many cars or roads or bridges. Locals took the *Hutigrute* for short distances, along with ferries and motorboats. The coastal steamer, sometimes delayed an hour or three by rough weather, was nevertheless a reliable way to travel. Most days you could set your watch to its incoming and outgoing horn blast. Its arrival and departure gave a structure to small coastal towns all year round, and in the summer months brought tourists to places that ordinarily they would never venture. These small towns had long histories, some of them, of captains who fished the winter seas for cod, of merchants who traded with Russia, of dreamers like Fridolf Nansen, who set off for the Arctic in his ship *Fram*. The towns had not yet become quaint. They were working ports, rough, cold, bare places backed up by spectacular snow-tipped craggy mountains.

In my day, the *Kong Olav* carried three classes of passengers. I knew them mainly by where they berthed and by what they ate. The first class guests had staterooms on the upper decks, with portholes, and their own dining room; they breakfasted and lunched off lavish cold and hot buffets, and dinner was several courses, with cocktails and wine. They were mainly Americans, Germans, and Italians. The second class passengers slept in interior rooms without portholes. Frequently Norwegians, they were served a menu of cod and potatoes drowning in white sauce or pork and gravy, with boiled carrots, not salads, for vegetables. They drank beer, not wine. The deck passengers brought sleeping bags and slept on the floor of the lounge or outside on deck chairs; they ate open-faced sandwiches of brown goat cheese or salami that they'd made themselves. Sometimes they got drunk and curled up in boozy corners surrounded by ashtrays and empty bottles.

Like most of the other crew, I shared a cabin deep in the bowels of the ship, near the engine. My roommate, Kari, was an eighteen-year-old who spoke the Trondheim dialect. Her job was to vacuum the dining rooms and lounges, the stairs and public places, to clean the bathrooms at night after everyone had retired. She slept till early afternoon, then spent hours polishing her nails, perfecting her makeup, and eating chocolate, smoking, and drinking beer. Our cabin stank of cigarettes and beer and sometimes sex, for various deckhands knew where to find her.

I worked eight or nine hours every day, seven days a week, scraping, rinsing, and putting into the dishwasher all the dishes of hundreds of people. The odor of fish and detergent seemed to settle into my hair and skin, along with the hot reek of greasy dishwater and the boiling-clean ceramic-and-glass scent of plates and glasses lifted rack by rack from the massive dishwashing machine. Most of the time I had two helpers, loutish boys of sixteen or seventeen, who spent a lot of their time rolling tobacco and smoking just outside the kitchen. One of my shifts began at six in the morning and went till three; the alternate schedule began at three and lasted until eleven. Thus there were twenty-four-hour periods of no work, as well as many short nights when I got to bed at midnight only to have to wake at five-thirty. It was a far cry from my easygoing days in Granada, when I passed my days reading, visiting friends, studying, and staying out half the night in bars.

At night when Kari was gone, I'd lie in my upper bunk reading Doris Lessing's Martha Quest novels, but during the day I often kept away. I'd go up on deck, to a wind-protected spot behind the smokestack, just so I could be alone. Occasionally, when my shift was over in the afternoon, I took a shower to get the grease and suds off and went up to the first class lounge for an hour or two to see if I could find British newspapers or American magazines. This was strictly prohibited, for crew to mingle with the guests, but I ignored that, and perhaps my boss realized that I had a terrible hunger to speak English and be with "my" people, for he never said anything about it, though the social director, Kirsten, glared at me whenever she found me outside the kitchen. The most powerful woman onboard, Kirsten wore a blue suit with a navel cut and had bleached blond hair and heavy makeup.

"We haven't seen you before," middle-aged men would say, buying me a drink.

"Oh, I got on at Bodø," I'd reply. Or, "It's taken me a day to find my sea legs."

To parental couples I'd sometimes confess the truth, that I washed their dishes, but I'd make it sound like a lark instead of the grindingly hard work it really was. I was a traveler, I'd tell them, and shipping out on the *Kong Olav* was just another in a series of big adventures.

"Well, aren't you the spunky one!" they'd say. "Where else have you been?" And I'd tell them how I'd worked in the Norwegian mountains last summer and then had gone to Granada in Spain to the university. I'd been in Europe for almost three years now, with only one trip home.

"Only twenty-two and you've been out on your own traveling for three years! What does your family think of all this gallivanting about?" an elderly pair from Durban, South Africa, once asked me.

I was breezy. "Oh, they're all for me seeing the world while I'm young." In reality, my father had almost no idea where I was.

"But don't you miss being at home? Where is your home, anyway? Are you going to stay in Europe?"

They were asking too many questions, questions I couldn't answer, questions that plagued me at odd times, when, enveloped in steam, I was scraping fish bones off a plate. What was I doing here? Where was I going? What would become of me?

But to the concerned and fascinated couples I only laughed and shrugged. "The time to see the world is when you're young." I played on my youth to them, and to the middle-aged men as well. Actually, I didn't feel all that young anymore.

The coastline of northern Norway slid by in gray rain and sea fog the first weeks of July. We wended our damp way through the Lofoten Islands and up to Tromsø, further north to Hammerfest and then around the forbidding North Cape to Kirkenes on the border to the Soviet Union. There we turned and retraced our passage back to Bergen. The coastal voyage took five days north and six days south. There were seven ships of the line, one departing Bergen or Kirkenes every day. We occasionally were tied up at the docks at the same time; more often we passed them at sea, and then the waitresses from each ship would grab tablecloths and run out to the deck and wave them at each other. Every third voyage we took an extra few days and headed across the wild Norwegian Sea from Tromsø to the large island of Svalbard or Spitsbergen. It was partly to entertain the tourists but even more to drop off supplies and pick up and deliver scientists to Longyearbyen and Ny Ålesund.

From time to time a strong wind would wrench the clouds away from the coastline and then the landscape of the snow-white mountain peaks and glaciers would become unbearably beautiful. When the sun shone there was no place I'd rather be than the top deck of the *Kong Olav*. I imagined the lines of stories as the fierce sea wind blew my hair streaming behind me: "Stephanie had run away to sea" and "With her Norwegian seaman's papers, Melissa planned after this summer on the coastal steamer to ship out for someplace even further away—Cape Town or Singapore." I also resurrected Alex from the pages of "The Travelogue" (the manuscript, along with a suitcaseful of journals and books, left behind for safekeeping at the Helland-Hansens'). In her youth, perhaps, Alex had worked on the coastal steamer—maybe she'd fallen from a set of outside stairs slippery with salt rain (I was always very careful myself) and had broken her leg. Now, on this voyage, I'd finally learn enough about ships and the sea to make Alex credible.

Whenever I was striding around the windswept decks with my hair in a wild tangle, occupied in imagining stories about my redoubtable heroines and their adventures at sea, I glorified my physical and emotional bravery and transformed my job of dishwashing into the more general term *seafaring*. But finding the time or even a place on the ship to write these stories of women seafarers was almost impossible, and the few times I managed to get my typewriter out, even tapping the keys felt hard. And then I looked at myself differently: a young woman scrunched in a tiny cabin that smelled of vodka and beer on a ship where no one understood her in the middle of nowhere.

If I let myself, I despaired. Most of my friends in the States had graduated from college and were probably well on their way to interesting careers. But I, for all my promises to myself to become a writer in Europe, seemed just as far from my goal as I'd been before I left. Further away, perhaps, in spite of the intermittent spurts of inspiration and even more intermittent stretches of disciplined creation. If I'd really been serious about writing, I brooded, why hadn't I stayed in Trondheim, where I had a place of my own and many free, if lonely, hours to work? Why had I jumped to take this job? What good was it to continue to pile up experiences if I never did anything with them?

Doris Lessing added to my worries. By the time I came to *A Ripple from the Storm,* the third Martha Quest novel, I was alternately frightened and outraged. Where was Martha's ambition? Where was her sense of personal destiny? Caught up in a colonial society she loathed, Martha spent all her time struggling to define herself against it. Very little she did ever seemed to be anything she wanted to do. Her dreams of freedom and independence were repeatedly dashed. She drifted; she sulked; she sat at home or ran about, but always on behalf of other people. After three books, Martha had learned only that she didn't want to be a wife, mother, secretary, or communist. There were dozens of passages in the novels about her lethargy, her inertia, her sense of being "landlocked."

Maybe Doris Lessing had experienced all those things early on, I thought, but at some point she'd made the leap from paralyzed young woman to prolific writer. Why didn't Lessing show Martha overcoming her passivity and becoming a writer? I already knew too much about the invisible paralysis of being a woman, of spending so much energy saying no to social roles that there was no will left with which to say yes. Why didn't Lessing show me, me and every other girl who desperately needed a role model, something of the nerve and spirit that had helped her write these books and get them published? Lessing was lauded for describing the reality of a woman's life. But I didn't want *that* reality. I wanted so much more.

There were many compensations for my kitchen confinement and the backbreaking work, including the *Kong Olav* itself. A sturdy workhorse, painted gleaming white, the ship had lacquered wooden trim around the interior windows and wooden planking in the public spaces. The outdoor decks had been painted a dark green mixed with sand. A polar bear skin hung in the small desk area, and a Norwegian flag flew off the stern. The captain wore dark blue during the day, white at night. Ship life had a Scandinavian simplicity and formality to it, born of the country's long association with the sea. The chain of command was very clear—the captain at the top, workers like me and my roommate, Kari, at the bottom. At the same time, there was that freewheeling spirit of the sea: A lot of drinking went on, a lot of practical jokes and rubbing up against each other in such close quarters. The fat cook provided for us in the mess, and although I was considered a mystery in some ways, I was liked and well taken care of. One seaman taught me oaths in the northern Norwegian dialect; another engineer took the time to give me a few navigation lessons—what shoals and whirlpools to watch out for, what landmarks to notice. The waitresses—temperamental, proud creatures—offered me candy bars and advice about men. Only Kirsten, the social director, actively looked down her nose at me.

The crew had their favorite ports; many times we all stood in a line at the railing to see Bodø come into view, or Tromsø: long stops, where they could make phone calls, buy clothes and necessities—liquor and cigarettes. For me, too, a city was a wonderful excuse to stretch my legs, mail letters and, in Trondheim and Bergen, where I had library cards, stock up on more books. In Bergen too I had friends: The lively Munck family had moved there last year.

The weather improved toward the end of July, and there were many brilliantly sunny days, especially past the North Cape, along Norway's north coast, which was sheltered from the western mists and storms. The latitude was so high, between seventy and seventy-two degrees north, that there were no trees, and the landscape in the sunshine looked bare as Baja, with brown hills and glittering, bright blue inlets with fresh whitecaps washing the flat shoreline. Up here was almost no darkness; the sun simply dipped briefly below the horizon only to reappear again. It could be warm too, when the wind died down; then the passengers, in the stern of the ship, lounged on deck chairs in T-shirts and shorts and turned red. One morning I woke boiling hot in my cabin to find the engines off, and the ship tied firmly to the wharf in Kirkenes. I got off and walked around the town, sweating in the surprising heat, noticing a woman in a bikini tending her flowers. It wasn't until I returned to the ship that I saw the time: four AM.

After a month I was no longer thinking so much about Spain; I had returned to Norway. I was where I was, and I began to crave the sensation of being at sea. When I was standing on a dock in one of the small towns, I liked to look at the *Kong Olav* and think, *That's my ship*. The sound of the horn as we came into port, the feel of the waves under us, the sense of leaving land behind—all those aspects of the trip I grew to love. Dishwashing never got much easier, but managing a crate of hot wineglasses just out of the machine while the floor was rolling in a storm wasn't such a problem. I grew stronger and tougher; never seasick, always doing what I was told, able to hold my own, swearing cheerfully at my two assistants. Life at sea suited me, and many years later I'd remember that and embark on a four-month trip around the North Atlantic, gathering stories about women and the sea for a travel book, *The Pirate Queen*. All through those weeks of salt rain and sea wind, of rocky coastlines and large ships and small boats, the memory of my summer on the *Kong Olav* would inform my curiosity and my research.

Although I got along with just about everybody, my only true friend onboard the *Kong Olav* was the woman who prepared the salads and sandwiches, a Hungarian named Agnes. Agnes' dark hair waved softly around a face that was both intellectually serious and intensely feeling. "The people here," she said sadly to me. "They're so *cold*, like their weather." Agnes spent much of her time making peace between her husband, Miklos, and the other servers, all of whom were Norwegian women. She explained, "He's a passionate man—his temper—well, and why should he always have to work in the second class dining room where there are no foreigners, only Norwegians, who will not give him tips?"

Miklos had a stiff brush of gray hair and a harassed air. Both he and Agnes had the bewildered, anxious look of older people rushed off their feet in a way that was not natural to them. In Budapest, Miklos had been a violinist with the national orchestra. Agnes had been a journalist. Six years before, they'd taken the opportunity to ask for asylum in Oslo when Miklos played in a concert there. They had found asylum but not jobs. "I knew I wouldn't find work as a writer," Agnes told me in the straightforward Norwegian in which we communicated, "but for Norwegian orchestras not to take Miklos— they said all the places must be filled by Norwegians coming out of music school—*that* we had not expected."

Occasionally Agnes and Miklos invited me down to their cabin, the same size as my own, and with great kindness and formality they brought out tiny painted glasses and a bottle of plum brandy and chocolates. Miklos sometimes took his violin out of its flannel cloth and case and played a little, but after only a piece or two, sometimes after only a phrase, he put it back. "No, no," he said. "Too many memories of Hungary. Of the old life."

I asked Agnes once, ignorant, "Why don't you go back to Hungary? Couldn't Miklos get his old job with the orchestra?"

"Oh, child," she said. She took my hand and squeezed it, something no Norwegian would do. "We'd both be punished. Maybe someday, if the Communists lose power . . . no, I'm afraid we're stuck here, not belonging anywhere. Not like you, so free to go where you like. . . . You have no man friend?"

"I had a boyfriend back in Spain," I said. "I don't think . . . he was quite right for me." It was the first time I'd acknowledged to myself that, wherever I ended up, it was not going to be on a communal farm in Marin.

"You're still young. But someday, you'll meet a nice man, you'll marry, you'll have babies. This I know."

"Someday, maybe, I'll find the right person," I said vaguely. Some of the things I'd been up to for the last three years didn't bear talking about. I burst out instead, "I don't want anyone stopping me from doing what I want to do!"

"What do you want to do that someone could stop you?"

"I want to be a writer, but I don't want to write about the same old things—women being stuck and miserable." I was mainly thinking about Martha Quest, but the same could have been applied to my characters Stephanie and Melissa, whose confusion about their purpose in life never propelled the story forward. "I want to write about women *doing* something. And I want to do something myself—something *large*. Something bigger than me."

"A good man doesn't stop you from doing something you want, whether it's large or small. A good man doesn't stop you from writing," she said, puzzled. But I remembered how it had been with Rob, how I'd gotten lost in his life, in his expectations and demands, and how hard I'd had to struggle just to keep who I was alive. I remembered how Tom had wanted to read "The Travelogue" and I'd hesitated, not wanting him to see the words "Alex was bisexual" and "Alex sometimes wondered if she were in love with Ruby." Neither of them had tried to stop me from writing—in fact, both of them had *wanted* me to write, both of them had been disappointed in me.

And yet, neither had inspired me to write, not the way Laura had. I couldn't explain that to Agnes because I didn't understand it myself.

I asked Agnes, "Did you leave Hungary because you wanted to or because Miklos did?"

"I followed him," she said simply. "I couldn't live without him."

"But here in Norway you can't work at what you were trained for. You can't be a journalist."

"I worked for a newspaper in Hungary, and every word I wrote, someone looked at and decided if it was correct or not. That wasn't what I was trained for either." She smiled at me, that lovely warm smile with so much sadness in it. "Don't look so gloomy, my young friend. I accept my life. I am with Miklos, which is all that matters. Miklos and I, we like you very much. Someday you will have the life you want as a writer. But don't forget about your heart."

Agnes was a reader, and one day she gave me a copy of the first novel in Cora Sandel's trilogy, *Alberta and Jacob,* in Norwegian. It was too hard for me, but it reminded me of the television program I'd watched last year. At the library in Bergen, I found the English translations that Elizabeth Rokkan had done of Cora Sandel's trilogy in the sixties and soon became completely absorbed in the story of Alberta Selmer, who'd fled the north of Norway for Oslo and then Paris. Yet the Alberta trilogy reminded me much of Doris Lessing's Martha Quest novels. For Alberta, too, from childhood through young adulthood, through marriage and motherhood, is always hoping for more from life, always encountering disappointment, always being thwarted by her yearning to be loved, by the perfidy of men, by her own biology. At more than eight hundred pages, the Alberta trilogy is one of the longest cases of writer's block on record;

yet at the end, Alberta finally leaves her marriage, takes a room of her own, and begins to write. That, at least, gave me some hope.

In retrospect, how could I expect Sandel and Lessing to write out of anything but their own experience? The Alberta trilogy had been published in the twenties, the Martha Quest novels in the fifties. The bitterness of social roles, the punishments meted out to women who overstepped their boundaries, the curious paralysis that affects both Alberta and Martha belonged to the eras they lived in. I was born in one era but lived to see another come into being while I was still young enough to have it stamp my personality. More importantly, I wasn't alone. Thousands of women were beginning to change the world we lived in.

From time to time, up in the first class lounge, I found *Newsweek*s and *Time*s, sometimes with news about court cases that involved women and ways in which relationships between the sexes were shifting. The articles seemed to hint that some vast force—"sisterhood," they called it in quotes—was awakening across the country. Germaine Greer, Kate Millett, Gloria Steinem, Robin Morgan, Flo Kennedy—all were new or newish names to me that summer. They'd eventually become so familiar I'd forget there had been a time when I had scrutinized mainstream magazines, trying to understand what was happening in my country. It was difficult to grasp that a grassroots movement was swelling in the heartland of America and that, for every small line in *Newsweek* about a woman suing for discrimination or the breaking down of another barrier, a hundred women left abusive marriages, started rape-crisis lines or battered women's shelters, founded newsletters and magazines, or began relationships with other women.

One day the purser gave me a letter that had found me, after several crossed-out addresses, from Laura. She and Georgiou were in San

Francisco and married—though she said it was only so he could get a visa. After I got over the shock of that, I became terribly happy. She hadn't forgotten me; she still thought of me often. She said her mind often went back to our time in Spain, to how unsophisticated she'd felt as a traveler. I'd opened her eyes to Europe, but she wished we could have traveled differently. She wasn't sure if I was still in Norway. Was I planning to come back soon to the States? She missed me. The women's movement seemed to have really taken off since she'd last been here. She was studying Transcendental Meditation and selling encyclopedias—for now. She'd love to see me. Was I writing? Was I still interested in bookbinding and the whole idea of printing? She still expected great things of me.

I took the letter with me out on deck. We were tied up at the dock in Bergen, very near the castle, not far from the Fish Market. It was gray, as so often along the coast, but the bright houses and orange roofs of Bergen made a colorful collage against the rich green hillsides. I felt as if I were suddenly whole; as if, for the first time in some while, I was seen. Laura's big, rounded script brought back a hundred memories. *She* thought of me as writer. *She* expected great things of me. *She* missed me. Tom had written that he missed me too, but it hadn't been enough to make me want to return.

And what did that mean, that the women's movement had taken off? Suddenly I felt strangely eager, for the first time in months, to be back in my country. So often this last year I'd wavered between Norway and Spain, between freedom and oppression as a woman, between dullness and gaiety, between north and south. Which was really me, I'd wondered: the woman who loved to be outdoors in the mountains, who'd discovered the snow and the sagas, and a language like singing, or the woman who read South American literature, drank *finos,* and danced the *sevillana?* The real choice, I understood, as I reread Laura's letter, wasn't between Norway and Spain but between living abroad and going home again. Was I going to join the "sisterhood"? Was I going to be part of history? Or was I was going to remain outside my country, a permanent expatriate? Suddenly that seemed a lonely choice, as if I were choosing to stay home from a party.

"You have a choice," Agnes had said to me once, when we were talking about writing. "If I were you, I wouldn't stay too long outside my country. After a while it won't be so easy to return. You might end up without a language to write in. That's sometimes how I feel. In Budapest I was a writer in conversation with other writers. Now I'm a Hungarian exile, a woman making sandwiches on a ship, talking bad Norwegian. Will I ever write Hungarian again? I can't just write it for myself. And so the language changes; it becomes private, not a conversation anymore."

I'd always thought the notion of exile sounded romantic, but now I thought about the possibility that by staying for a long time outside my country, I'd lose connection with the language. I wanted to forget the past, but that didn't mean I didn't want to be part of the future. I'd told Agnes I wanted to do something large. Could I do a large thing in a foreign country? Or would I always be on the sidelines, wondering what life could have been like back in America? Always the foreigner, just outside the conversation. If I stayed in Norway, one future awaited me; if I returned to Spain, another. If I kept traveling, still other futures beckoned. "I miss you," wrote Laura in the letter I was holding. "When are you coming back?"

Toward the end of the summer, on the last voyage to Svalbard of the season, before the pack ice enclosed it again, we hit rough weather.

That night I woke to the headache of being slammed against something hard and unyielding. I was on the top bunk, and it was

the ceiling of my cabin banging my head as I was thrown up against
it. Through the porthole I saw sky, then water, as the ship rolled
back and forth in the heavy sea. The light outside was gray and
threatening, the sea the color of thick green mud. I could hear the
engine straining and out in the corridor the sound of people groaning
and crying out in fear.

I pried myself out of my bunk. I'd never been seasick and had been
sure it would never happen to me, but I still wanted to get out of the
cabin. Up in the kitchen, I found a horrible mess. One of the cupboards
had opened, and a sack of sugar had spilled on the floor. A glass jar of
beets that hadn't been stowed away properly had fallen off a counter
and broken into the sugar. The red beets slithered like body organs and
there was something hideously bloody and granular about the disaster.

I was retching into the sink when Agnes found me. The ship was
rolling so hard it was almost impossible to walk, but Agnes led me
back to my bunk. In a motherly way she washed off my face with a
wet towel and then handed me a suppository. "Try this. It should
help you with the seasickness. It will make you sleep." For the rest of
the voyage to Svalbard, I was dead to the world.

When I finally woke up, it was about noon, and sun was streaming
through the porthole. I peered out and saw land, barren and treeless, with
a few rough buildings on a rise near the wharf. Everything looked just
washed and clean. The *Kong Olav* was just docking at the tiny village
of Longyearbyen, Svalbard's largest settlement. Kirsten was herding her
tourists together. "Now, remember, we only have a few hours, and I don't
want you to get lost. If we sail without you, remember we don't come
back till next summer! I think you might get cold and hungry, yes?"

They chuckled appreciatively. They adored her. Kirsten shot
me a look that said, "What the hell are you doing here? You're not
coming with *us*."

Agnes was up on deck, too, and some of the other crew members. We were just standing around, relieved not to be in motion, in a holiday mood. There wasn't much work to do. Almost no one had eaten breakfast, so there were no dishes. After the passengers were down the gangway, the rest of us could go, too, to swarm into the duty-free store and load up on cigarettes and liquor. Although there was a limit on how much the crew could purchase, there was no limit on how much they would sell us, and ingenious ideas abounded about where to hide the stuff from the inspectors who would search the ship in Tromsø. I bought a carton of cigarettes for Leanne and hid them in a vacuum cleaner bag.

When we left Longyearbyen later that day, we headed north, to the very small settlement of Ny Ålesund, where the ship sent over provisions in a small dinghy and the dinghy came back with a meteorologist who'd spent six months there. The *Kong Olav* kept sailing north, to the edge of where the sea turned solid ice, the beginning of the polar ice pack. We reached latitude eighty at about four in the morning. Everyone was up on deck, including a group of Italian tourists in heavy fur coats who set up tripods. We'd been passing through a sea of icebergs, silver and blue in the morning light. Where the sun shone through the mist it touched the huge, sculptured icebergs with unearthly gleams and lusters. The ship moved slowly now, carefully among the bergs.

I had a sudden memory of having looked down from an airplane, years and years ago it seemed now, at icebergs floating in the sea. That was the December I'd left home for Europe, telling Rob I'd be gone two months.

> For long years a bird in a cage:
> Now flying along with the clouds of heaven.

Agnes had come up to the top deck with me again, and we watched in silent wonder the stately procession of bergs. We were coming to the ice pack, a flat plain of glittering white broken by rivers of blue. This was as far north as we could go.

I joked to Agnes, "Maybe I should have just stayed in Longyearbyen. I'm not sure I can bear the crossing back to Tromsø." I tucked my hands in my armpits, for I didn't really have warm enough clothes for the icy wind.

Sometimes she took me literally. "You couldn't stay here in Svalbard," she said. "*Brrr.* You'd freeze. You'd be frozen in for the winter. Those people left there for the season have to just stay there."

"Well, I've got to go somewhere in September when this job ends," I said. "At least if I stayed on Svalbard I wouldn't have to think what to do next. I wouldn't be able to leave."

"You should go back to your country is what I think," Agnes said, rubbing her hands against her cheeks. "If you want to be a writer, you should go home. You must have language to be a writer. You can't be a writer without a language. You need to be part of a *conversation.*"

"I do want that conversation," I said. "I just—I don't want to lose the person I've become as a traveler. I don't want to lose—all this!" And I gestured, to the hugeness of the icy snow pack and the icebergs all around us, which were lit up like candles in the morning light.

She repeated, "Maybe I only say this because I lost my home. Or because I'm old and wise. Go home while you still can, and carry all this with you. Remember it."

The *Kong Olav*'s engines reversed, and now we backed away from the pack ice and turned. From this moment, we were on the homeward voyage.

❧ SEVENTEEN ❧

O Pioneers!

I LEFT THE *Kong Olav* around the first of September and worked a few weeks in Bergen in a laundry to save up the rest of the money I needed to get back across the Atlantic. Nothing happened those last weeks to make me change my mind and stay. Only when I came to Hamar on the local train did I feel a pang of loss.

Lake Mjøsa sparkled blue against the russets and golds of the heathers and the birches, and the town was quiet as I walked the familiar streets from the train station to the big yellow farmhouse, where Elisabeth made me a cup of Earl Grey tea and where I buried my face in Buster's neck and swung Knut up in my arms. A part of me would have liked to keep living with the Helland-Hansens for the rest of my life, safe in the room at the top of the stairs.

I stayed with Leanne in her new apartment on my last night in Norway. Over the past year she hadn't learned much more Norwegian, but she'd found a job where that wasn't a necessity, in the field of computing science. Her data-processing work in Raleigh now turned out to be useful. She asked my advice about her married lover and told me more details than I wanted to know about their sex life. Late in the evening he came over, forty-five and balding, with a gold medallion flashing in the chest hair of his open shirt. I heard them making love in the other room, and then he left. In the morning Leanne said, "What should I do? Do you think he'll leave his wife? You gave me such good advice once, in London. You were such a great listener."

I didn't seem to be any longer; I was bored with her love life. I'd always be grateful—and amazed—that it was Leanne who'd brought me to Norway, but it was clear we weren't close any longer, if we'd ever been. I left a few things with her, since my bags were over the weight limit—some clothes, some books, my high-heeled boots from Spain—and said I'd retrieve them on my next visit. But I didn't come back to Norway for six years and by that time I felt I'd changed so much that I wouldn't have known what to say to her. I couldn't imagine, returning in Birkenstocks, that I could fit into my old Spanish boots either, even assuming she'd kept them.

I went first to northeastern Connecticut, where my friend David now lived and where a number of other artists had also settled. I rented David's spare room and worked in a button factory in Putnam to save up more money to get across the country. I read *Sexual Politics* and *Sisterhood Is Powerful,* and my first copies of *Ms.* Suddenly the world seemed full of new writers and new ways of writing about being female. Along with stories about women who left home and were changed, I wrote a few about women who stayed put and tried to change the world around them. I also wrote poetry, stirring manifestos against the patriarchy, which David found annoying.

In Connecticut I met some other writers and many visual artists. I turned twenty-three. I joined a writing group and hesitantly began to read aloud the stories I was beginning to write. In *Ms.* I found a notice about a journal called *Amazon Quarterly* and sent away for a copy of this early lesbian literary magazine. I began to mail out my poems and stories and started collecting rejection slips. I was thrilled to get a letter from Patricia Hampl, the editor of a journal in Minnesota, *Lamp in the Spine*. She kindly critiqued one of my poetic diatribes against Western civilization, composed after reading Elizabeth Davis' *The First Sex*.

I corresponded frequently with Laura, who by now had parted from her Greek actor and had moved to Phoenix with her boss and his wife, to continue selling encyclopedias door-to-door. In March I took the Greyhound to Phoenix. En route I read Virginia Woolf's essays and visited Battle Creek, where my uncle now lived with his new wife, Margaret May, in the house on North Broad Street.

For several days I slept in my grandmother's old carved walnut bed, slept late into the morning the way I used to do as a teenager. My uncle was in one of his good periods, taking his medication and working at the VA hospital in the laundry room.

"I'm sorry I never met your grandmother. I know from your uncle that she was a strong-minded woman," said Margaret May one morning as we sat in the kitchen, which had not changed in the nine years since I'd been there last. The house still smelled just the same, and all the same furniture was in the parlor. I could almost imagine my grandmother's heavy step moving impatiently toward the ringing phone and her clear, firm admonition to sufferers to sit up, stand up, stop coughing and whining, and recognize that God had already healed them.

"My father used to say she was the stubbornest woman in the world."

"Too stubborn, perhaps?" said Margaret May. Some flakes of March snow flew by outside. Margaret May was from Flint and had met my uncle through the personals. She knew of his schizophrenia but had decided to love him anyway. I might not have stopped in Battle Creek if she hadn't warmly invited me, saying she wanted very much to meet some of my uncle's relatives. I wouldn't have stopped because I was a little frightened of my uncle.

"I thought she was mean when she used to come to our house in California," I said, looking out the window at the bare cherry tree. "But I think she was just trying to help my mother, in the only way she knew how. She had ideas about how things should be. Firm ideas."

Margaret May gave me many photos, of my mother as a child, of my Irish grandfather with my mother in Brooklyn, of my grandmother at the age I remembered her: big-nosed, strong-chinned, decisive. But there were also photos of Faith Lipscomb as a younger girl, willowy and determined. I remembered how Grandma Lane had told me she'd gone out west as a young nurse, how she'd said, "Well, why shouldn't you go to Europe?"

Although it was chilly March, I walked around Battle Creek for hours every day, recalling my childhood. In 1974, the center of town was in decline, with many storefronts boarded up. People had, as everywhere else, moved out to suburban developments, and the Kellogg Foundation hadn't begun to refurbish the town with a new sports arena and hotels. The bustling main streets I remembered were quiet now. I walked past the Post Building, where my grandfather had had his practitioner's office, and the Bank of Battle Creek. For just a moment I was tempted to go in and confront Mr. Butterworth face to face. But in fact, I had a guilty conscience about those letters I'd sent him from London, which seemed now to have been written by a child.

I revisited the library and handled the same books I'd once checked out from the D row of fiction: *Hard Times, Little Dorrit,* and, of course, *Bleak House*. I sniffed at their spines, turned their pages, and was astonished to realize I now could picture in much greater detail the London that Dickens was describing. I'd been there. I remembered lying on the horsehair sofa reading *Bleak House* on a muggy summer day, with dust of the parlor in my nose and sweat on my brow. I remembered Grandma Lane lumbering into the room and sitting down, telling me, "You are certainly strong-willed enough to make your way in the world. Only time will tell if you have any talent as a writer. Talent is nothing without persistence."

I'd told her I wanted to go to Europe, and I had. In fact, she'd made that possible. I had flailed around and made mistakes and had adventures and tried to learn to write, and now (I felt, standing at the D shelf, shocked at the passage of time) I was grown-up.

What was next? I couldn't imagine myself in Phoenix, and though I had hopes about Laura, something in her letters also warned me that her feelings were not—had never been—the same. I wished my grandmother were still alive, wished I could go back to the house on North Broad and ask her what to do now with my life. I didn't expect her to be sympathetic. I imagined her saying, "Now you've spent all my hard-earned money, and all you have to show for it is a pile of notebooks, maps, and memories. You better figure something out, missy, because I am certainly not going to be handing out anything more. You're on your own now." But after her lecture, she would have slipped me a $10 bill and said, "Never give up."

That day in the Battle Creek library, I happened to see a bulletin board with a review of a book called *The Publish-It-Yourself Handbook* and an interview with its author, Bill Henderson. The interview spoke of a tradition of self-publishing and small presses in the U.S. and Europe and talked about how the new technology of small offset presses now made it feasible for anyone to learn to print—for anyone with interest to start a small publishing company. He'd just founded the Pushcart Press and he didn't look, from his picture, so much older than me.

Something clicked into place, perhaps his references in the interview to Anaïs Nin and Virginia Woolf, both of whom had set type and run off limited editions. I made a note of Bill Henderson's book and resolved to buy it. I seemed to know all of a sudden that starting a small press would be the action, the thing bigger than myself that I'd been longing for. That printing books would give me a place to put my energy and a way, along with writing, to be part of the conversation about women's literature and women's changing roles in society. I didn't know how that would happen, until I moved to Seattle and met Rachel da Silva at a party two years later. I was studying commercial printing at Seattle Central Community College, and Rachel, who worked as a printer, had just bought a Chandler & Price printing press. By the end of 1976 Seal Press had its first book, a letterpress poetry chapbook that we typeset and printed by hand.

That summer in Seattle, in 1976, in her mother's old garage in Eastlake, the first thing I handset and printed was a small broadside with the famous quote from Kafka that ends "a book should serve as the ax for the frozen sea within us."

It would be a very long time before I could write such a book, a very long time before I could crack that frozen sea within me, which was the memory of my childhood. Yet I must have had a clear notion, even then, of what I eventually would need to do as a writer. On the last page of one of my journals from Europe, titled "Record of Work 1971–73," full of ideas for stories and novels, I find this surprising note to myself:

These are the things someday I will write about—
I will write about my father's life, the terrible
tragedies and misfortunes of it & I will write
about my grandmother & uncle & and about my
mother's religion & her death. I will write over
& over about Rob & Ruthie & what they were
to me. I will write about Laura. I will write of the
experience of foreignness, of exile, of language
& travel.

I never did write much about Rob and Ruthie, nor about Laura
as Laura. She haunts some of my fiction instead as a kind of ghost:
the early love, the unrequited love, the friend who believed in me at
a time when nobody else seemed to. Most of my fiction in the years
to come would focus on women and politics; the novels and stories
were part of the conversation of the women's and gay movements.
Some of those narratives have a European backdrop and do focus
on foreignness, exile, and language through the eyes of characters I
invented. It took a long time before I could make myself the narrator
of my own travels and relish the role of interpreter and guide. As for
writing the truth about my family—for many years the hard work of
excavating loss would be too difficult.

It would be almost twenty years before I'd have the courage to
return to Battle Creek and to memories of the past. Again I'd walk
the streets and go to the library and the Christian Science church,
this time for research in writing my memoir, *Blue Windows*. By that
time my uncle was back in the VA as a patient and Margaret May
was living in Florida. The house on North Broad had long been sold.
Still, there were people who remembered my grandmother very well.
"When Faith told you to stand up straight and stop complaining,
that you were a child of God and already whole and healed, by
gum, you believed her. And you stood up straight. And you did feel

better. Immediately. She was a stubborn, stubborn woman. And we loved her."

In Phoenix, Laura told me that while she *liked* me, even *loved* me, she was probably not really a lesbian and didn't feel that was something we should pursue; in fact, she was having an affair with her boss. She and Len were to live together for many years, until she left him for her women's studies professor when she went back to school in her thirties. Still, I stayed with her for some time, reading Virginia Woolf and continuing to write the short stories I'd begun in Connecticut, before heading to Seattle. I gradually moved away from the notion that I could be attracted to only one woman.

In fact, I already knew that. Sitting in the restaurant of the Greyhound station in Detroit, while I waited for the bus that would take me back across the country I'd left so long ago, a woman looked over at me. She had short dark hair and wore jeans and a T-shirt that said NATIONAL ORGANIZATION FOR WOMEN. She was reading *O Pioneers!* I was in the midst of the first *Common Reader*. She asked if I'd like some coffee and flirted with me.

I flirted back. Yes, something had changed in America while I was gone.

I was glad to be home.

Acknowledgments

This book owes everything to my grandmother, Faith Lane.

I would like to thank my editor, Marisa Solís, who pushed and prodded and never failed to be encouraging, as well as Jill Rothenberg and Laura Mazer of Seal Press, and the book's designers, Kimberly Glyder and Megan Cooney. Thanks to Betsy Howell, for love and support, and to Nancy Pollak, Michele Whitehead, and Jan Wright. Every writer needs such readers.

❧ ABOUT THE AUTHOR ❧

Barbara Sjoholm is the author of *The Pirate Queen: In Search of Grace O'Malley and Other Legendary Women of the Sea,* a finalist for the PEN USA award in creative nonfiction. Her essays and travel journalism have appeared in *The American Scholar, The Antioch Review, The Harvard Review, The New York Times, Smithsonian,* and *Slate,* among other publications. As Barbara Wilson, she is the author of *Blue Windows: A Christian Science Childhood,* the winner of a Lambda Literary Award and a finalist for the PEN USA award. She is also the author of two mystery series, one of which, featuring the translator-sleuth Cassandra Reilly, takes place abroad in Spain, Italy, Romania, and other countries. Her Cassandra Reilly mystery *Gaudi Afternoon* won the British Crime Writers Award for best crime novel set in Europe, as well as a Lambda Literary Award. It was made into a film starring Judy Davis and is set in Barcelona. As Barbara Wilson, she is also the translator of several books from Norwegian, including *Cora Sandel: Selected Short Stories,* which won a Columbia Translation Award.

Barbara Sjoholm co-founded Seal Press in 1976 with Rachel da Silva, and was an editor and publisher there for eighteen years. She also founded the imprint and, later, the publishing house Women in Translation, which published fiction in translation by women from around the world. She lives in Port Townsend, Washington.

SELECTED TITLES *from Seal Press*

For more than thirty years, Seal Press has published groundbreaking books. By women. For women. Visit our website at: *www.sealpress.com*

The Pirate Queen: In Search of Grace O'Malley and Other Legendary Women of the Sea by Barbara Sjoholm. $15.95, 1-58005-109-X. A fascinating account of one of history's most intriguing women, along with tales of cross-dressing sailors, medieval explorers, storm witches, and sea goddesses.

Italy, A Love Story: Women Write About the Italian Experience edited by Camille Cusumano. $15.95, 1-58005-143-X. In this thrilling and layered collection, two dozen women describe in loving prose individual infatuations with a land that is both complicated by and adored for a rich tradition. Also available, *France, A Love Story: Women Write About the French Experience.* $15.95, 1-58005-115-4 and *Mexico, A Love Story: Women Write About the Mexican Experience.* $15.95, 1-58005-156-1.

Es Cuba: Life and Love on an Illegal Island by Lea Aschkenas. $15.95, 1-58005-179-0. This triumphant love story captures a beautiful and intangible sense of sadness and admiration for the country of Cuba and for its people.

Reckless: The Outrageous Lives of Nine Kick-Ass Women by Gloria Mattioni. $14.95, 1-58005-148-0. An entertaining collection of profiles which explores the lives of nine women who took unconventional life paths to achieve extraordinary results.

The Risks of Sunbathing Topless: And Other Funny Stories from the Road edited by Kate Chynoweth. $15.95, 1-58005-141-3. From Kandahar to Baja to Moscow, these wry, amusing essays capture the comic essence of bad travel, and the female experience on the road.

Stalking the Wild Dik-Dik: One Woman's Solo Misadventures Across Africa by Marie Javins. $15.95, 1-58005-164-2. A funny and compassionate account of the sort of lively and heedless undertaking that could only happen in Africa.